MURDER BEYOND THE GRAVE

TRUE-CRIME THRILLERS

JAMES PATTERSON

with ANDREW BOURELLE
and CHRISTOPHER CHARLES

As Seen on Investigation Discovery's *Murder Is Forever*

GRAND CENTRAL
PUBLISHING

NEW YORK   BOSTON

Dear Reader,

Above all else I'm a storyteller. I craft stories for insatiable readers. And though my books may seem over-the-top to some, I find that I am most often inspired by real life. After all, truth is stranger than fiction.

The crimes in this book are 100% real. Certain elements of the stories, some scenes and dialogue, locations, names, and characters have been fictionalized, but these stories are about real people committing real crimes, with real, horrifying consequences.

And as terrifying and visceral as it is to read about these crimes gone wrong, there's something to remember: the bad guy always gets caught.

If you can't get enough of these true crimes, please watch the pulse-racing new television series on Investigation Discovery, Murder Is Forever, *where you'll see these shocking crimes come to life.*

I hope you're as haunted by these accounts as I am. They'll remind you that though humans have the capacity for incredible kindness, we also have the capacity for unspeakable violence and depravity.

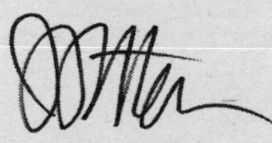

CONTENTS

MURDER BEYOND THE GRAVE

JAMES PATTERSON

WITH **ANDREW BOURELLE**

CHAPTER 1

THE MAN GASPS FOR air and claws at the plywood siding of his prison. He's inside a coffin that is six feet long and three feet wide.

Rivulets of sweat pour from his brow. His shirt is soaked. His heart is thumping like he's just run up a flight of stairs. His skull is throbbing with a nauseating headache.

He has been buried alive.

At gunpoint.

A stranger, disguised with a ski mask and motorcycle helmet, had kidnapped him, had clipped handcuffs around his wrists, and later, when he forced him into the box, he cut the chain between the cuffs but left the circles of metal clasped tightly to his wrists.

The kidnapper left three items in the coffin: a gallon jug of cloudy water, a pile of candy bars, and a car battery attached to a caged lightbulb. He has gulped half the water already but hasn't touched the candy bars. He isn't sure how long he's been in here. The lightbulb is starting to dim.

He looks up at a small piece of PVC pipe sticking through the plywood, and he puts his mouth over the tube, trying to draw big gulps of fresh air. But though he's in good shape, his lungs strain. No matter how much air he pulls in, his chest is still heaving, still gasping for more.

He knows what's happening. He's running out of oxygen. The pipe isn't doing enough to circulate fresh air into the chamber.

He pushes up against the plywood and pounds on the wood with his fists.

"Help!" he screams.

But his vocal cords are raw from yelling so much. And he can barely catch his breath as it is.

He tries to calm his panicked breathing, taking long, slow breaths. His head is pounding.

Keep it together, he tells himself. *Calm down!*

He remembered what the masked man said when he put him in here, that this is all about money.

Everything's going to be fine. I've worked out all the details. You're not going to die.

But he is beginning to think his kidnapper is never coming back.

The air smells of sour sweat, plywood, and caulk. And hidden behind those odors, barely noticeable, is the smell of freshly dug soil—the smell of his grave.

He presses his trembling hands against the plywood again. This time, when he pushes upward, straining with all his strength, he feels some give in the earth. He feels a moment of hope. But when he releases the pressure, the board sags inward, like a mineshaft nearing its inevitable collapse.

The light flickers. He takes deep breaths. Long inhalations. Slow exhalations. He tries to calm his nerves.

He closes his eyes and, as he waits for the light to die and the darkness to envelop him, he thinks of the faces of his children and the woman he loves. He hopes they know how much he loves them.

CHAPTER 2

January 1987
Eight months earlier

DANNY EDWARDS WALKS DOWN a sidewalk in Chicago, his head down, his fists buried in his coat. Flakes of snow drift in the air. Danny's breath comes out in bursts of visible vapor. Cars drive by, slicing through gray slush.

Danny is thirty years old, well dressed, and handsome. Under ordinary circumstances, he would seem like a friendly guy, but today he has a determined look on his face. He's anxious.

He pushes through the door into a steak house and is greeted by a rush of warm air, a cloud of cigarette smoke, and a barrel-chested host who lights up when he sees him.

"Yo, Danny," the man says, his Chicago accent thick. "Long time no see, eh?"

When the man opens his arms to give Danny a hug, Danny awkwardly thrusts a hand out for a shake instead.

"How've you been?" Danny says, feigning a smile.

"Oh, you know," says his longtime associate, who,

unfazed by the rebuffed embrace, claps Danny on the shoulder. "Same ol', same ol'."

Danny opens his mouth for more small talk, but the host cuts him off with a nod toward the kitchen.

"He's waiting for you in the back. Told me to send you in straightaway."

Danny makes his way toward the rear of the restaurant, walking through tendrils of cigarette smoke. The room is full of low-hanging lamps and checkerboard tablecloths. He enters a redbrick hallway and walks past the kitchen, where white-clad cooks shout over a flaming grill, and then past the dish room, where a kid with pimples on his face and a cigarette between his lips is blasting dirty plates with a high-powered spray nozzle.

In the very back of the restaurant is an oak door, standing ajar, and Danny knocks gently and pokes his head inside.

"Hey, Mitch," Danny says, trying to sound nonchalant.

"Sit down," Mitch says to Danny without any of the good cheer the host displayed when Danny entered the restaurant.

Danny sits in a leather chair across from Mitch, who is leaning over a white platter. There are no vegetables on the plate, no sides whatsoever. Just a sixteen-ounce porterhouse barely seared on the outside and as bloody as a bullet wound on the inside.

Mitch, an intimidating sixtysomething man with silver-streaked hair and cold, dark eyes, saws into the meat and pops a dripping bite into his mouth.

"How's it going?" Danny says.

"Cut the crap," Mitch says, his voice like a garbage disposal filled with broken glass. "Where's my money?"

Danny's façade breaks. He nervously glances around the room. "Here's the thing, Mitch," he says, and then hesitates to continue.

Mitch stares at him. He holds his fork in one hand and a steak knife in the other, but his meal is forgotten. His attention is focused on Danny.

Danny takes a deep breath and then rips the Band-Aid off.

"The cops nabbed my cocaine," Danny says. "The whole supply."

Mitch's expression is unreadable.

"I'm lucky they didn't get *me*," Danny says.

Mitch continues to stare, saying nothing. Danny fidgets in his chair.

"Listen," Danny says. "I've got it all worked out. My buyers are still interested. They're hungry for product. I just need another kilo. I'll give all the profits to you. It will cover what I owe you *and* the new bag. You know I'm good for it."

Mitch returns to his steak without speaking. Danny waits. He can't sit still. He pulls at the collar of his shirt and wipes a bead of sweat from his brow. Mitch takes his time cutting off another bloody hunk of steak.

"So you're going to pay me double?" Mitch says, without looking at Danny.

"Of course."

"And a penalty fee?"

Danny hesitates. "If that's what it takes. I want to make things right."

"What's up with you?" Mitch says, raising his eyes and fixing them on Danny. "You seem a little bit off. Why are you sweating so much?"

CHAPTER 3

OUTSIDE IN A NONDESCRIPT panel van, two police officers listen with headphones.

"Damn it," says the first officer. "He's been made."

"Wait," says the other. "This guy Danny is a slick operator. Let's see what he does."

High-tech equipment lines one side of the van's interior, and the first officer adjusts a knob to try to hear the conversation better.

"I seem a bit off?" Danny asks.

"Yeah," Mitch says, his gravelly voice particularly jumbled in the earphones. *"Jumpy."*

"Jumpy?"

"Yeah," Mitch says, getting frustrated now. *"You gonna repeat everything I say?"*

"Sorry," Danny says.

"What I'm wondering is if the cops nabbed the cocaine you were selling, how is it that they didn't nab you?"

The two cops look at each other.

"Get ready to call in the team," the first one says. "I don't want a dead informant on our hands."

The detectives spent weeks putting this operation together. After they busted Danny Edwards, they convinced him that they wouldn't charge him if he wore a wire and helped them bring down his supplier.

Danny Edwards is a little fish—they want the Big Kahuna.

The plan is simple: once Mitch shows Danny the drugs, Danny is supposed to say a code phrase. Then the police will come rushing in. The only other reason they would come rushing in would be if Danny seemed to be in danger. Danny's a low-level hoodlum, but they don't want his blood on their hands.

"I'm making the call," the first officer says, picking up a walkie-talkie.

"Wait!" the second says, and they both go quiet as they listen.

"How is it that they didn't nab me?" Danny whispers.

"I swear to God you better stop repeating everything I say."

"Okay, okay," Danny says. *"Here's what happened."*

Danny explains how he's been keeping his supply of drugs at a construction site down the road from where he does most of his deals, not in his own home. The house is a skeleton of two-by-fours and plywood flooring. Just now, the roof is getting shingled and the walls are being covered in drywall. But the central air ducts are installed, and it's a convenient place to keep a brick of coke hidden and dry.

"That part of the house has already been inspected, you see. No one looks in there."

"Why don't you just keep your coke at your own house like a normal drug dealer?" Mitch asks.

"Are you kidding?" Danny says. *"My girlfriend would have a fit. I'd be sleeping on the street if she found out there were any drugs in the house."*

Danny goes on to explain that he was selling to a couple guys he hadn't seen before. They were asking for more than he had on him. He should have known better, he admits, but he told them to wait and he'd be back in thirty minutes. He walked to the construction site without realizing he was being followed. Once he'd reached into the vent and pulled out the brick, two other guys came running from the corner of the house waving guns and badges.

Danny took off on foot and lost them when he hid in the rafters of another half-finished house at the construction site.

"I saw them grab the coke," Danny says, *"and then I snuck off."*

"And these cops don't know who you are?" Mitch asks.

"No way, man. That's why I walked to the construction site. They don't have my plate number. They don't know the car I drive. They saw my face, but I never ended up selling them anything. Even if they found out who I was, they couldn't do anything. They've got nothing."

The two police officers listen as the conversation in their headphones goes quiet for a moment.

"You were right," says the first officer.

"Told you he was a slick operator."

"That was such a convincing story he almost fooled *me*," says the first cop.

"If I give you more," they hear Mitch say, *"are you going to be careful?"*

"Thank you so much," Danny says. *"I'm so happy I could kiss a pig."*

"Did you hear that?" says the first police officer.

The other officer nods and barks into his walkie-talkie, "Move! Move! Move! The drug deal is going down!"

CHAPTER 4

"DON'T GO KISSING ANY pigs just yet," Mitch growls at Danny. "You're still in hot water."

Danny dabs more sweat from his forehead.

"This is your last chance." Mitch points his knife toward Danny. "You know what happens if you mess this up?"

A drop of red juice drips off the blade of the knife.

Danny opens his mouth to answer, but then they hear a commotion going on outside the office door. There's yelling, then the sound of pans clattering and glass breaking. Then comes an earsplitting crash, as if someone dropped a whole tray of dinner plates outside the office door.

"What in the holy hell is going on out there?" Mitch snarls.

Mitch stands to his feet just as the door bursts open, crashing against the wall with a bang. In seconds, the office is full of police officers pointing shotguns and pistols at Mitch and Danny.

"Hands up!" a cop yells.

Danny obliges. Mitch ignores the request.

"What's going on here?" he barks. "What do you think you're doing?"

"You two are under arrest," one cop says, leveling a pistol at Mitch's forehead.

Another cop grabs Mitch and shoves him against his desk. He kicks Mitch's legs into a wide stance and begins patting him down. Another officer shoves Danny against the wall and begins patting him down as well.

"Where are the drugs?" one of the officers asks Mitch.

"What drugs?" Mitch says. "This is a family restaurant. It's a law-abiding business."

The cop gets close to Mitch's ear and says, "You're the biggest drug dealer in the city. You know it. We know it. Everybody knows it. And now you're finally going down for it."

"Where's your evidence?"

The cops glance around the room, as if they're expecting to see a brick of coke sitting out in the open. There isn't anything but Mitch's half-eaten steak.

"Don't worry," the cop says, pulling Mitch's hands behind his back and cuffing them. "We'll find the evidence, even if we have to tear this place apart."

A cop yanks one of Danny's arms behind his back, fastens a cuff around it, and then pulls his other arm back and locks them together.

"Ouch," Danny mumbles.

"What's wrong?" a cop says. "Don't like being locked up? Get used to it. We're going to lock you up until you're old enough to collect social security."

The police begin searching the office, flinging open

drawers on the desk and turning over furniture. Danny watches them search, then raises his eyes to look at Mitch.

Mitch is glaring at him, his eyes focused and murderous.

A cold chill slithers up Danny's spine. Mitch doesn't say a word, but his expression tells Danny everything he needs to know.

Mitch's expression says, *I know it was you.*

CHAPTER 5

DANNY SITS IN THE rear of an unmarked police car as it rolls past the welcome sign for the city of Kankakee, Illinois. In the front seats sit the same officers who were in the panel van earlier, his handlers for the undercover operation. They are detectives with KAMEG—the Kankakee Area Metropolitan Drug Enforcement Group. Danny has forgotten their names. Both were friendly to him before, but now things are different. Ever since the bust went awry, they've been alternating between cold indifference and fiery antagonism.

"You know you could have taken these damn handcuffs off me," Danny says, shifting his body to find a comfortable way to sit in the seat while his hands are still locked behind his back.

The officer in the passenger seat—a fortysomething man with blond hair, sideburns, and a mustache—shifts around to look at Danny. His eyes glare at Danny with nearly the same rage that had been burning in Mitch's eyes.

"You're lucky we're not throwing your ass in jail," the officer says.

"Hey," Danny says, shrugging his shoulders, "I did my part."

"You were supposed to say the code phrase *after* you saw the coke. Not before."

"He was about to pull it out," Danny says. "I was sure of it."

"It's our fault," says the driver, a man about Danny's age with a buzz cut that made him look as if he just got out of the marines. "We assumed this high school dropout knew the difference between *before* and *after*."

"My three-year-old knows the difference between before and after," says the officer with the mustache.

"Yeah, but your son's human." The driver looks in the rearview mirror and fixes his eyes on Danny. "Not a rat."

"Very funny," Danny says. "You weren't calling me a rat when I agreed to help you."

"That was back when we thought you were actually going to help us," the cop says. "Not screw us over."

"If it was up to me," the mustached officer says, "I'd put your lying ass in jail. You reneged on your agreement as far as I'm concerned."

"Well, it's not up to you," Danny says, unable to hide a smile. "The state's attorney says I fulfilled the terms of my deal."

The cop in the passenger seat looks over at the driver. "I told you he was a slick operator."

The driver says nothing, and quiet overtakes the car. Danny looks out the window. The car crosses a bridge over the Kankakee River. Its water is gray in the January light, and the trees lining the banks are leafless and lean.

Soon they're driving through downtown Kankakee, a short strip of old brick storefronts. With a population of about twenty-five thousand people, Kankakee is a nice little town—quaint, quiet, and close enough to Chicago that residents can get their big-city fix whenever they need to.

Danny watches the storefronts roll by, remembering growing up here. He'd ridden his bike into town on summer afternoons. He'd gone swimming in the river. He'd snuck into train cars at the old depot and smoked marijuana with his friends.

His parents were well off, and he'd never been left wanting. As an adult, he'd done well for himself—just not by obeying the law. Up until recently, he'd been making four thousand dollars a week selling cocaine. He'd owned a riverfront house in an upscale neighborhood, and he'd also been making enough to lease a split-level town house for his girlfriend, Nancy. He paid for her place because he didn't want her and her eight-year-old son, Benji, to be close to his drug-dealing operations.

Life had been great. He'd been planning to buy a boat.

But then KAMEG agents raided his Aroma Park home, seizing ten thousand dollars in cash and two hundred grams of cocaine—with a street value of twenty thousand. The story of the narrow escape that he told to Mitch was a complete fabrication. The truth is he'd been busted red-handed.

A month ago, he'd had the world at his feet. Now he's sleeping in Nancy's town house, trying to figure out how to make the monthly payment. All the money he had in the world is gone. Life as he once knew it is now over.

"Why are you looking so gloomy?" the officer in the

passenger seat says to him. "You just lucked into a get-out-of-jail-free card."

"It doesn't feel that way," Danny says. "What am I supposed to do now?"

As the police car rolls up in front of Nancy's town house, the two officers look at each other, incredulous. The driver turns around and glares at Danny.

"Why don't you try getting a job like everybody else."

CHAPTER 6

August 1987

DANNY SWINGS HIS HAMMER and drives a framing nail into a two-by-four. He stands inside the skeleton of a house under construction, sweating in the summer humidity. He reaches into his tool belt, pulls out another nail, and lines it up. He takes a swing and misses the nail—hitting his thumb instead.

"Damn it!" he shouts, throwing his hammer down onto the plywood floor.

He shakes his hand, trying to wring out the pain. He checks his watch. It's not quite quitting time, but close enough.

He collects his hammer and heads over to the foreman, who hands him a check. Danny stares in disbelief at the numbers on the paystub.

"Uncle Sam sure takes a bite, don't he?" the foreman says.

And people say I'm a crook, Danny thinks.

He almost opens his mouth to ask for more hours. He

sure could use the money. But he hates the work. There's got to be an easier way to make money.

He climbs into his van and heads home. At a stoplight, he examines the palms of his hands. The soft flesh is full of blisters. He keeps waiting for calluses to form and for his skin to toughen up, but it hasn't happened yet.

I'm not cut out for this type of work, he thinks.

The only problem is that the one type of work he is cut out for is illegal. He's been walking the straight and narrow since January because he knows that another bust will put him in prison for who knows how long. There will be no leniency this time. No deal.

No get-out-of-jail-free card.

He pulls up in front of the town house, which is in need of a new paint job.

Inside, he finds Nancy crouched in the kitchen behind the dishwasher, which she's slid out from the counter. A slick of soapy water covers the linoleum floor. Her son, Benji—oblivious to the difficulties of the world—is playing in the puddle. Nancy has a roll of duct tape and is wrapping it around a pipe.

"What the hell are you doing?" Danny says.

"The damn thing's leaking again," Nancy says without looking up.

Nancy Rish is a knockout. Twenty-five years old. Petite. Platinum blond. When she dresses up for a night on the town, she looks like a Barbie doll.

But right now, her hair is damp and hanging in her eyes, her sweatpants are soaked with soapy water, and she has grease on her hands and forearms like she's an auto-shop mechanic instead of a stay-at-home mom.

"That should do it," she says, and stands up.

She presses the button to start the dishwasher again. The motor begins to hum, and they watch for more water leaking out. It appears she fixed whatever was wrong.

She grabs a mop and starts to clean up the floor. Danny knows he should help, but he's dog tired after working all day, so he just watches her.

When she's finished mopping, she leans against the handle and says, "You know, I've been thinking. It's time I go back to work."

"No," Danny says without considering it.

"Honey," she says. "We need the money."

Benji is walking around the kitchen, searching for puddles. There's no more water for him to splash in, but his shoes are wet and he keeps leaving dirty footprints on the linoleum.

"I'll think of something," Danny says. "I'll get back on my feet. I promise."

Nancy approaches him, and even in her soaked sweatpants and dirty tank top, she is still beautiful. She puts her arms around his neck and pulls his face down for a long kiss.

"I'm so proud of you for not dealing anymore," she says. "Times are tough right now, but they're going to get better. You're doing the right thing. Let me help you."

Danny shakes his head. When he first met her, Nancy had been working two jobs and somehow taking care of Benji in what little free time she had. She'd gotten pregnant and married as a teenager and ever since she divorced her husband, she'd worked odd jobs: waitressing, selling makeup, cleaning houses. He'd been able to take her from that life. He'd be damned if he was the reason she had to go back to it.

He wraps his arms around her and embraces her. She closes her eyes and rests her head on his chest.

They hear Benji splashing in a puddle.

"I thought I got it all," Nancy says, opening her eyes.

The dishwasher is leaking again.

CHAPTER 7

DANNY DRIVES DOWN THE tree-lined streets of the tony neighborhood where his parents live. His van's window is down because even though it's only midmorning, the day is hot and humid.

Danny parks his van in front of his parents' home, a big two-story house with a large front porch with columns flanking the front door. He cuts through the grass and takes the porch steps two at a time.

He raps on the door and waits. He can hear a lawn mower down the street and somewhere kids are playing and laughing. He feels a pang of nostalgia for his own childhood, a time when life was simpler and easier.

When his father comes to the door, Danny expects to be invited in, but instead George Edwards steps out onto the porch and closes the door behind him. His hair is grayer than the last time Danny saw him. His eyes look weary.

"What do you want, Danny?"

Danny frowns. "How about a 'Hello, son, it's good to see you'?"

His father crosses his arms and leans against the porch railing. He repeats his question. "What do you want, Danny?"

Danny huffs. "It's nice to see you too," he says sarcastically.

When his dad doesn't say anything else, Danny says, "Look, Dad, I need a loan. I just need some help getting on my feet. I promise I will pay you back."

"No."

"I've cleaned up my act," Danny says. "I'm staying out of trouble, making important changes in my life. Nancy and I need a little help, that's all."

"No," his father says. "I'm done helping you."

Danny opens his mouth to object, but his father doesn't give him the chance.

"I offered you a place in the family business," his father says. "But you didn't want to be an electrician. Then I offered you a job at the grocery store I own. You didn't want anything to do with that either."

Danny doesn't have a defense. He's always preferred easy money to hard work and started selling marijuana in high school.

"May I also remind you," his father says, "that when you dropped out of high school and married Peggy, I gave you a house—a *house*, Danny!"

Danny lowers his head. After he divorced his wife so he could be with Nancy, he and his ex-wife had sold the house, and he'd used his share to get in the door of the cocaine business.

"Look," Danny says, trying to sound sincere, "I understand why you don't want to help me. I've screwed up in the past. But I'm really trying to do the right thing here."

His father takes a deep breath, and Danny feels relieved that he's finally gotten to the old man.

"I hope that what you say is true, Danny. I hope you've cleaned up your act. But I won't help you anymore."

Danny's hope evaporates.

"You've hurt me too many times in the past," his dad says.

With that, his father opens the front door and walks back inside. Danny can hear the click as his father throws the dead bolt.

"Well, to hell with you," Danny mutters, "you old son of a bitch."

He climbs back into his van and begins driving through Kankakee. He isn't ready to go home and face Nancy. He knows the city well, and he guides the van through the nicest neighborhoods. He looks at the big houses, with vast green front yards and shiny sports cars parked in the driveways.

His parents were never millionaires, but they were well off. He was born with a silver spoon in his mouth. He wishes now he could reverse the decisions that led him to where he is today. If he had finished high school, he could have gotten his electrician's union card. He could be running the business with his older brothers. Or the grocery store—he could be managing it now.

But selling drugs was too easy.

He passes a particularly opulent house with an expansive front yard and a wraparound front porch. There is a red Ferrari parked in the driveway in front of a detached garage. Three barefoot boys are running through a sprinkler, a teenager and two younger boys who look like twins.

A man wearing glasses, a polo shirt, and a pair of khaki shorts steps out on the front porch. The guy has a smile on his face like he has it all.

"I wish I had that guy's life," Danny says to himself, and he drives on.

CHAPTER 8

STEPHEN SMALL DOESN'T EVEN notice the white panel van driving past his house, let alone the scraggly haired man behind the wheel who is leering covetously at his home. He only pays attention to his boys, who are taking turns running through the sprinkler.

His twins, Barrett and Christopher, are laughing as they dart through the water. His older son, Ramsey, tries to do a cartwheel over the spray, but slips and falls into the grass, howling with laughter.

Stephen chuckles to himself and heads toward the Ferrari parked in the driveway.

"Oh, Stephen," his wife, Nancy, calls from behind him.

Stephen turns to see his wife holding up a set of keys.

"Forget something?" she asks.

Stephen laughs and heads back toward the porch. His wife of eighteen years has a bright friendly smile that he fell in love with early in their courtship.

"Thanks, hon," Stephen says, giving her a hug and a kiss on the cheek.

"Where are you going, Dad?" Ramsey calls out to him.

"I've got to go to the boat shop and pick up a few things," he says.

"Then can we go out on the river?"

"You bet," Stephen says.

He fires up the Ferrari and pulls out of the driveway. The two-hundred-thousand-dollar car has a V8 engine, but Stephen doesn't push the car too fast, especially in residential areas. He is a careful driver.

He takes a slight detour on his way into town and cruises down Kankakee's Riverview Historic District. He slows and creeps past a large, unusual-looking house on a spacious lot. There are a handful of workers going into and out of the building.

The twelve-thousand-square-foot house is a historic fixture in the community. Built in 1901, the house was designed by famed architect Frank Lloyd Wright. It has twelve bedrooms and more than a hundred windows.

Just this month the house was placed on the National Register of Historic Places. In Stephen Small's view, the house is the jewel of the Riverview Historic District.

But Stephen isn't just another sightseer slowing down to admire the house.

He owns it.

A year ago, he bought the house with the intention of renovating it and perhaps one day turning it into a bed-and-breakfast. The B. Harley Bradley House, named for the original owner, is Stephen's passion project.

He doesn't stop the Ferrari, just slows down, checks

to make sure the house is okay, and then speeds along toward his destination.

He has faith in the workers, but he can't help himself. Stephen keeps an eye on the house whenever he's in the area.

If anything happened to the house, he isn't sure what he would do.

CHAPTER 9

DANNY PULLS HIS VAN into a parking space at the local boat shop and strolls in through the door. The air-conditioning feels refreshing on his clammy skin.

"Hey there," the manager says. "What can I do you for?"

Danny explains that he needs his deposit back on a boat he put a down payment on.

"I don't have the riverfront property I did when I planned to buy the boat," Danny explains.

After his arrest, Danny moved out of the river house he had used as the base of operations for his drug deals. Not only could he not afford it anymore, but he was also afraid that Mitch would find him there and exact revenge for Danny leading police to his restaurant. He hoped Mitch wouldn't hold a grudge since he'd led the police astray. He'd known Mitch didn't keep any drugs in the restaurant, but he wasn't sure Mitch would see what he'd done as a favor.

"You want your deposit back?" the manager asks.

"You know you don't get all your money back, just a portion. It says so in the agreement you signed."

Danny scratches his head and reluctantly says that he understands.

"I need the money," Danny says. "There's no way I can buy a boat any time soon."

The manager walks into a back office to collect the paperwork and write Danny a check, and Danny stands and waits, looking around. He studies the selection of skis, life jackets, and boat-maintenance tools. He feels a wave of depression come over him. There is such a difference between the life he lives now and the life he had a year ago— the life he thought he would continue to have forever.

As if he needs another reminder of the difference between what he has and what he wants, Danny watches as a red Ferrari zips into the parking lot and parks next to his van. The two vehicles couldn't look more different. His van is dingy and dented, with rust growing on the doors and a filthy film on the windshield. The Ferrari is gleaming and red, as if its owner washes and waxes it every time he takes it out for a spin.

When the driver steps out, Danny can't believe it— it's the same man he'd seen on the drive here. The preppy man with glasses at the house where the kids were playing in the sprinkler.

The man walks in the door and starts down the aisle, whistling without a care in the world. Danny stares at him.

When the man comes to the counter with a few bottles of cleaning products and a package of sponges, he nods at Danny and says, "Afternoon."

The manager comes back to the counter and tells

Danny that he'll ring the customer up quickly and then take care of Danny's refund.

"Getting your boat cleaned up?" the manager says politely.

"Yes, sir," the man says enthusiastically. "Gonna take my boys out tubing this afternoon."

The man says he has a thirty-foot, five-hundred-horsepower speedboat.

"The kids love it," he says, taking his receipt and heading out the door.

Danny and the manager both watch as the Ferrari glides out of the parking lot.

"I wish I had that kind of money," Danny says.

"You and me both," the clerk says, handing Danny a check. "Do you know who that is?"

Danny shakes his head.

"Stephen Small."

"I've heard the name."

The clerk explains that the Small family just sold its media empire for sixty-four million dollars. He doesn't know how much Stephen Small got, but it has to be a decent chunk. He says that Stephen Small recently bought the B. Harley Bradley House.

"You know, that fancy house over in the historic district? The one Frank Lloyd Wright designed?"

Danny knows the one.

"Some people have it all, don't they?" the clerk says, shaking his head in wonder.

"Not me," Danny groans, and tucks the measly refund into his jeans.

As he walks out the store, the manager calls after him, "Gotta make your own destiny, man."

CHAPTER 10

DANNY DRIVES AROUND, THINKING.

He has no destination in mind. He just doesn't want to go home yet. He can't stop thinking about why some people have so much and other people have so little. Why does a guy like Stephen Small get to drive around in a Ferrari and take his family out on a speedboat when Danny has to swing a hammer under the hot summer sun for meager wages?

Danny doesn't stop to consider that he was born into a life of privilege and squandered his opportunities. He focuses only on how little he has now and how his father won't even give him a loan.

It's not fair, Danny thinks.

At a stoplight, he glances in his rearview mirror and notices a black sedan two cars behind him. The windows are tinted, and he can't see the driver.

Didn't he see that car earlier today?

He can't be sure, but he thinks he spotted the car on

his way to his parents' house. He quickly takes a right, and the sedan does, too, even though its signal wasn't on while it sat at the light.

Could it be Mitch's guys?

Or the cops?

Danny takes another quick right and looks in his rearview mirror. The car rolls through the intersection without taking the turn. Danny breathes a sigh of relief, still studying the rearview mirror. He looks up in time to slam on his brakes to avoid hitting a car stopped in front of him.

Am I just being paranoid? Danny thinks.

When traffic begins moving again, Danny speeds out of the neighborhood, checking and rechecking his rearview mirror. He takes a circuitous route to make sure no one is following him anymore.

By the time he pulls up in front of the town house, Danny has made a decision.

Gotta make your own destiny, the manager had said.

Danny plans to.

He finds Nancy sitting on the couch watching a videotape of *Crocodile Dundee.* Their air conditioner isn't working, and she looks miserable in short cutoff jeans and a tight T-shirt. Her hair is damp around her forehead, and there are sweat stains on her shirt. There is fresh polish on her toenails and wads of cotton wedged between each toe.

"Honey," she says. "Do you want to go get some ice cream? It's hotter than blue blazes in this house."

"I need to run to the lumberyard," Danny says. "We can get ice cream along the way, if you'd like."

"What do you need at the lumberyard?" Nancy asks, pulling the cotton balls out from between her toes.

"I've got an idea for a new woodworking project."

"Is it something you can sell?" Nancy asks, standing up and slipping her manicured feet into a pair of flip-flops.

"Not exactly," Danny says. "But I think it could make us some money."

CHAPTER 11

WHILE DANNY IS LOOKING for the supplies he needs, Nancy wanders through the hardware store. She passes through the paint section, imagining a new color for Benji's room. Then she looks at some trim and imagines it lining the floor in their living room. She arrives at the appliance section and examines a row of dishwashers, looking at the prices. She wants badly to ask Danny if there's any way to buy a new one. Layaway? A credit card? She hates washing dishes by hand. But she knows what Danny will say.

The same thing he says when she suggests she go back to work.

No.

No, no, no!

There's no talking to him. It's always his way or the highway.

She wanders through the store, looking at faucets. They could use a new one of those too. Theirs is always leaking all over the kitchen counter. She exhales deeply, thinking about all the things she can't have.

Life had been so easy when Danny was dealing. He'd always had plenty of money for anything she wanted. Dinners in nice restaurants. Jewelry and flowers. It was a good life—much better than working two jobs before Danny came along—but it was a life that always made her feel guilty. She'd made mistakes in the past, and she liked a good party as well as the next gal, but she was trying to be a good mother. What kind of mother lets her drug-dealing boyfriend pay for the roof over her child's head?

The answer: yours truly, Nancy Rish.

The guilt had eaten her up, and she'd pushed for Danny to quit dealing. She isn't sure why he finally decided to quit, but he did. She'd initially been skeptical that he would be able to stay clean, but so far he has. It's been seven months, and times have been tough for them. But it looks like Danny isn't going to backslide to his old ways.

She tells herself she got what she wanted. She needs to be okay with washing dishes by hand and doing without the unnecessary purchases she used to make. She decides she'll tell him that they don't need to go get ice cream. She doesn't want him to stress about money. She can do without.

She finds Danny in the plumbing section talking to an employee about plastic tubing. What the hell is he planning to build?

Danny tucks three long pieces of PVC tubing under his arm and grabs a couple elbow joints. The pieces of plastic pipe flop under his arms as he walks to the front of the store. On his way, he grabs a package of caulk and a set of door hinges.

At the counter, Danny charges the purchases to his boss's account. Nancy isn't sure if Danny worked this out with his boss ahead of time. It occurs to her that it's possible that his boss purchases so many supplies at the store that he won't even notice an extra charge. She chooses to believe Danny has turned over a new leaf. She needs to stop doubting him.

As they're walking out the door, Nancy tells him that she has decided she doesn't want ice cream.

"Fine," he says, pulling the van around back to the store's lumberyard.

She wants him to recognize the sacrifice she's trying to make, but he seems too preoccupied. It hurts her feelings and she almost blurts out that she's changed her mind and wants ice cream after all. But just because Danny doesn't appreciate the sacrifice she's trying to make doesn't mean she shouldn't make it. She needs to be supportive, whether he notices or not.

Danny shows an employee his receipt. The two men load two sheets of plywood and six two-by-fours into the back of the van.

"What the heck are you building?" Nancy asks when he climbs back into the driver's seat.

"You'll see."

CHAPTER 12

NANCY DUMPS SPAGHETTI NOODLES into a pot of boiling water. The water bubbles up and spills over the side, hissing as it hits the open flame of the burner. Next to the pot on the stove is a pan of simmering marinara sauce. She dips a wooden spoon in and gives it a taste.

Satisfied, she turns to Danny, who is sitting at the kitchen table next to Benji, and says that dinner will be ready in ten minutes.

Both Benji and Danny are drawing. Using crayons, Benji is drawing a dinosaur fighting a robot. Using a mechanical pencil, Danny seems to be drawing designs for whatever it is he hopes to build. He takes a slug of his beer—his third since they got home—but doesn't take his eyes off the illustration.

Danny and Benji look cute together, both locked in concentration. Nancy's heart swells. She has long had her doubts about Danny as a father figure. But now that he is no longer dealing drugs, she feels like he could be a better role model for her son.

It is nice to see him engrossed in something. She doesn't know what the heck he is planning to build—he still hasn't told her—but it's a relief just seeing him focused on something besides how difficult life has been lately.

Curious about what he's doing, Nancy tries to sneak a peek at the drawing. He's sketched out some kind of box, with the two-by-fours serving as the frame and the plywood serving as the walls. Danny has no background in technical drawing as far as she knows, but it looks like he's done a decent job of illustrating his design. He's even included measurements for the dimensions of the box. Next to the box, he's drawn what appears to be the PVC pipe. She can't quite figure out what the PVC pipe is for. It looks like it comes out of the box, but there's nothing in the drawing to indicate what it connects to.

"Honey," Nancy says, placing her hand on Danny's shoulder, "did you hear me? Dinner's almost ready."

Danny jerks his head up, as if coming out of a trance.

"I'm not hungry," he says. "I'm going to skip dinner tonight. I want to go ahead and get started on this."

He grabs his piece of paper and rises. He opens the refrigerator and pulls out two more bottles of beer. Before heading to the garage, he stops and gives Nancy a peck on the cheek.

At first, she feels a stab of resentment. If she'd known he wasn't going to eat with them, she and Benji could have just eaten leftovers. She wants life to be as normal as possible around here. She wants them to act like a family. If Danny is running off to do something without explanation, that seems more like the Danny of old. But the kiss on the cheek—that quick act of tenderness—erases her bitterness. Despite all the pressure he's under, Danny can still take the time to make her feel special.

As she and Benji eat their spaghetti, they can hear a power saw running in the garage, biting through plywood and two-by-fours. Then Danny begins driving nails into the wood. Nancy tries to make Benji laugh by slurping her noodles up. He gives her a half-hearted smile, but he keeps looking distractedly toward the garage.

After dinner, Nancy and Benji decide to watch a movie. They turn the movie up loud so they can hear it over the racket. At some point halfway through, Nancy realizes that the banging and sawing have stopped. After she tucks Benji into bed, she goes out into the garage to investigate.

Danny is nowhere to be found.

But the box he was building is there. It's about six feet long, three feet wide, and two feet deep, with a hinged lid. The edges are caulked, so the box will be watertight, except for a two-inch hole in the lid where it looks like the PVC pipe will connect.

Nancy can't figure out what Danny could possibly mean to use it for. What is he planning to put in it?

The damn thing's big enough to hold a person.

She presses the button and raises the garage door. Danny's van is missing from the driveway. She steps out onto the concrete and looks up and down the street. The heat has finally broken, and the cool air feels refreshing. But Nancy has a sinking feeling. Again, disappearing in the middle of the night without explanation is behavior typical of the old Danny.

She forces the doubt away.

You just need to trust him, she tells herself.

CHAPTER 13

DANNY SITS IN HIS van down the street from Stephen Small's house. His eyes are bloodshot. He has a cigarette between his lips. The van's window is open, but the smoke pools in the ceiling. Danny takes a drag and jettisons the butt out the window.

He glances around to make sure no one is watching him; then he lifts a pair of binoculars and spies the Small house. The Smalls aren't particularly careful about closing their shades at night. Danny can see into their house quite well. Through an upstairs window, he sees both parents tucking their twins into bunk beds.

Danny can't stand the look of this guy, with his receding hairline and goofy aw-shucks smile. He's probably never had a hardship in his life. His wife isn't bad-looking. Maybe a little homely. But she could do better than him, if he wasn't rich, that is. That has to be the reason she's with him.

After they tuck the boys in, they go to their other son's

room. Danny can't see well into this one, but he imagines them going through a similar ritual.

One big happy family.

It makes Danny sick.

He has two children from a previous marriage, and now Nancy wants him to be a surrogate father to her son. He loves his children, and Benji is a cute kid. But the responsibility that goes with children is just exhausting.

He had liked living in a separate house from Nancy. He was able to go back and forth between the houses whenever he wanted. It was the best of both worlds. He had a girlfriend, but he could live like a bachelor half the time. If he had Stephen Small's kind of money, he'd pay someone to tuck his kids into bed at night so he could go out and party.

After the other son's light goes out, Nancy Small heads to what Danny assumes is their bedroom. Stephen trots downstairs and appears briefly in front of the glass window on the front door. He's checking to make sure the door is locked, Danny thinks.

Stephen makes the rounds through the house, turning off lights; then he heads upstairs. He joins his wife in their bedroom and closes the curtains. Danny can't make out anything but blurs behind the white drapes. Then the lights go out. The house is dark. Quiet.

Danny moves the binoculars over the rest of the property. He studies the detached garage. To leave the house, Stephen Small has to walk from one building to the other.

Danny wonders if the side door to the garage is unlocked. He doesn't want to risk checking. There's too much at stake for him to get caught snooping around the property.

Danny starts the engine and slowly drives down the street.

He doesn't turn on his headlights until he is well past the house he's been spying on.

CHAPTER 14

September 1, 1987

NANCY SITS WITH BENJI at the kitchen table, helping him read a picture book. Their empty dinner plates have been pushed aside, and it's nearing Benji's bedtime. But school hasn't started yet, and she wants to cherish this moment. This is a new book they picked up from the library, one that's more challenging than books Benji read in the past. He needs her help as he reads.

Nancy doesn't mind helping him. In fact, she enjoys it. She has already promised that once school starts, she will help him with his homework whenever he asks. She wants to set a good example for the school year.

When they get to the last sentence, Benji looks hard and then carefully sounds out the words.

"You did it!" Nancy says, grabbing him by both shoulders.

Benji has a sheepish smile.

Nancy tells him to go put his pajamas on and brush his teeth. She'll be in to tuck him in soon.

She takes their dinner plates and scrapes the remnants into the garbage. She debates for a moment whether to let them sit in the sink overnight or wash them by hand now. The dishwasher is still broken. She takes a deep breath. No point putting it off until tomorrow.

As she's filling the sink with soapy water, she hears a noise and turns to see Danny sauntering in. She hasn't seen him all day.

"Hey, hon," she says. "There's still a little bit of dinner. Want me to make you a plate?"

He doesn't answer, and Nancy takes a moment to really look at him. His skin is flushed, and his eyes are dilated and wild. It doesn't look like he has brushed his hair in days. For that matter, it doesn't look like he's slept in days.

At first she thinks he must be high on cocaine, but she isn't sure. She's seen him stoned plenty of times, but he's never looked quite like this. He seems stressed out—to the point he's about to snap.

He opens the refrigerator and scans its contents.

"Hon," Nancy says, this time louder. "I made dinner."

"I'm not hungry," he says dismissively.

He grabs a half-full gallon of milk and walks over to the sink. He starts pouring the milk into the soapy water.

"What are you doing?" Nancy says.

She's going to have to drain the sink now and start over.

"I need some water," Danny says, as if that is explanation enough.

He begins to fill the empty jug at the tap. The water in the container is cloudy from the milk residue.

"Danny," Nancy says softly, "is something wrong?"

"Don't worry about it," he says, without taking his eyes off the milk jug.

"You're not dealing again, are you?"

She regrets the words as soon as they come out. Danny's head jerks toward her, and he fixes her with bloodshot eyes.

"No, I'm not dealing again, goddamn it!"

He slams the jug down on the counter, and milky water sloshes out of it.

"If I was dealing again, would we have to live in this crappy little house?" he shouts. "Would we have a dishwasher that leaks all over the goddamn place?"

"I'm sorry. I just don't want you doing anything…" she says, trailing off.

"Anything what?" Danny growls. "Anything *stupid*?"

Nancy steps back. "I didn't say that."

"No, but that's what you were thinking," Danny says, leaning over her. "You think I'm stupid?"

She cowers against the countertop between the stove and the dishwasher. He raises his hand to slap her but holds back.

"You should be thankful for what I do for you," he says.

Nancy feels a burst of courage, and she stands up straight and glares at Danny with tear-filled eyes.

"Don't you love me anymore?" she says.

This snaps him from his trance. He lowers his raised hand, looking at it as if he doesn't know how it got there. He takes a few steps back and leans against the counter, his shoulders slumped.

"I'm sorry," he says. "I'm just really stressed out right now."

Nancy takes a deep breath, steadying her voice. "Let's go to bed," she says. "You look exhausted."

"I just need a little space right now," he says, grabbing the milk jug and putting the lid back on. "I've got an errand to run."

He heads to the door, and Nancy stares at the empty space he left behind. She has the feeling of being watched. She turns to see Benji standing at the threshold of the kitchen, wearing striped pajamas. His chin quivers as he tries to stop himself from crying.

Nancy kneels and embraces him. His tiny body trembles in her arms.

"It's going to be okay," she whispers into his ear. "It's going to be okay."

She hopes her son believes her more than she believes herself.

CHAPTER 15

AFTER PUTTING BENJI TO bed, Nancy walks through the house to make sure the doors are locked. She peeks into the garage and sees that the weird box Danny built is gone. She feels a twinge of relief and isn't sure why.

She pours herself a glass of wine and goes to her bedroom. She pulls off her jeans and blouse, and she puts on one of Danny's T-shirts she uses as a nightgown. The shirt is big on her, hanging halfway down her thighs. The shirt smells of him, and the odor gives her mixed feelings. She loves him, but she knows he's not good for her.

She stands at the window and looks down onto the street. Part of her wants Danny's van to pull into the driveway. At least that way she would know he's safe. But another part of her doesn't want that. In fact, part of her hopes he never comes home again.

She crawls into bed and grabs the telephone from her bedside stand. She dials her friend Julie's number. Nancy takes a long drink of wine while she waits for Julie to answer.

"Are you okay?" Julie says right away.

Nancy opens her mouth to say yes, but she can't let the lie out.

"No," she says, and she starts to cry. "It's Danny."

"What did that bastard do to you? Did he hit you?"

"No. Nothing like that." Nancy pictures Danny raising his hand to strike her, but she doesn't tell Julie how close he came. "He's just acting really weird. He's up to something."

"Is he cheating on you?"

Nancy considers this. She wouldn't put it past him. He'd been married with two kids when he started pursuing Nancy. She'd met him at a bar, but she'd avoided him because she knew he was married. He'd been relentless and she finally gave in. They'd dated, but she wouldn't let things get serious until he started divorce proceedings.

She remembers how he'd made her feel special, how he claimed that he couldn't stay away from her. His persistence had been flattering. But times have changed. They have no money, and Danny sleeps on the couch more often than he sleeps in bed with her.

Maybe that's what this is all about. He's out there chasing women again, and he's found a new pretty young thing to replace her.

Nancy talks this theory through with Julie, but it doesn't feel right. If he was cheating, he'd probably be on his best behavior at home—not on the verge of hitting her.

"He's keeping a secret from me," Nancy says. "That's for sure. But he's still motivated to take care of me. He doesn't seem to want to leave this life with me—he just wants to make that life better."

With this statement, Nancy feels guilty for doubting him. Danny is far from perfect, but he's always had the best intentions when it comes to Nancy. She can't imagine the stress he is under. He's given up a life of crime and is struggling to make ends meet.

Julie keeps talking on the other end of the phone, but Nancy's mind is focused on that thought: he's given up a life of crime.

Nancy feels a cold chill.

Has he given up his life of crime?

CHAPTER 16

DANNY'S VAN CRAWLS THROUGH a desolate area in eastern Kankakee County known as the sand hills. Danny's headlights illuminate the sandy ground, barren except for weeds and gnarled bushes. He finds a place that looks perfect—there are no tire tracks, no footprints, no evidence that anyone comes here.

Welcome to the middle of nowhere, he thinks.

Danny climbs out of the cab and circles around to the back of the van. Inside sits the wooden box he built, the PVC pipe, a cloudy jug of water, an assortment of candy bars, a car battery, and a shovel. Danny reaches for the shovel and circles back to the front of the van, where the headlights illuminate a section of sandy ground.

Danny stabs the blade of his shovel into the loose dirt. He tosses a shovelful of sand aside. Then another. And another. Particles of dust float in the headlight beams. He works hard, breaking a sweat. His hands start to ache. He takes a break to smoke a cigarette and then gets back at it.

When the hole is big enough, he turns the van around and backs up to it. He grabs ahold of the box and drags it out. It fits snugly in the hole. Once he shovels the dirt back on top, there will be a good two feet of earth between the box and the outside world.

Danny puts the car battery into the box, along with the water jug and the candy bars. He closes the lid and admires his craftsmanship—and his plan.

But Danny isn't done yet. He takes the shovel and begins scraping a trench in the dirt, starting from the hole and working his way toward a cluster of weeds about twenty-five feet away. Once he's satisfied with the trough, he takes the PVC tubes out of the van and begins connecting them. He lays them in place and then shovels back over the trench until the only pipe visible is a stub sticking into the hole that he will connect to the lid once he seals the box. The other end of the air tube is hidden in the weeds.

Danny sits in the back of the van and lights a cigarette. His hands are filthy, his shirt sweat-stained.

To the east, the dark horizon is beginning to turn blue with the first hints of sunrise.

Danny smiles to himself. *It's a good plan,* he thinks. *It's going to work.*

CHAPTER 17

September 2

NANCY WAKES UP TO the sound of the shower. Warm sunlight floods the room. She sits up and notices that a cup of coffee and a doughnut are sitting on her nightstand.

Danny comes out with a towel around his waist, his hair wet and dripping. He smiles and gives her a firm kiss on the lips. She looks at him skeptically. Does he not remember what happened last night?

"I've got an idea," he says, more chipper than she's seen him in months. "After we drop off Benji at his dad's, let's go for a drive. We can go look at horses."

Nancy can't help but smile. She loves taking drives and looking at horse ranches. She's tempted to stop him and say they need to talk about what happened last night, but Danny seems to want to move past it. She decides to let it go. He's under a lot of pressure, and this is his gesture of making amends.

Thirty minutes later, they're zooming out of town

toward the countryside. Danny whistles. Nancy lets her hand dance in the breeze. They pass farms and horse paddocks, and Nancy feels relaxed. They don't need a lot of money. All they need is each other and a nice scenic drive—when Danny isn't acting weird, that is.

They're approaching the area known as the sand hills, where the vegetation isn't as lush. Danny pulls over next to a railroad crossing. He parks the car in a pullout, and Nancy has the thought that he's going to lean over and kiss her, the way he used to when they couldn't keep their hands off each other.

Instead, he looks her in the eyes, suddenly serious, and says, "Do you know where we are? Could you find this place if you came back without me?"

Nancy nods, uncertain what's going on.

"I need you to do me a favor," Danny says. "I need you to pick me up here at three o'clock tonight."

"Three o'clock?" she says, incredulous. "In the morning?"

"Yes."

Nancy feels sick. All morning she'd been thinking he'd turned over a new leaf. Things were finally going to change. But he is up to something.

"This whole morning wasn't so we could spend time together," she says, hurt. "You've got some kind of scheme going on, and you're trying to rope me into it."

Danny looks at her sincerely. "Listen, Nancy. I need you to do this for me. Don't ask me why, but I'll need a ride from this place at three o'clock."

Nancy looks out her window, thinking. They're in the middle of nowhere. She can't imagine what Danny will be doing here in the middle of the night.

Unless he's making a drug deal.

"You promised me that you were done with anything shady," she says.

"Just this last thing," Danny says. "I have to do this, and then I promise I'm done forever."

"Just tell me one thing," she says. "Is it drugs? Are you dealing again?"

Danny takes her hand in his and looks earnestly into her eyes.

"I promise I am not dealing drugs," he says.

"Okay," she says, taking a deep, nervous breath. "I'll do it."

As they drive away, the mood in the car has changed. Danny seems agitated again, stressed. Nancy is quiet. She tries to convince herself that as long as Danny isn't dealing, then whatever he's up to can't be too bad.

It doesn't occur to her that it might be worse.

CHAPTER **18**

STEPHEN SMALL AND HIS wife, Nancy, sit in their bed talking about plans for the upcoming Labor Day weekend. It will be the kids' last big hurrah before school starts again, and they want to make it memorable. As they wrap up their conversation, Stephen leans over, kisses Nancy good night, and then takes off his glasses and sets them on the nightstand. He reaches to turn off the lamp, but stops. Downstairs, the telephone begins to ring.

"Who is calling at this hour?" Stephen says.

It's after midnight.

Stephen pulls his legs out from under the comforter and slides his feet into a pair of slippers. The phone stops ringing.

"Ramsey got it," Nancy Small says. "He's up watching a movie, remember. It's probably one of his friends."

Stephen is putting his legs back under the blanket when Ramsey knocks gently on the door and pokes his head into the room.

"Dad," the fifteen-year-old says. "The police are on the phone."

"The police?" Stephen says.

"Yeah. He said he needs to talk to you. Said it's important."

Stephen gives Nancy a perplexed look and then heads downstairs to the phone.

"This is Stephen Small," he says. "How may I help you?"

"Sir," says a male voice, "I hate to bother you at this hour, but there's been a break-in at the Bradley House. You own the house, correct? The one in the historic district?"

"Yes," Stephen says, his heart pounding.

"We've caught the intruders," says the voice on the other end. "We've got them at the Kankakee Police Station. But we need you to come down to the Bradley House and assess the scene, see if there's any damage or anything missing we don't know about."

"Of course," Stephen says. "I'll be right there."

He hangs up the phone and jogs up the stairs.

"I've got to run down to the Bradley House," he tells his wife. "Apparently someone broke in."

He explains that the perpetrators have been caught, but the police need him to take a look at the house and make sure everything is okay.

Stephen pulls on a pair of blue jeans and a T-shirt. He slips his feet into a pair of loafers and grabs his eyeglasses off the nightstand.

"I love you," he says, kissing Nancy on the cheek.

"Be careful," his wife says.

Stephen hurries through the yard toward the detached

garage. He unlocks the side door and steps inside. He presses the button to raise the garage door. When he opens the door to his Mercedes, he catches movement out of the corner of his eye.

A dark figure ducks under the opening garage door and bounds to the side of the Mercedes. He points a gun directly between Stephen's eyes.

Stephen can't see the armed man's face. It's covered with a motorcycle helmet. Stephen looks at his own terrified reflection in the helmet's visor.

"What's this all about?" Stephen says, his voice trembling.

"We're going for a ride," says the man with the gun.

His voice is muffled because of the motorcycle helmet, but Stephen still recognizes it. The voice is the same one he just spoke to on the telephone.

CHAPTER 19

September 3

DRIVING HIS MERCEDES WHILE the mysterious man sits behind him, Stephen has trouble gripping the steering wheel because his hands are shaking so much. The back of his T-shirt is soaked with sweat.

The streets of Kankakee are empty, the shops closed up for the night. Stephen keeps hoping he'll see a police car and be able to get the officer's attention somehow. But there's no one around. The streetlights illuminate vacant parking lots, storefronts with their lights turned off, empty sidewalks along the roadway.

Stephen checks the rearview mirror to look at his kidnapper. He notices the man has a ski mask underneath the helmet. Whoever he is, he's gone out of his way to disguise his identity, which gives Stephen a flicker of hope. If the man planned to kill him, he wouldn't have bothered hiding his face. At least Stephen hopes that's the case.

"I'm a rich man," Stephen says. "I can give you money, if you just let me go."

"I know you're rich," the kidnapper says, but that's all.

Stephen drives for a minute without speaking, and then he decides to try again.

"What are you going to do?"

"If you don't shut up," the man says, lifting the gun and aiming it at the back of Stephen's head, "I'm going to splatter your goddamn brains all over the windshield."

Stephen's breath catches in his throat. He feels his insides constrict.

"Turn here," the man says, and Stephen does as he's told.

They pass the *Welcome to Kankakee* sign and head out of town. Soon the residential streets turn to rural countryside. There are no streetlights, just patches of forest and fences lining pastureland.

The kidnapper tells Stephen to pull off the paved road onto a dirt road. Soon after, he directs Stephen to leave the dirt road altogether, and Stephen finds himself navigating around trees and brush and patches of weeds.

Stephen's hands start shaking even more. He thought the man didn't plan to kill him, but what other purpose could he have for bringing him out to the middle of nowhere? This is the perfect place to bury a body.

"If you kill me," Stephen blurts out, "you won't get your money. I'm rich. I can pay you. Please just let me go."

"Calm down," the voice behind the helmet says, sounding much more relaxed than he did while they were in the city. "Everything's going to be fine. I've worked out all the details. You're not going to die."

"Then let me go."

"Not just yet," the man says. "Stop here."

Stephen parks the car, its headlights illuminating

nothing but sandy, weed-filled ground. Stephen starts to shake uncontrollably.

"Turn off the lights," the man says.

Stephen presses the button, and then the two of them are sitting in blackness.

"Shut the engine off."

Stephen can hardly grip the key because of his trembling hands, but he finally gets his fingers to cooperate.

"Hand the keys to me."

Stephen reaches behind him, and the man takes the keys.

"Now get out of the car," the man instructs him. "If you want to tuck your kids into bed or kiss your wife good night ever again, you'll do exactly as I tell you."

CHAPTER 20

THE MASKED MAN ORDERS Stephen to hold out his arms and then clips a pair of handcuffs around his wrists, squeezing the metal rings tight against his skin.

"Walk," the man orders, pressing the barrel of the pistol against Stephen's lower back.

Stephen staggers forward. The moon is out, but it's far from full, casting barely enough light for Stephen to see by. He isn't dressed for this kind of cross-country trek. His loafers quickly fill with dirt. It's a hot, muggy night, and Stephen's skin is sticky with sweat. He hears insects chirruping, and somewhere in the darkness a bullfrog croaks.

The man follows a pace behind, holding the gun in one hand and carrying a duffel bag with his other arm.

"Please," Stephen says, turning his head slightly to look at the man over his shoulder. "Whatever you're planning, you don't have to do it. I've already told you I'll give you money."

"I'll get my money, all right," the man says, poking Stephen with the gun again.

Stephen jerks as if he's been burned by a hot poker. His foot collides with a clump of dirt and he stumbles forward, landing on his hands and knees. His glasses slip off his sweaty face and fall into a patch of weeds. He gropes for his glasses with his cuffed hands, but his kidnapper grabs him by the back of the shirt and yanks him to his feet.

"Wait," Stephen says. "My glasses."

"You'll buy another pair," the man growls, shoving Stephen.

Stephen almost falls again, but he catches himself. Without his glasses, the world is a blur. Between the darkness and his own impaired vision, he can make out almost nothing, just clumps of vegetation or the occasional tree.

"Stop here," the man orders.

Stephen squints. He can make out a large discoloration in the sandy ground in front of him. It looks like a large hole in the dirt. Stephen hunches over and tries to look more closely.

He sees an open coffin sitting in the hole.

"No," Stephen says, wheeling around and collapsing to his knees. "Please don't kill me. I have a wife, three kids. They need me."

"Shut up," the voice says, sounding annoyed. "I'm not going to kill you. There's a breathing tube. As long as your family does what they're supposed to do, you're going to live. Okay? Relax."

The kidnapper orders Stephen to stand in the box. Then the man removes a handheld tape recorder from the duffel bag and hands Stephen a handwritten note. He points a small flashlight onto the text.

"Read the words as they're written," the man orders, and he presses record.

Stephen squints again. Without his glasses, he can barely make out the words.

The man presses the gun barrel against Stephen's skull and nods his head toward the note.

"Nancy, this is, this is, umm, this...I...that...I thought this was a joke or something, but it's no joke. I'm...there's somebody and I've got handcuffs on, and I'm inside some, I guess, a box."

Danny interrupts: "You got two days of air and that's it. And it's going to get real stuffy in there."

Stephen can make out enough of the note to relay the kidnapper's demands to Nancy. He says to get one million dollars in fifty- and hundred-dollar bills. No consecutive serial numbers.

"You've got forty-eight hours of air," the man says, speaking toward the microphone.

"I love you," Stephen says. "I really do, and the kids. That's all I know. This hurts like hell."

The masked man presses the stop button and puts the recorder back in his bag, then pulls out bolt cutters and severs the chain between the handcuffs. The kidnapper points out the amenities inside the box: There are candy bars, light, water, and even an air tube.

"I'll be back out as soon as your family ponies up."

"You don't have to do this," Stephen says as he first kneels and then lies down in the box.

The man slams the lid closed. Then he adjusts the air tube sticking through the plywood.

Stephen calls out to his kidnapper, telling him it's not too late to let him go.

The kidnapper says nothing. He answers by throwing a shovelful of dirt on top of the box. Stephen cries for help as dirt rains down onto the lid. He tries to shift positions, but it's almost impossible to move—and the temperature inside the box is sweltering.

He feels like he can't catch his breath, and he strains his neck toward the air hole. In doing so, he knocks the car battery and the light flickers. He feels on the verge of panic.

This can't be happening.

He adjusts the battery. At least he has light now, but he can't control his breathing. He gets his mouth as close to the air hole as he can and tries to take slow, deep inhalations through the pipe.

The wooden roof starts to sag under the weight of the dirt.

CHAPTER 21

NANCY RISH WAITS FOR Danny at the railroad crossing, as she was instructed. She looks around, nervous, unsure if whatever Danny is up to is illegal. She thinks about firing up the engine and driving away, leaving Danny to whatever trouble he's gotten himself into this time.

But she can't bring herself to do it. She loves him. She wants a life with him.

A normal life.

Is this a normal life? she asks herself. *Waiting by a railroad track in the middle of nowhere at three in the morning? No, this is far from a normal life.*

But Danny has promised this is the last time he'll do something like this. And at least it—whatever *it* is—is not drug dealing.

Even if this isn't a normal life, maybe a normal life is right around the corner. A little voice inside Nancy's head tells her she's just fooling herself. But she's already here, already waiting. What would Danny do if she drove off without him?

He almost slapped her the other day. Whatever he is into is stressing him out to the point that he was almost willing to hurt her.

It probably wouldn't be a good idea to abandon Danny now. If she did, she might as well go home and grab Benji out of bed and run away. But where could she go?

The answer is simple: nowhere.

If she runs away from Danny, she has nowhere to run to.

She bites her fingernails and looks around impatiently.

Danny comes walking toward the car, emerging from the darkness like a phantom. He is carrying a duffel bag slung over his shoulder.

Nancy scowls at him as he opens the door.

"There aren't any drugs in there, are there?"

"No," Danny says, irritated. "I already told you I'm not dealing."

"Then what are you doing?"

Danny leans his head back against the headrest like he's worn out from a hard day's work.

"You don't want to know," he mutters.

Danny is filthy. His pant legs are dusty, and his hands are caked in what looks like a muddy mix of dirt and sweat.

Nancy opens her mouth to speak, but Danny cuts her off with a curt "Let's get going already."

Nancy starts the engine and drives away. The headlights slice through the darkness. They drive in silence for several minutes.

"Pull over up here," Danny says, pointing to a gas station. "I need to make a phone call."

"At this hour?"

Danny doesn't answer, and Nancy doesn't press him. She pulls off into the gravel parking lot and stops the car. She leans back and closes her eyes as she waits.

She doesn't see Danny pull a tape recorder out of the duffel bag when he gets to the pay phone.

CHAPTER 22

September 3
3:00 a.m.

NANCY SMALL IS ASLEEP and dreaming when she hears a telephone ringing. She sits up, looks around, tries to orient herself. She's sitting in a recliner in the living room. She sat down to wait for Stephen to return home and ended up dozing off.

Now she checks the clock in the kitchen and sees how late it is. The phone is still ringing. She hurries and grabs it.

"Hello," she says.

"Nancy," she hears her husband say, but his voice is distorted, muffled. It's hard to hear him, but the voice is still recognizable as her husband's. *"This is, this is, umm, this...I...that...I thought this was a joke or something, but it's no joke. I'm...there's somebody and I've got handcuffs on, and I'm inside some, I guess, a box."*

Nancy's mind reels as she tries to keep up with what Stephen is saying.

He's locked in a box?

I'm supposed to come up with a million dollars?

"Slow down," she says. "What is going on?"

She hears another voice, even more distorted, say something about forty-eight hours of air. Then she hears Stephen's voice again.

"I love you. I really do, and the kids. That's all I know. This hurts like hell."

"Wait, Stephen—"

Another voice comes on the line.

"We have your husband."

This voice isn't distorted or muffled. It's clear and cold, and hearing it sends chills down Nancy Small's spine.

"Get the money together," the voice says. "If you don't give me one million, your husband is dead."

"I don't know if I can get that kind of money," Nancy pleads.

"Your husband is buried in a box, and only I know where it is," the voice says. "He has forty-eight hours of air. If I don't get what I want, I'll leave him there to rot. You'll never find him."

"I need some time."

"I'll call back," the voice says. "And don't you dare go to the cops."

The line goes dead.

Nancy's heart is jackhammering in her chest. Tears fill her eyes. She paces the room for a moment, trying to process what is happening.

She considers not calling the police, trying to do this alone. Could she assemble that kind of money? Could she do what the caller asks in exchange for Stephen?

There is no guarantee that Stephen will be allowed to

live. She only has the kidnapper's word, and she can't trust him.

No, Stephen's best chance of survival is for her to call in the authorities.

She grabs the phone and dials the operator.

She clears her throat and says in as confident a voice as she can muster, "Please connect me to the FBI."

CHAPTER 23

IN THE LATE MORNING, Danny Edwards cruises down the residential street where Stephen and Nancy Small live. He is driving slowly, trying to look for anything suspicious, but also trying not to look suspicious himself. Everything seems normal. A man is trimming his lawn with a push mower. A teenager is riding his bike. An elderly woman is kneeling in a planter of flowers, clipping roses.

Danny pulls over near the Small house and pretends to consult a piece of paper. Really, he's looking around for evidence of law enforcement. He doesn't see any marked cars or uniformed officers. The Small house looks like it does any other day, except the blinds are pulled and there are no kids running around in the yard playing in the sprinkler.

Danny is about to put the van in drive when he sees one of the curtains shift. A man in a suit looks out, glances around, and then pulls the curtain shut again.

"Damn her," Danny growls, firing up the engine and speeding down the street. "That bitch called the goddamn cops."

Danny heads out of town, careful to make sure he isn't followed. He drives to the sand hills, finds the spot where Stephen Small pulled off the road last night, and follows the tire tracks.

The Mercedes is just where he left it, hidden in a cluster of bushes and trees. He keeps going and pulls up to the place he buried Stephen Small. It's easy to see that the dirt has been disturbed here, but because the air tube sticks out of the ground twenty feet away, Danny doesn't think anyone who might wander upon the spot would think that a person is buried alive down there.

He heads over to the place where the pipe is sticking out of the ground. The sunlight seems unusually bright and oppressive. The air is hot and humid. A mosquito buzzes around his ear, and he swats it away.

Danny leans over the tube sticking out of the ground and calls out, "Hang in there, man. This is almost over."

He stops and listens for Stephen Small to say something.

"Stephen, you in there, buddy?"

There is no response.

Danny opens his mouth to call out to Stephen again, but he hears something in the brush nearby. He freezes and stares. He sees no movement. Was it a bird? A rabbit?

Or something else?

You're just being paranoid, he tells himself. *Keep it together.*

He hurries back to his van and spins the tires in the sand trying to get out of there. When he gets to the blacktop, he keeps looking around, checking his rearview mirrors.

Is someone following him?

He doesn't see anyone who looks suspicious, but he just can't shake the feeling that he's being spied on.

Maybe this is how I'll feel the rest of my life, he thinks. *Like someone is after me.*

CHAPTER 24

September 3
5:00 p.m.

FOURTEEN HOURS AFTER SHE first talked to her husband's kidnapper, Nancy Small's phone begins to ring.

Everyone in the house—the Kankakee police, the FBI, her lawyer—all go quiet. One of the FBI agents gives Nancy a nod.

She looks at the recording device next to her phone, trying to remember how they told her to operate it. She presses the record button and slowly lifts the receiver.

"Hello," she says, attempting to sound as calm as possible.

"I told you not to call the cops," the voice on the other end growls. "Do you want your husband to die?"

Nancy inhales sharply. Tears spring to her eyes. She tells herself to remain calm.

"I have the money," she says coolly.

This statement seems to relax the man a bit.

"How much?" he says.

"All of it—one million," she says. "It's in hundreds and fifties, no sequential serial numbers. Just as you asked."

"I'll call you back with instructions," the man says.

One of the FBI agents gestures to Nancy with his hands: *Keep him on the phone.*

"I want to talk to my husband," Nancy says, her voice beginning to lose its composure for the first time.

"You called the police," the man snaps. "You messed everything up. It's more complicated now. I'll call you back."

"I want to talk to Stephen," she pleads, her voice breaking.

There's no answer. The line is dead.

Nancy Small lowers the phone to its cradle. Her hand is shaking. Her whole body is numb.

The head FBI agent in charge puts a gentle, reassuring hand on her shoulder.

"You did good," he says. "We traced the call."

Relief floods through Nancy's body.

The agents start frantically discussing what to do. The call came from a pay phone at a Phillips 66 gas station in Aroma Park, about thirty miles outside of Kankakee.

"I want four stakeout teams," the agent in charge says. "One for that gas station and three more for the closest pay phones. The next time the kidnapper makes a call, we're going to pounce on that son of a bitch."

CHAPTER 25

NANCY RISH AND DANNY EDWARDS are sitting on the couch, watching the rest of *Crocodile Dundee*. Nancy sneaks a glance at Danny, who can't sit still. He keeps looking toward the window and his leg keeps fidgeting. His skin seems flushed, and she can tell he isn't paying attention to the movie. His eyes might be looking at the TV screen, but his mind is a million miles away.

"Are you okay?" Nancy asks.

He doesn't say anything.

"Danny?"

"I'm fine," he snaps.

After a few minutes, the telephone rings, and Danny jumps out of his seat as if he's heard a gunshot.

"What is going on with you?" Nancy says, walking toward the phone stand. "Hello?" She holds the receiver to her chest and says to Danny, "It's Julie."

She sits down and begins talking to her friend. Julie

wants to know what her plans are for Labor Day weekend.

Danny's legs bounce restlessly. Finally, he bursts out of his seat and storms out of the house.

"Is Danny still acting weird?" Julie says.

"Weirder than ever," Nancy says.

After a long conversation about everything from Benji's school clothes to the weather, Nancy finally hangs up. She goes looking for Danny. He isn't anywhere in the house. She peeks into the garage and sees him pacing around. She opens her mouth to ask what he's doing when he spots her.

"Hey," he says, excited. "I've got an idea."

Nancy looks at him skeptically as he explains. Since Benji is at his dad's tonight, Danny says, they should take Nancy's bicycle over to his friend Jerry's house to get the brakes fixed.

"At this hour?"

"He's a night owl," Danny says. "He won't mind."

Without waiting for a response, Danny opens the garage door and wheels the ten-speed into the driveway.

"Let's take your car," he says. "We'll put the bike in the trunk."

Nancy steps out onto the driveway in bare feet. The night air is muggy. Danny is trying to wedge her bicycle into the trunk. The brakes haven't worked in months. Every time she mentioned getting the bike fixed to Danny, he said he had a friend who could do the work. But he never got around to calling him and asking for the favor. It seemed to be the lowest item on his priority list. She can't imagine why, at eleven o'clock tonight, he unexpectedly wants to get this done.

"Danny," she says, "what's really going on?"

Danny can't get the trunk closed, so he leaves it ajar, with the handlebars sticking out.

"I just want to go for a drive with my girl," he says. "And I thought we'd get an errand done while we're at it."

She purses her lips and folds her arms, trying with her body language to send the message that she doesn't believe a word he's saying.

"Nancy," he says, putting his hands on her shoulders. "I've told you a hundred times. I'm not dealing anymore. I've learned my lesson. I've got a second chance, and I'm not going to blow it."

Then he wraps his arms around her in a tight hug and adds, "Besides, I would never put you in a situation where you could get in trouble for something I've done. Trust me, okay?"

She doesn't answer. She wraps her arms around him and sinks into his embrace, and that says it all.

CHAPTER 26

NANCY DRIVES HER BUICK on the same route they'd gone the other day when they were looking at the scenery, and then again last night when she picked Danny up at three o'clock in the morning. Her bicycle is poking out of the open trunk, rattling around behind them.

Danny isn't talking. He's fidgeting in his seat, just as he was at home.

So much for our nice evening drive as a couple, Nancy thinks.

"Pull over here," Danny says. "Let me call Jerry, just to make sure it's okay if we swing by."

"You said he's a night owl."

"He is. I just want to make sure he's there."

Nancy eases the car into the gravel driveway of a bait shop, and she parks near the pay phone. She turns off the engine. There's no telling how long Danny will be.

Danny hops out and looks around. The shop is closed. There are signs in the windows written in Magic Marker advertising fresh worms and inexpensive fishing lures, but the store itself is dark. The neon Budweiser sign is turned off. The parking lot is lit only from a single street-light. There are no other cars in the lot. Danny looks up and down the road and sees no headlights. He listens and hears only crickets and the rustling of tree leaves.

He dials the number of Nancy Small.

"Hello," the woman says after two rings.

"Take Route 17 east," Danny says.

"What?" she says. "Wait. I want to talk to my husband."

Danny continues giving directions, telling her to leave the money by the railroad tracks where he had Nancy pick him up the other night. But the woman can't keep up and asks him to repeat what he said.

"Wait a minute," she says, her voice panicked. "I'm not getting this."

CHAPTER 27

AS NANCY SMALL PLEADS with her husband's kidnapper over the telephone, the police and FBI whisper to each other in the background.

"We've traced the call to Aroma Park," someone reports to the special agent in charge.

"We've heard from all four stakeouts," another agent says. "No one is using any of the phones."

"How is that possible?" someone asks.

"There must be another phone in the area."

The special agent in charge has a radio in his hand with a surveillance team on the other end.

"We spotted one more pay phone down the road," the surveillance officer says, his voice crackling through the radio.

"Go check it out," the agent in charge says. "Go, go, go!"

On the telephone, Nancy Small is still trying to make sure she understands the directions correctly.

"I'm not getting this," she says, panic overtaking her voice.

Then she hears another voice on the phone. It takes her a moment to realize it's her husband's voice, muffled and distorted again like it was the other night.

"If everything is okay," Stephen says, *"if he gets the money, he'll tell you where I'm buried. He seems serious."*

"I'm not doing this for nothing," the other voice says. Now it is distorted too. *"I'm not coming back to dig you up. If I don't get my money, you're dead."*

Nancy opens her mouth to call out to her husband, but before she can speak, the line goes dead.

She collapses to the floor, weeping loudly, relieved to know Stephen is still alive.

She doesn't realize that his voice was on a tape recorder.

CHAPTER 28

DANNY PRESSES STOP ON the tape player and hangs up the phone. His whole body feels tense. He turns back to the Buick, and just as he does, he sees a black sedan driving down the road. It has a large antenna sticking up from the trunk, and it looks a lot like an unmarked police car. Danny should know—he spent some time in them when he was working with the Kankakee drug-enforcement agents last winter.

"Goddammit," Danny mutters, and hurries to Nancy's car.

"Let's go," he says, practically shouting. "Come on. Come on!"

"Jeez," she says. "What's wrong with you?"

Danny doesn't answer.

The sedan slowly passes the bait shop. Once the car has passed, Danny watches as it attempts a three-point turn in the middle of the road.

"Was Jerry home?" Nancy asks.

"He can't do it," Danny snaps. "Go this way. Hurry up."

Nancy drives the Buick onto the road. Danny watches in the rearview mirror as the car begins to follow them. He checks and rechecks the mirror, squirming in his seat as if it's a bed of nails.

The car is behind them, its headlights far away but clearly visible. But then the car turns off the road, and the lights disappear.

Danny collapses into his seat.

"Sorry," he says. "It just seemed like that car was following us."

"You're being paranoid," Nancy says. "Why would anyone be following us?"

Danny has an idea. He sits up and rolls down his window and zips open the duffel bag.

"Keep your eyes on the road," he says to Nancy.

"What are you talking about?" she says, but she keeps her eyes forward, fixed on the yellow lines in the center of the road.

Danny pulls out the tape recorder and launches it out the window into the weeds. Then he rolls up the window and sinks back into his seat, exhaling loudly.

"Are you going to tell me what the hell is going on?" Nancy says.

"I'm telling you for the last time, Nancy. For your own good, stop asking so many goddamn questions."

Nancy says nothing more, just keeps driving. She doesn't know what Danny has gotten himself into—and doesn't want to know.

When she passes another gas station up on her left, there is a car sitting in the lot, waiting to pull out. When she passes the car, she looks out her window and, under a parking lot lamp, makes eye contact with a woman behind the wheel.

The car pulls onto the road behind Nancy's Buick and begins following them at a distance.

CHAPTER 29

NANCY SMALL SITS ON the couch, her legs pulled up underneath her, her arms wrapped tightly around her body. It's as if she's trying to become smaller, squeezing into as tiny a space as possible. The room is dark except for a pool of light cast by a reading lamp next to her. The windows in the room are curtained, but the darkness outside seems to press against the house. She can't wait for the sun to rise. Somehow she associates the dawn with an end to this nightmare she's living.

This is the couch she normally shares with her family. She sits on one end, Stephen the other, and the boys—all three of them—squeeze in between them. Now the couch is empty. She's in her normal spot, but the boys are staying with her parents. And Stephen...she doesn't know where Stephen is.

No one does.

At least no one besides his kidnapper.

Their house—their warm house that holds memories in every corner—is now full of FBI agents and police detectives.

It's the middle of the night, and no one has slept, least of all Nancy Small.

Her mind is a fog. To her, the men in suits are just blurs in the background. They move around doing whatever they're doing, but her mind is elsewhere.

She is trying to remember the last time she saw Stephen. He left in a hurry, running out of the house because he believed there had been a break-in at the B. Harley Bradley House. She can't remember if she said she loved him as he was walking out the door. Or if he said it to her.

It was their habit to say the words whenever they parted, but he'd been in such a hurry to get out the door, they might have forgotten.

It seems very important to remember whether she said it or not. She wants to remember Stephen's face as he said the words.

She shakes her head, trying to clear it of her spiraling thoughts.

But then she notices something is different in the house. The atmosphere has changed. The police officers are talking with more urgency, speaking into radios, discussing what to do. Their voices are louder as they call out ideas to each other.

Nancy wants to ask what's happening, but she feels paralyzed on the couch. How can she inquire about what's going on when she can't even rise to her feet?

Finally, the agent who seems to be in charge—she's forgotten his name—approaches her and sits gently on the couch next to her, where Ramsey usually sits. The FBI agent wears round glasses and has a paunch. He looks like a nice man, and, from the start, she has believed him when he told her that he will do everything he can to bring her husband home safe.

"Nancy," he says. "We've caught a break."

"Do you know where Stephen is?"

"Not yet," he says, "but we're getting close."

He explains that the surveillance teams spotted a car leaving the location where the telephone call was made. An undercover officer followed the car to a home in Kankakee.

"We've run the plates," he says. "Does the name Nancy Rish mean anything to you?"

Nancy is stunned for a moment—the absurdity that Stephen's kidnapper is a woman with the same first name as hers? Then she thinks hard, traveling through her mind looking for any reference to the name.

"No," she says. "I have no idea who that is."

"Well," the agent says, "we believe she is one of the kidnappers, working with at least one accomplice. We're assembling a SWAT team now. We're going to bring her down. If all goes well, we'll have Stephen home by dinner tomorrow."

Nancy feels her heart swell with hope. But then a cold needle pops her balloon of optimism, and she fills back up with apprehension.

The kidnapper said Stephen had forty-eight hours of air.

If he isn't home by dinner, as the agent suggested, then he'll soon be running out of oxygen.

CHAPTER 30

NANCY RISH IS DREAMING.

In the dream, Benji is graduating from high school. She is sitting in the stands with Danny. They're older. Danny's hair is going gray at the temples. She's put on a little bit of weight and has a few wrinkles around her eyes. But she's still pretty. And they are happy together.

There's a gold wedding band on Danny's ring finger and a pea-sized diamond on hers. As Benji takes the stage and receives his diploma, Danny reaches over and takes her hand. They smile. This is it: the life she always wanted.

Then a loud noise—like a car crashing into the house—jolts her awake. She sits up, trying to orient herself to where she is. She's in her bed. The room is dark, but the curtains of her window are pulled back, casting a bluish light into the room. The sun isn't up yet, but it's close. She can tell by the soft morning glow.

She feels for Danny in the space next to her. He's not there.

She hears yelling coming from downstairs. Lots of voices—deep and loud and full of authority. Danny's voice, defiant but scared, is mixed in with the other voices.

Nancy's first thought is that the drug dealers Danny used to work for have come for him and they're going to kill him.

She is frozen with fear, unable to get up.

She thinks of Benji. She must protect him. Then she remembers that he is at his father's.

Thank God, she thinks.

But her relief is short-lived. Loud footsteps stomp up the stairway. The bedroom door bursts open, slamming against the wall. Nancy jumps and lets out a short, clipped scream.

Two men step into the room. They're dressed in black, with combat boots and bullet-proof vests. Both are holding military rifles, and they aim them at Nancy's face.

"Danny!" Nancy screams.

She doesn't know what else to do.

She gets no answer from Danny.

Instead, one of the SWAT agents pulls her to her feet. He is forceful but doesn't hurt her.

"Ma'am," he says. "You can put on some clothes before we take you in."

Clothes? she thinks. *Take me in?*

She doesn't understand what is going on.

She looks down at herself and sees she's wearing Danny's T-shirt, the one she uses as a nightgown. She has no bra, no underwear.

She looks around the room, trying to find some clothes to wear. She grabs a pair of jeans lying on the floor. Then something out the window catches her eye.

She walks to the edge of the window and looks out. The road is filled with police cars. Blue and red lights flash in the dim morning light. Two officers dressed like the ones in her room are leading Danny across the lawn to a police vehicle. His hands are cuffed behind his back.

A female officer arrives in the bedroom and keeps an eye on Nancy as she gets dressed. Nancy pulls on the pair of jeans and puts on a blouse. The officer is wearing street clothes and her black hair is in a ponytail, but she has a pistol clipped to her belt. Nancy thinks she looks familiar. She just isn't sure from where.

Then it hits her like a bucket of cold water dumped over her head. She saw the woman last night driving the car that was behind them.

Danny was right. They were being followed. Now Nancy is more confused than ever.

"Can you at least tell me what's going on?" Nancy says.

The woman answers by instructing Nancy to put her hands behind her back. The woman clips on handcuffs and leads her down the stairs and into the yard. Blue and red lights flash from the police cars.

The garage door is open, and police are inside, looking around. One uniformed officer is standing before a man in a suit, showing him a sawed-off hunk of two-by-four and a short length of PVC tubing. Two plainclothes detectives are kneeling over Danny's duffel bag. They pull out a motorcycle helmet Nancy has never seen before. Then a pair of bolt cutters. A flashlight.

Finally, one man pulls out a pistol. He holds it between his thumb and forefinger, like it's something he doesn't want to touch.

"Someone tell me what's going on," Nancy says, practically shouting.

"As if you don't know," the female officer says, opening the back of a police cruiser and gesturing for her to get in.

CHAPTER 31

THEY PUT NANCY IN a room with cinder-block walls and into a cold metal chair in front of a stained metal table. On the other side is another chair that sits empty.

For now.

"I want to see Danny," she says. "I think we can clear up this misunderstanding if I can just see him."

Instead of answering, they slam the heavy steel door on her. She tries the handle.

Locked.

She settles into her chair. The room is so silent she can hear her own heartbeat. The room has a dankness to it, like an underground basement. The air has the faint sour smell of body odor. And perhaps there's the stink of urine.

Nancy doesn't know how long she can stand being in here. Panic starts to creep through her bloodstream.

Thank God Benji wasn't home, she thinks.

But this thought leads to another thought. She needs to get out of here before Benji comes home from his dad's. She wonders how long this will take before whatever has led to her mistaken arrest becomes clear.

She hears the bolt slide free, and the door swings open. She feels relieved to know they're not going to make her wait. That must be a good sign, right? That they're not going to make her sweat before talking to her?

But as the agents walk into the room, the expressions on their faces quell her relief. These men are tired and haggard, with loose ties and circles under their eyes.

The first man, who settles into the chair across from Nancy, has sideburns and a pair of circular eyeglasses. Under ordinary circumstances, he would probably look like a very nice man, but right now he looks like someone you wouldn't want to cross. The other man has a mustache and is going bald. Both men have five-o'clock shadows, and their suits hang from their bodies like they haven't been changed in a couple days.

"I'm going to make this really easy on you, Nancy," the one with the glasses says to her. "Where is Stephen Small?"

Nancy looks back and forth between him and the other man, who leans against the wall with his arms crossed.

"Who?" she says.

The agent slams his palm down on the metal table and makes Nancy jump.

"Don't play stupid with me!" he snaps. "A man's life is at stake. Don't you understand that?"

His actions are so rapid that his glasses slide down his nose. He pushes them back up the bridge of his nose with his index finger.

"Stephen Small?" Nancy says. "You mean the millionaire?"

"That's who you kidnapped, isn't it?"

"No, no, wait," Nancy says, shaking her head. "There's some kind of misunderstanding. Kidnapped? What is going on?"

Nancy knows who Stephen Small is, of course. He's one of the wealthiest people in town. He bought that antique mansion designed by Frank Lloyd Wright. Everyone in Kankakee has heard the name Stephen Small. But she's certainly never met him. And she doesn't understand what they're talking about.

He's been kidnapped?

And they think she had something to do with it?

The agent sitting at the table points toward the door and says, "Down that hall, there's a room just like this that Danny Edwards is sitting in. Before I came in here, I was talking to him. And when I'm done here, I'm going to go back. We're going to get the story out of one of you. And whoever cooperates is going to get some leniency from the judge."

"You think Danny kidnapped Stephen Small?" Nancy says.

The agent continues, as if he hasn't heard her. "Your boyfriend has a reputation around here. He's a snitch. I'm guessing that it's not going to take long for him to turn on you and try to save his own skin. If I were you, I'd start talking now."

"Can I see Danny?" Nancy asks. "I think we can clear this up if I could just—"

"So you two can get your stories straight? We're not stupid, Nancy."

"But you are," the other agent adds, "if you think you can get away with kidnapping a millionaire."

"I'm not trying to get away with anything."

"Why should we believe you, Nancy? You're driving around making ransom calls in the middle of the night—"

"No I'm not."

"—and you're living with a drug dealer."

"He's not a drug dealer. He's cleaned up his act. He's a carpenter now."

"Well, carpenters make a lot less than drug dealers, don't they?" the agent with the glasses says. "Money must be pretty tight right now. That can make people desperate, can't it?"

Nancy opens her mouth to speak but stops herself. She thinks of how strange Danny has been acting, how stressed out he's been.

She wonders if he could have something to do with what the police are talking about. But then she pushes the thought out of her mind. There is no way Danny could be involved in something like this.

Sure, he sold drugs in the past. He isn't perfect.

But kidnapping?

That isn't Danny. He is a good person, deep down.

"I asked you a question," the agent says forcefully.

Nancy snaps back to the present.

"What?" she says. "I'm sorry I didn't hear you."

"Did you or did you not stop at the bait shop in Aroma Park last night and make a phone call?"

"Sure," she says. "Danny made a call. He was calling his—"

"And the night before," the agent says, "where were

you at approximately three a.m.? You were making another phone call, weren't you?"

Nancy thinks. She can't keep pace with all that's happening. She remembers picking up Danny at the railroad crossing. She remembers him making a phone call.

But if they think he's mixed up in this, then she doesn't want to get him in any trouble. She wants desperately to talk to him.

I can't tell them anything, she thinks. *Not until I talk to Danny and figure out what's going on.*

"I was home," Nancy says.

"We know you're lying," the agent says with deadly earnestness. "And if you keep lying, the grave you're digging for yourself is only going to get deeper."

CHAPTER 32

September 4
7:00 p.m.

AFTER HOURS OF QUESTIONING—a whole day practically—they lead Nancy out of the room in handcuffs. She is hungry and tired. Her skin is clammy with sweat. She wishes she could go home, take a warm bath, and curl up in bed and sleep for about twelve hours.

Instead, they lead her down a narrow corridor to a series of jail cells. Once she's inside, they have her turn her back toward the bars so they can unlock her handcuffs.

"I want to see my son," she says, rubbing her wrists. "He needs his mother."

The agent with glasses glares at her.

"I'm sure Stephen Small wants to see his sons too," the agent says. "I'm sure his boys need their father."

With that, he turns and leaves. A female police officer in uniform remains standing outside the cell.

Nancy can't imagine why they think they need a guard posted outside her jail cell. She isn't a dangerous criminal. She isn't going to escape. But then she understands why the officer is there. They want someone nearby in case she decides to tell them something important.

She can't imagine what they think she might know.

There is a bed in the room, nothing more than a cot really, and a metal toilet with no seat. The cinder-block walls are painted a drab yellow. The room stinks like its last occupant didn't know what a shower was.

Nancy doesn't particularly want to touch the mattress— who knows who has slept on it?—but it's the only place to sit besides the floor, and she figures that must be even more gross.

She lies down. The thin mattress provides very little comfort. The wire springs press against her back.

She tries to ignore the discomfort and stares at the ceiling, thinking. This is the first opportunity she's had to really let her thoughts catch up with what's been happening. The FBI agents bombarded her with questions for hours. The only time they left her alone, she assumes, was when they were down the hall doing the same to Danny.

She thinks she stuck to her story, but they kept catching her in inconsistencies. She didn't want to tell them about picking Danny up at three o'clock in the morning or about any phone calls he made that night. But at first she told them she was sleeping and later said she was watching a movie.

It doesn't matter, she thinks. *Once they find Stephen Small and all of this gets sorted out, then I'll be free to go.*

She didn't do anything wrong. So this nightmare can't go on much longer. Can it?

She thinks of Danny, wherever he is. He must be scared too. She wishes she could comfort him.

But then she stops herself. It seems more and more clear that he's involved in this mess somehow. His behavior has been so weird lately. There was the box he built in the garage. The way he disappeared for hours in the middle of the night. The strange late-night drive to supposedly get her bike fixed. And the three a.m. pickup at the railroad tracks.

Danny's erratic behavior should have been a telltale sign that he was up to something. The way he snapped at her. The way he almost hit her. The way his mind has seemed a million miles away for the past few days.

Nancy thinks that he must have been roped into being involved. Maybe the drug dealer he used to work for coerced him because Danny still owed him money. Maybe other past associates tricked Danny.

This couldn't be Danny's idea.

But then she remembers him sitting in the kitchen, next to Benji, drawing designs on paper. He wouldn't tell her what he was building. But it had been him who built the strange box in the garage, him who drew the designs, him who went to the lumberyard and bought supplies.

Danny wasn't following anyone's orders, doing anyone else's bidding.

Now Nancy's mind turns to Benji and the memory of him sitting next to Danny, drawing pictures. She'd liked the sight of the two of them together. She remembers thinking that Danny could be a good father figure for Benji.

Could she have been that wrong about him? She has the desperate need to see her son, to hold him in her arms.

When I get out of this mess, she thinks, *I'm going to be the best mother I can possibly be.*

She vows to love him and hold him and stay away from any bad influences.

She'll stay away from men like Danny, she swears to herself.

She suddenly recognizes how stupid she's been, lying to protect Danny. Her concern should be for Benji. She needs to get out of here. She needs to be with her son. Let Danny worry about himself. She needs to worry about her child.

Down the hall from her jail cell, Nancy hears a commotion. Urgent voices. The female officer posted outside her cell glances Nancy's way, then heads down the hall to find out what is happening.

Wait, Nancy thinks. *I'm ready to tell the truth.*

CHAPTER 33

DANNY EDWARDS SITS IN an interrogation room similar to the one Nancy was questioned in. His eyes are bloodshot, with dark circles underneath. He doesn't know how long the questioning has gone on, but they've finally given him a break.

And a cigarette.

He takes a drag. The room is so quiet he can hear the flame eating away at the paper and tobacco. He tilts his head back and exhales a long stream of smoke that puddles against the ceiling, creating a hazy cloud around the yellow fluorescent bulbs.

Danny isn't worried. He hasn't told them anything. He's denied everything. He knows they know he is lying, but he also knows how the police and FBI work. Just because they know he did it doesn't mean they can prove he did it. It doesn't matter if there are inconsistencies in his stories or if they know he's lying.

They have no evidence.

He's worked the police before, and he'll work them again this time. He knows he holds the cards here. He isn't going to tell them anything they need to know—not unless there's something in it for him.

He hears the bolt being pulled back on the other side of the door. The agent who was questioning him earlier, the one with glasses, swings the door open and looks in at Danny.

"The clock is ticking, Danny. What side of this thing do you want to be on?"

Danny stubs the cigarette out on the table. He flicks it into the corner defiantly.

"How many times do I have to tell you?" he says, shaking his head. "I don't know what you're talking about."

The agent steps inside. He leaves the door to the interrogation room hanging open behind him. A uniformed police officer stands behind him, so it's not as if Danny can escape, but still this is something different. Something has changed. They're not coming in for another marathon round of questioning. This is going to be quick.

Maybe Danny doesn't hold all the cards after all.

The FBI agent holds up a police radio and rotates the volume knob so Danny can hear it. Static crackles, and voices talk back and forth.

"...all available units..."

"...Pembroke County..."

"...Mercedes matching the description..."

"...keep the plane in the air until we get officers in the area..."

"...let's try to find it before the sun goes down..."

The agent turns the volume back down, then leans close to Danny's face and says coolly, "An airplane with infrared sensors found Stephen Small's missing Mercedes, Danny. I'm guessing Stephen is stashed somewhere nearby. We're getting closer. If you want any chance of leniency, you better cooperate now."

Danny sits back, takes a deep breath. All day he's been calm, but now his limbs start to tremble.

The agent says, "On the phone, you said Stephen had forty-eight hours of air. We're approaching forty-eight hours, Danny. Kidnapping is a serious charge, but it's not the same as murder. If this thing turns into murder, you're looking at the death penalty."

Danny tries to swallow, his throat suddenly very dry.

He's been wrong all day. He has no cards in his hands. He's only been bluffing. It's time to fold.

"Okay," Danny says. "I'll take you to him."

CHAPTER 34

NANCY STANDS AT THE bars of her cell, trying to look down the hallway. She can't see anything, but she hears commotion. Lots of voices and static from the police radio. She hasn't been able to make out everything, but she understands enough. The police are going somewhere. They think they know where Stephen Small is being kept prisoner.

A knot of people begins walking down the hall toward Nancy's cell. A group of cops and FBI agents are clustered around Danny. He is in handcuffs. His head is hanging low.

"Danny," Nancy says, her voice a whisper full of fear. "What's happening?"

Danny looks up at her.

"I'm sorry, honey," he says. "I didn't mean to hurt anyone."

As he passes by, she stares at him. The yellow lighting makes his skin look pallid, his hair greasy, his eyes red with burst capillaries. More than just his appearance disgusts her. The way he carries himself, as if he doesn't care what's going on, as if all of this is some kind of inconvenience to *him*. His apology to her lacked any sort of conviction in its tone. He's not sorry.

She sees him in a way she's never seen him before.

He's a thug.

A selfish, no-good narcissist who only cares about himself.

A criminal who would rather sell drugs than get a job.

How could she have ever fallen for him?

Tears fill her eyes as Danny and the rest of his entourage disappear down the hall. Nancy turns her head and the woman cop returns and stands outside the jail cell.

There is no sympathy in the woman's face.

"You better hope they find Stephen Small alive," the woman says. "If he's not, you're going to get the electric chair."

"But I didn't know," Nancy says, sobbing.

"They shave your head, you know," the woman says. "So your hair doesn't catch on fire."

Nancy collapses to the floor, weeping. She hears the woman's boots retreat down the hallway, leaving her alone with her tears.

"I want to see my son," she wails.

Her cries echo down the empty hallway.

No one is listening.

CHAPTER 35

"STOP HERE," DANNY SAYS.

The FBI agent driving the car pulls to a stop and puts the vehicle in park. They are in the sand hills outside of Kankakee. The sun is low in the sky, coating the clouds in red and casting a pink, bloody hue onto the sandy ground.

The driver and the agent in the passenger seat get out. The one with the glasses opens the back door of the sedan for Danny, who steps out. His hands are cuffed.

The irony is not lost on Danny that two days ago he was the one leading a handcuffed man down this same path.

This time, instead of just Danny and Stephen Small, Danny is joined by an entire contingent of FBI agents, police, paramedics. There are people all around him, waiting for him to take them to the place where he buried Stephen Small.

"This way," Danny says.

He walks through the sandy soil.

Danny's stomach is knotted, as if someone has taken his intestines and twisted them into a tight ball.

Off to his left, Danny hears a crunch. He pauses and looks over. One of the cops lifts his shoe and looks down. Beneath his foot is a crushed pair of eyeglasses.

The glasses that had fallen off Stephen Small's face.

"Hurry up," one of the agents says, shoving Danny forward.

Danny continues until he spots the PVC pipe sticking out of the ground.

"There," he says.

From the tube sticking out of the ground, it's easy to see the disturbed segment of ground where the rest of the pipe is located, leading to a large swath of disturbed earth.

"He's buried down there," Danny says, then adds, "I gave him food and water."

Officers come in with shovels and get to work. One of the agents leans over the pipe and calls to Stephen Small.

"Mr. Small, it's the police," he shouts. "We're almost there. Just wait a little while longer."

There's no answer.

Danny stands back. His heart hammers in his chest.

He remembers pointing the gun at Stephen Small and the fear he saw on the man's face. Later, when Stephen didn't want to get into the box, Danny had assured him he would live.

Danny had believed his own words.

The cops work furiously, throwing shovelfuls of dirt. Several of them are digging, but the work is slow.

Hurry up, Danny thinks. *Hurry.*

Finally, one of the shovels strikes wood. The officers double their efforts, trying to clear the lid.

"Hang in there, Mr. Small!" one of the agents shouts.

They get enough room around the edge of the box, and an officer kneels and wedges his fingers underneath the lid. He pulls up, and the still partially buried plywood groans under the weight.

Then he pries the lid open so everyone can see inside.

CHAPTER 36

STEPHEN SMALL IS LYING in a curled ball, like a fetus.

He isn't moving.

An EMT kneels down next to him, placing two fingers on his neck, searching for a pulse from the carotid artery. Another EMT leans next to the hole, ready to help.

After only a few seconds, the EMT closest to Stephen looks at the agent in charge and shakes his head.

"He's dead," the EMT says.

Danny's legs go wobbly. He feels like he could throw up. He begins taking deep breaths—long and slow—trying to get himself under control.

Then it occurs to him. What he's doing—breathing deeply—was exactly what Stephen Small couldn't do. Danny had buried a man underground and he had suffocated.

The EMTs step away from the hole, and a new process begins. This is no longer a rescue mission—it is a homicide scene. Detectives begin photographing the body. Others start taping off the perimeter.

The agent in charge approaches Danny. He's furious. Danny can tell by looking at him. But there's something else in his expression too. Sadness. They've solved the crime, but it's too late. There's no satisfaction in the resolution, only anger and sorrow and confusion about why this had to happen at all.

The agent takes Danny by the arm and leads him close to the grave.

"Take a good look," the agent says. "I want you to see what you've done."

Stephen Small's skin is gray. His milky eyes are vacant, staring at nothing. His loafers are in the corner of the box, and his bare feet are contorted with the toes curled up. Up until this moment, Danny had thought perhaps the EMTs were wrong. He had thought there was still a chance that Stephen Small might sit up, yawn, and look around with sleepy eyes.

But seeing the body this close, there is no mistaking it. A dead man looks different from someone who's sleeping. There is no air inflating his lungs. There is no blood pulsing through his veins.

Stephen Small is not asleep.

The man Danny kidnapped is gone forever.

Another officer approaches them, holding up a length of PVC pipe.

"This diameter is way too narrow for how long it is," the agent says to his colleague. "There was no way for him to expel his carbon dioxide out of the box. And no way to pull in adequate oxygen from the outside. We'll have to wait on the autopsy, but judging by the rigor mortis, I'd say he's been dead for at least a day. I doubt he survived more than a few hours with this ridiculous contraption."

The agent looks at Danny. "He might have been dead before you ever made the first phone call to request a ransom."

With that, the agent walks away, getting back to work.

"What made you think he had forty-eight hours of air?" the agent in charge asks Danny.

Danny stares at the body of Stephen Small.

"I don't know what I was thinking," Danny says, and it seems to him that it's a blanket statement that could describe the ill-conceived air pipe as well as the whole kidnapping scheme. It is a statement that might encompass his entire life, practically every decision he has ever made.

I don't know what I was thinking.

"How does it feel to be a murderer?" the agent asks Danny.

"I never meant to kill him," Danny says. "I'm no murderer."

"Even now," the agent says, gesturing to the body, "you're unwilling to take responsibility for your actions. Unbelievable. You, Danny Edwards, are the most reprehensible human I've ever met."

Danny doesn't argue.

"You *and* your accomplice," the agent adds.

"Accomplice?" Danny says.

CHAPTER 37

NANCY IS BACK IN the interrogation room.

It's late at night. Earlier today, she told the female police officer that she needed to talk to someone, but hours passed before the woman led her down the hall, back to the interrogation room.

The agent in charge is already there, waiting.

His tie and suit jacket are gone, and his collar, now open, has yellowed with sweat and dust. His hair is disheveled, and his eyes have dark crescent moons beneath them. Despite how exhausted he obviously is, his expression is as alert as when she first spoke to him.

"I'm ready to tell you everything I know," Nancy says. "I didn't do anything and I didn't know what Danny was up to."

The agent gives her a look that silences her.

"We found Stephen Small," he says.

"Good," she says. "Thank God."

"He's dead."

"Oh no," she says. "That's awful."

"When you and Danny concocted this scheme, whose idea was it?"

Nancy stares at him, dumbfounded.

"I told you," she says. "I had no—"

"Yeah, yeah," the agent says. "You just happened to go for a ride with Danny late at night to get your bicycle fixed. And then he called the guy and it turned out he couldn't fix the bike after all. You expect us to believe that?"

"It's the truth," she says, and then clarifies, "That's what Danny told me anyway."

The agent leans in and puts his elbows on the table. His glasses have gotten progressively dirtier as the day has gone on, and he stares at her through smudged lenses.

"Okay," he says. "Let's talk about the truth. Danny told us that you picked him up after he buried Stephen Small alive."

Nancy goes cold.

"That's true," she says quietly.

"So you knew he was burying Stephen Small out in the sand hills?"

"No!" she says, practically yelling. "I picked him up. I didn't know what he was doing."

The agent smirks and shakes his head disapprovingly.

Nancy knows how ridiculous it sounds. She picked Danny up late at night in the middle of nowhere, and the agent is supposed to believe she didn't know what she was doing there. She can hardly believe it herself. What was she thinking trusting Danny?

"You told us before that you were sleeping. Oh, wait."

He consults his notes. "You told us you were watching a video. Oh, wait, you told us both lies."

"I'm sorry," she says, flustered, unsure what more to say.

"Which is it?" the agent says. "Were you sleeping? Watching a video? Or helping your drug-dealing boyfriend commit felony kidnapping?"

"No," Nancy blurts out. "None of those."

"So what's your story now?"

Nancy takes a deep breath.

"I picked Danny up," she says. "I didn't know what he was doing. I didn't want to know. If I had any idea he was kidnapping someone, I never would have gone along. I would have run as far away from him as I could."

"Lady," the agent says, "you should have gotten as far away from him as you could a long time ago. But you didn't. You knew he was a drug dealer and you stayed with him. Why would I believe you didn't know about this?"

The agent rises and clears his throat.

"Nancy Rish, you are under arrest for the kidnapping and murder of Stephen Small. You have the right to remain silent—"

"No," Nancy says, tears spilling down her cheeks. "I didn't do anything."

"Yes, you did," the agent says. "You helped Danny Edwards kidnap and murder Stephen Small."

He continues reciting the Miranda rights, but Nancy doesn't hear him. She's too preoccupied crying. She puts her head in her hands and sobs.

She can think of only one thing.

Her son growing up without a mother.

CHAPTER 38

10 years later

NANCY SITS IN THE visitation area of the Logan Correctional Center. Around her, other women, all wearing the same prison-issued jumpsuits, wait for their family members. Husbands enter and hug their wives. Sons and daughters come in and either embrace their mothers or sit down in a huff, glaring at the women.

Nancy knows some of the women. Others are just faces in the halls of the prison. Some of them are nice; others are mean. Some are tough and scary, and others cry at night, weeping for what they've lost.

Nancy keeps craning her head toward the entrance. She is especially anxious today. She always expects him to look younger than he is, as if time will have stopped on the outside world while she's been locked away. She expects an eight-year-old boy to run and leap into her arms like she's just been away for the weekend. But then the real Benji strides in—a man now, no longer a boy—

wearing a button-down shirt and tie. Today, he holds a black square object in his hand and grins sheepishly.

Nancy's mouth bursts into a wide, uncontrollable smile. Tears pool in her eyes.

"I did it, Mom," Ben says, holding out the object.

It's the cap from his graduation regalia, complete with a yellow tassel marked with the words *Class of '97*.

She throws her arms around his neck and grips him in a tight hug.

"I'm proud of you," she says, unable to keep herself from crying. "I wish I could have been there."

"Me too," he says, and begins to cry too.

A guard walks toward their table and tells them to separate. Wiping her eyes, Nancy sits. Ben does too. She wants to hold his hand, but that is against the rules also. It's hard to sit this close to him and not touch him, but she'll try to sneak another hug before he leaves.

Ben tells her about the graduation ceremony, which fills her with joy and sadness. She wants to hear all about it, but hearing him speak of the ceremony—a milestone event in his life that she couldn't be there for—is also like pressing on a bruise that never heals.

She's been locked up for ten years, and still the frustration over her powerlessness never ebbs, never weakens. She can't be there for her son and can't imagine a more painful way to live her day-to-day life.

Inevitably, as it does every time Ben visits, their conversation turns to the status of her appeals. Her lawyer is getting ready to file the papers, she says.

Nancy was sentenced to life in prison for murder, with another thirty years tacked on for aggravated kidnapping. In short, she is supposed to spend the rest of her life behind bars, without the possibility of parole. If she can't overturn her conviction, she will die in prison of old age.

It could have been worse. Because the murder was committed during the act of a felony, the crime qualified for the death penalty. That's the sentence Danny Edwards received.

There is a rumor going around that the state plans to abolish the death penalty, which would commute Danny's sentence to life in prison without parole, essentially the same as Nancy's.

But Nancy is confident that her appeal will overturn her conviction.

It has to. She's already missed her son's childhood. She doesn't want to miss the rest of his life.

"I promise you," Nancy says, reaching out and breaking the rules by grabbing his hand, "I will spend however long it takes to get out of here. I will come home to you."

Ben takes this cue to hug her. When a security guard heads their way, they split up and Ben heads for the door, holding his graduation cap at his side.

Tears streak Nancy's cheeks.

As she heads back to her cell, she thinks about what landed her here. Not the murder of Stephen Small, but what she is actually guilty of—blindly loving the wrong man.

She thinks about Danny and wonders where he is. She imagines him sitting in a cell, thinking somehow that he is a victim in all this. It wasn't fair he couldn't make ends meet. It wasn't fair other people had so much money. It wasn't fair that Stephen Small died from asphyxiation when Danny never actually wanted to hurt him. Danny always blamed everyone else.

She wonders if Danny feels any guilt for the lives he destroyed. Not just those of Stephen Small and his family.

But her life too.

She settles back into her cell and sits down on the bunk. Her cell is similar to the first one she was locked in all those years ago: metal toilet, metal sink, cinder-block walls. It makes her long for the leaking dishwasher and chipped paint of her old town house.

The cell also has a small desk in the corner, and taped above it are pictures that Ben has sent her over the years. She missed his first day of middle school, his first day of high school. She wasn't there for him when he was getting ready for prom. She didn't help him study for his SATs. She won't be there to see him off to college.

So much has been taken from her.

It isn't fair, she thinks.

Then she stops herself and wonders for a moment if she is just like Danny, putting all the blame on someone else.

She knew Danny was up to something. She didn't know it was kidnapping. She didn't know it was murder. But she knew something bad was happening, and she went along with it. She wasn't just ignorant of what happened. She *chose* ignorance despite warning sign after warning sign.

A man died.

A wife lost her husband.

Three boys lost their father.

Could she have stopped this from happening if she'd done anything differently? Could she have at least protected herself and her son by getting as far away from Danny as possible?

What could she have done differently?

She lies down on her bunk and stares at the ceiling, thinking.

She won't come to any answers today, nor anytime soon. As she looks around her prison cell, she knows there will be plenty of time to ponder these questions.

Finally honest with herself, Nancy Rish knows she will be in prison for a long, long time.

MURDER IN PARADISE

JAMES PATTERSON
with CHRISTOPHER CHARLES

PROLOGUE

1990

A FLASH OF COLOR broke in on her dream and startled her awake.

I knew I shouldn't have had that second Vodka Collins, Bonnie thought.

Hard alcohol always made her jumpy, restless. She rolled onto her side, shut her eyes, felt a faint mountain breeze coming through the cracked window.

But then she heard what sounded like a man clearing his throat, and she knew it was this sound, and not her dream, that had woken her. The noise hadn't come from the man lying beside her, who wasn't so much asleep as passed out, but from somewhere farther off in the room. She sat up, reached for the lamp on her nightstand.

"Don't bother," the intruder said. "This will be over real quick."

Bonnie's first instinct was to pull the covers up around her neck. She looked toward the voice and squinted. A large silhouette emerged from the darkness. She couldn't be sure, but she thought the man was smiling. Maybe this was a joke. Another prank being played by one of the patrons from the bar.

"I don't know who you are, but this isn't funny," Bonnie said. "In fact, it's criminal. If you're still here by the time I switch this light on, I will press charges."

Her own words sounded strange to her, like she'd borrowed the phrasing from her schoolmarm mother. Maybe, she thought, that's how people cope with terror: by channeling someone else.

"He don't wake easy," the intruder said, gesturing to the other side of the bed with what Bonnie now saw was a long-barreled revolver. "Must be all that Jack D," he added.

So he had been watching them at the bar. Another local who didn't want an Orange County developer — especially a female developer — scooping up property on *their* mountain. She would just have to show them that she was here to stay, that she hadn't bought Camp Nelson Lodge on a whim: she'd fallen in love with the place. She sat up straighter, reached for the light. The porcelain base of the lamp seemed to explode before she heard the shot. She screamed, slammed her back flat against the wall.

The man beside her stirred, then came fully awake. He threw the covers back, swung his legs out of bed, and stumbled forward, still drunk. A second shot and he staggered, grabbed the dresser, brought it down on top of him.

The room went silent just long enough for Bonnie to realize she was going to die. Somehow the setting felt all wrong. Or rather the setting was right, but the timing was wrong. She was supposed to finish raising her kids here.

Grow old here. Spend her waning years sharing the back-woods with her grandchildren.

She tried to call for help but couldn't find the air inside her. The man raised his gun. Bonnie shut her eyes.

It was over.

CHAPTER 1

1989

"WE DROVE FIVE HOURS and he's the one who's late?" Jim said.

"By five minutes," Bonnie said. "Besides, the drive along that gorge was as beautiful as anything I've ever seen."

"Made me carsick."

Bonnie climbed atop the picnic table and turned in a slow circle, craning her neck to see the tops of the sequoias, taking deep breaths of mountain air. Jim sat on the bench, brushed a pine needle from the flannel shirt he'd worn to blend in with the locals.

"I feel like the Marlboro Man," he said.

Bonnie didn't hear him, or at least pretended not to. Jim scanned the property. With its stone façade, the lodge appeared sturdy enough, but the two-story motel looming in the background looked like it might topple from one well-placed kick, and the small cabins, set at random distances along the periphery of the main clearing, were bordering on disrepair. Nestled among the world's tallest trees, with the Sierra Nevada rising to the east, it was, as Bonnie said, a beautiful spot. But there were a lot of beautiful places in the world, and Jim didn't see the point in anchoring yourself to just one.

"That must be Rudy," Bonnie said, nodding at the short, squat man exiting the main building.

"About time," Jim said.

"Shush now," Bonnie told him.

Rudy waved as he walked toward them. Jim stood, looked at his watch.

"Mr. and Mrs. Hood?" Rudy called.

Bonnie nodded.

"Welcome to Camp Nelson Lodge. I'm really sorry about the wait. The plumbing in the lodge got cranky. I'm not going to lie: that happens pretty regular these days."

Bonnie shook his hand, then turned to Jim: "You see? I told you we're blessed to have a realtor who doesn't work Sundays. We're going to get the inside story."

Now that Rudy was up close, Jim noticed a fresh grease stain running across the man's ratty polo shirt. Rudy had muscular forearms, a barrel chest, and a gut that suggested long nights in the saloon. His salt-and-pepper hair was in bad need of a shampooing. Jim pegged him as a ne'er-do-well: a middle-aged man who'd attached himself to a near-vacant lodge in order to keep a roof over his own lazy head.

"What exactly do you do here again?" Jim asked.

"I'm the caretaker."

Jim glanced around.

"No offense," he said, "but it doesn't look like you've been busy."

Bonnie gave him a sharp jab with her elbow.

"It's okay," Rudy said. "More honesty: I'm a staff of one with no budget. I've been hoping someone would come along and sink some money into this place."

"Sink?" Jim asked.

Rudy grinned.

"I mean invest," he said. "Look around. There isn't another parcel of land like this one anywhere in the world. Every morning I step outside and I remember that life is a miracle. If I had kids, I'd raise 'em right here."

"Maybe you *should* have been a realtor," Jim said.

"Nah," Rudy said. "I'm not trying to sell you anything. Truth is, it's sad what's happened to Camp Nelson Lodge. It used to be bustling with city folks whose souls needed a rest. They'd show up looking like they'd been wound so tight their nerves were snapping, and within a couple of days you'd see all that tension just leave their bodies. This place can be magic that way. But now it's just part of the Edwards Group's portfolio, and they've let it rot. We haven't taken a guest in two years. The saloon is still open for locals, but that's it. Like I said, I've been praying Edwards'd sell. I'd buy the place myself if I had the money."

"I used to come here with my parents when I was a kid," Bonnie said. "I never stopped dreaming about the sequoias. You're right: Camp Nelson is magical."

Rudy gave a solemn nod; Jim sniggered.

"I'd settle for functional," Jim said.

* * *

Rudy took them on a tour, beginning with the lodge. The lobby was a long, open space with twin stone fireplaces, one at either end. The ceiling beams were made of solid logs ("This is a logging community," Rudy pointed out), and the floor of ceramic tile. The walls were covered with unfinished wood panels, which Jim thought gave an otherwise stately room the look of a semifinished basement.

"It's real wood, Jim," Bonnie said, "not laminate."

The dining room/meeting hall featured wraparound windows and looked onto a small meadow separated from the forest by a stream.

"The view's not bad—I'll give you that. But even my grandmother wouldn't have put up with this wallpaper," Jim said.

"You can change the wallpaper," Bonnie said. "The view is for keeps."

Jim rapped on one of the windows with his knuckle.

"You'll have to change these, too, if you plan to be open for ski season," he said.

Rudy seemed amused by their back and forth. He led them out the back door and on to the motel. With its wooden shingles and log pillars it looked exactly like the saloon-hotel combo from countless Western flicks. There were signs of termites on the porch, and the foyer smelled of mold. The doors to the large but utterly bare rooms all hung open.

"Nothing for folks to steal," Rudy said. "Might as well air the place out."

Jim started to say something, then stopped when he noticed his wife smiling like a little girl on a trampoline.

"I have such incredible memories of this place," she said, then turned and ran up the stairs.

Jim and Rudy followed. They found her standing on a rickety balcony, staring out at a large, overgrown meadow.

"They used to stage Civil War reenactments there," she said. "Afterwards, there'd be a Southern-themed buffet."

"I hope you'll let that tradition lie," Jim said.

Rudy chuckled. Once again, Bonnie didn't seem to hear.

CHAPTER 2

RUDY WALKED THEM THROUGH the cabins, which were more like the skeletons of cabins, and then on to the bar: a standalone log structure situated on the access road to the resort. There was an unpaved parking area out front. Jim pointed to crisscrossing, single-tire tracks.

"Bikers?" he asked.

Rudy rolled his eyes.

"Harleys are the loggers' vehicle of choice up here," he said. "No gangs, though, if that's what you're worried about. But I won't lie: it's noisy at closing time."

He dug out his keys and led them inside. It was more saloon than bar, with swinging half-doors, sawdust covering the floor, and nothing hanging on the walls save a silver-framed mirror above the shelves of whiskey. The wooden tables and hardback chairs seemed, like the cabins, to be arranged in no particular order.

"This place turns a profit?" Jim asked.

"There's a small crowd most nights—bigger on week-ends. The Edwards Group isn't getting rich off it, but I'd guess they're breaking even. They'd have cut bait before now if they weren't."

Bonnie walked up to the bar, ran her fingers along the zinc.

"This is vintage," she said. "Real mahogany. With a little polish and elbow grease, it might be worth some-thing."

"A diamond in the rough," Rudy said.

He smiled. Bonnie smiled back. The exchange both-ered Jim: it was like watching adolescents bond over some pop band he'd never heard of.

"So what do you think?" Rudy asked when they were back outside.

"You know what I think," Bonnie said, still smiling.

"We'll get back to you," Jim told him.

* * *

"I've been developing other people's properties for up-wards of twenty years," Bonnie said. "I want a project of my own."

They'd left Rudy and were following the Camp Nelson Trail through a forest of giant Sequoias and mountain streams. Despite the mild temperature and perfect blue sky, they had the trail all to themselves.

"Okay, but why *this* project?" Jim asked.

"Why? Just look at these mountains, Jim."

"Just look at that property. One well-placed kick and half those buildings would fall right over."

"We came here every summer when I was a kid. You know that."

"So you're nostalgic?"

"Look, I know the lodge has been in decline for years, but you couldn't ask for better bones. Just imagine what this place *could* be. Hiking, horseback riding, swimming, fishing—it's all right here. We'll replace those old, rickety mattresses with waterbeds, give each cabin a private sauna. And we'll bring that god-awful bar into the twentieth century."

"The locals seem to like that god-awful bar. You heard your caretaker friend: it's the only thing keeping the place afloat."

"They'll learn to like the new one, too. Just think what a day could be like up here. Think about breakfast at altitude. Stacks of homemade pancakes and fresh fruit and those venison sausages you like. And after breakfast, a nice stroll into the mountains while the air is still cool and the deer are active."

"I'd rather sleep in and go for brunch. You know, there's something to be said for museums and concert halls."

Bonnie stopped midstride, gave him a pointed look.

"Really? How many symphonies have you seen in the last year?"

"I'm thinking about our kids."

"So am I. I don't want them to grow up all urban and neurotic, like me."

"They're only halfway through the school year."

"So they'll finish it out. I'll stay up here, get the place ready. We can talk on the phone every night. You guys'll visit on weekends. That way they get a slow introduction to the place. Think about it. It's a dream life."

They came to a small footbridge, paused to look at the stream below, then stood facing each other, leaning against opposite railings.

"We've got two healthy kids and all the money we could ever spend," Jim said. "I thought we were living our dream life."

"Maybe *you* were."

"What does that mean?"

"This place is the first thing I've asked for—the first thing I've really wanted in all the time we've been married. You, on the other hand—you get everything your heart desires and I never say boo about it."

"Like what?"

"How about that little trip to Spain with your buddies so you could run with the bulls on your forty-fifth birthday? Without me, of course."

"I was gone a week."

"Okay. What about your little trek through the Amazon? Also no wives allowed."

"Again, that was two weeks, not the rest of our lives."

Bonnie rolled her eyes, sucked in a deep breath.

"The point is you needed those trips to get through your midlife crisis, or whatever it was. And I let you have them. Well, I need this. I'm not saying you have to give up the place in Newport, but I *need* this. Our marriage needs this."

Jim started to object, then stopped himself. He bent down, picked up a rock, turned it over in his palm like a prospector appraising the soil.

"I guess it's settled then," he said.

CHAPTER 3

1990

BONNIE SAT FLIPPING THROUGH a wildflower guide on a brand-new porch swing outside the Camp Nelson Lodge, glancing up anxiously at the road. It was only five days since she last saw her husband and children, but it felt longer. It felt like they belonged to another life, maybe another lifetime—back when she drove a Lexus instead of a Jeep, back when all she could see from her porch was a cluster of suburban mansions and lawns decorated with hydrangeas and plastic flamingos. She didn't miss her lawn, didn't miss anything at all about the 'burbs. It may have taken her forty-seven years, but she'd finally landed where she was meant to be.

She spotted Jim's Mercedes, tossed aside her book, and ran to greet her children. Jim Jr., who'd just turned thirteen, was asleep in the front passenger seat, his mouth hanging open. He'd never in his short life been able to stay awake in a moving vehicle, and Bonnie was already worried about the prospect of him one day getting his license. The car pulled closer, and she saw eleven-year-old Mindy in the back seat, too engrossed in her *Illustrated Mythology* to look up. Bonnie knew this was a snapshot of the last five hours in her family's life: Jim listening to talk radio, making snarky comments about the hosts and callers; Jim Jr. snoring away with his head slouched against the window; Mindy quietly reading, tracing the pictures with her fingers. It was like Bonnie might as well have made the trip with them.

Jim was the first out of the car.

"You're looking a little crunchier every week," he said, referring to her leather hiking boots, her long ponytail, the beaded necklace he'd never seen her wear before.

"Nice to see you, too," she said, giving him a peck on the cheek. "Maybe you'd better wake up Rumpelstiltskin."

Jim banged on the hood of the car with an open palm.

"Hey, buddy, come on now," he called.

Jim Jr. raised his head, looked around, seemed to want to retreat back into his dream. Mindy ran up and grabbed her mother around the waist.

"It's so beautiful here, Mommy," she said.

"There's my girl," Bonnie said, giving her daughter a squeeze. "God, I missed you."

And Bonnie realized that this was true. She'd had her hands full looking after the guests, renovating the final cabin, supervising the bar, fitting in the occasional hike—but beneath all of that there had been an ache. The nightly phone calls weren't cutting it: she wanted her children there with her. *Soon enough*, she thought. Only a few months left in the school year.

She leaned into the backseat, the smell of bubblegum

momentarily replacing the smell of pine, and pulled out Mindy's duffel bag. When she turned around, Rudy was standing there. He reached for the bag, and she felt his hand on hers, felt it linger there a beat too long. Bonnie spun her head, found Jim lifting luggage from the trunk. Oblivious.

* * *

Once the family had unpacked and settled in, they gathered in the dining room around two extra-large ice cream sundaes.

"So what do you kids think?" Bonnie asked. "Maybe some kayaking later? Or a hike?"

Jim cut in before they could answer.

"I'm anxious to baptize that new in-ground pool," he said.

"You hate swimming," Bonnie said.

"Yeah, but I like sitting in a lounge chair with a gin and tonic in my hand."

"Swimming!" Mindy said. "I want to go swimming."

Jim Jr. nodded enthusiastically.

"All right," Bonnie shrugged. "Swimming it is."

She shot her husband a pointed look. She was sure he'd prepped them. For Bonnie, the pool was the least interesting part of the property—the only part you could find back in "civilization," as Jim called it. She'd only had one installed because it seemed to be something guests expected.

The door to the dining area opened and Rudy appeared. Jim watched him walk up to the table. He'd cleaned himself up since that day he first showed them around. Instead of a grease-stained polo shirt he wore a plaid button-down with short sleeves that showed off his bulging forearms. He was younger than Jim originally thought, too—maybe thirty-five or thirty-six? A good ten years younger than Bonnie, but still Jim wondered if he should worry.

"Excuse me," Rudy said. "Sorry to interrupt. I just wanted to bring you the mail before I run my errands in town."

She can't get her own mail? Jim thought.

Bonnie took the small pile, and Rudy left. Her eyes were drawn to a pale-blue envelope addressed in a shaky cursive. The kids started squabbling about whether or not Jim Jr. had spotted a black bear during the drive up ("So you can see in your sleep?" Mindy asked), and Jim took the opportunity to attack the remains of their sundae. Bonnie set aside the flyers and bills, slit the envelope open. Inside, she found a brief note written in block letters on a sheet of matching blue paper:

GO HOME WHILE YOU STILL CAN, YOU RICH BITCH.

She smiled to keep herself from shuddering, then folded the paper in thirds and slid it back inside the envelope.

CHAPTER 4

THAT NIGHT, BONNIE AND Jim stayed in one of the newly updated cabins. Bonnie had set it up with a vase of wildflowers, a chilled bottle of white wine, a hand-stitched duvet. They sat out back in the hot tub, looking up at the stars.

"This isn't so bad," Jim said.

He slid closer to her, put an arm around her shoulders, kissed her neck. Bonnie didn't move a muscle. She didn't seem to know that he was there.

"Goddamn it, Bonnie," Jim said, "what's the matter with you?"

"What do you mean?"

"The cabin, the wine, the hot tub—wasn't that all your idea?"

"I'm sorry, Jim," she said. "It's just...I've got a lot on my mind."

"I thought you came out here to clear your mind. Get away from the stress."

She frowned.

"Maybe not in the first year, Jim. There's a ton to do. To be honest, the place is taking off faster than I thought possible. Any chance we've got the cash flow to build two more cabins?"

It was true that she'd already found herself turning people away, but the suggestion that they expand was a whim. She'd figured out years ago that the best way to distract Jim was to give him what he most enjoyed: the power to say no.

And she needed to distract him. She had no intention of sharing what was really on her mind: another anonymous death threat on pale-blue stationery. Jim would insist at once that it was time to come home, give up this experiment in the woods. Only, as far as Bonnie was concerned, this was home—hers and her children's—and she was prepared to fight for it if need be.

"I don't know," Jim said. "I've got a lot of irons in the fire right now. Our money is spread pretty thin. Maybe in the fall?"

Not an outright no, but Bonnie knew why: Jim was feeling randy. Once again, the world boiled down to what he wanted. It made her so furious that she forgot about the letter for a minute.

"You're so obvious," she said.

"Obvious?"

"You're like a teenage boy."

"Excuse me for wanting a little affection from my wife."

"Affection?"

"Is that so hard to believe?" Jim asked. "I miss you. I miss our life. A year ago we were the glamour couple.

The real estate queen and king of SoCal. Now I feel like I'm second fiddle. Maybe not even second."

Bonnie took a long sip of wine.

"That's the problem, Jim: you think of me as your queen. An extension of the business, with side benefits. It's like I'm one-stop shopping. Maybe I just got tired of being convenient."

Jim sat up straighter, was on the verge of saying *Well, there's nothing convenient about you now* when Rudy came bolting around a corner of the cabin.

"Jesus," Jim said. "You might want to put up some fences."

"Sorry," Rudy said. "I tried knocking, but no one answered."

"I wonder why," Jim said.

"What is it?" Bonnie asked.

"There's trouble at the bar. Some of the customers are asking for you."

"Splendid," Bonnie said. "Exactly how I hoped this evening would go."

She reached for a towel, wrapped it around her torso as she stood.

"Tell them I'll be there as soon as I can," she said.

"You mind if I finish your glass?" Jim asked.

CHAPTER 5

ON A SATURDAY NIGHT, Bonnie found the Camp Nelson Saloon, the only watering hole for thirty miles, crowded with locals from every corner of the county. Most of the patrons seemed to be having a good time, laughing, drinking, smoking, bopping to the country music on the jukebox, playing cards or backgammon at the tables. But a cluster of bikers at the bar, their voices drowned out by the general din, appeared to be giving the bartender a hard time.

Rudy greeted Bonnie at the door.

"Thanks for coming," he said. "They wouldn't take no for an answer."

"What was the question?" Bonnie asked.

"Hey, there she is," one of the bikers yelled, waving her over with a gesture that looked like a command. He was well over six feet, ruddy faced, wore a heavily patched denim vest and a red bandana. Bonnie started forward, took her time crossing the floor. Rudy followed close behind.

"What seems to be the problem?" Bonnie asked.

She counted five of them altogether. They hopped off their stools, formed a semicircle around her and Rudy.

"I was hoping you could tell us," the one who'd called her over said. "Did we offend you somehow?"

"I don't understand," Bonnie said.

"Seems the prices have been raised, but only on what we like to drink."

"You mean the draft beers?" Bonnie asked.

"Yeah, that's exactly what I mean."

Bonnie knew this was coming. In fact, she'd hoped it was coming. The man wasn't wrong: she wanted him and his entourage gone. They were rowdy, coarse. Their motorcycles disturbed her guests. They disturbed *her*.

"I'm sorry," she said, "but the distributor raised his prices. I had no choice."

"He gouges you, so you gouge us. Is that it?"

"It's business," Rudy said. "You'd have done the same."

"Don't tell me what I would've done."

The bikers surrounding them folded their arms, shifted their weight back and forth. Bonnie sensed a wrong turn coming.

"Look," she said, "I'm sorry for the inconvenience. How about a pitcher on the house?"

"How about you keep the prices where they were?"

"Sorry, can't do it," Bonnie said.

To her dismay, she realized she was guilty of the very complaint she'd just leveled against Jim: she had the power to say no, and she was enjoying it.

"Well, then you and your little houseboy are in for a tough time."

Rudy stepped forward; Bonnie put a hand on his chest.

"If you can't be civil, then you need to leave now," she told the man.

He grinned.

"Sorry, you prissy skank," he said, "but we were here first."

He reached behind him, took his drink from the bar, held it out toward Bonnie, then slowly and deliberately let go. The glass exploded at her feet. Beer soaked her sneakers and jeans. She jumped back just as Rudy sprung forward. The whole bar was watching now. Before Bonnie could register what was happening, Rudy had the man's arm up behind his back and was running him outside. The entourage followed on their heels.

Kelly, the tall and emaciated bartender who'd come with the place, handed her new boss a rag while making only the slightest attempt to hide her smirk. *Well*, Bonnie thought, *it's clear whose side you're on.*

Rudy came back. His hair was disheveled but he appeared otherwise unscathed.

"Are you all right?" Bonnie asked.

Rudy nodded. They heard the bikes firing up in the lot.

"I wouldn't count on this being over, though," he said.

He put a hand on her shoulder. She was about to take it when she noticed that all eyes remained fixed on her. She cupped her hands around her mouth, shouted: "Next round is on the house."

* * *

"I'm telling you, it was nothing," Bonnie said. "A simple misunderstanding."

They were lying in bed under the skylight with a fire winding down across the room.

"Really?" Jim said. "Because you came back drenched in beer and looking white as a sheet."

He seemed genuinely worried, and Bonnie felt a pang of guilt as she realized she didn't even want that much from him anymore.

"I promise, it's all fine," she said. "But now I really need to get some sleep."

She rolled onto her side, fought back a gasp when she spotted what looked like a male figure watching them through a part in the curtains. She leapt out of bed, started for the window, watched the figure dart off.

"What is it?" Jim asked.

"Just shutting the curtain," she said.

CHAPTER 6

BONNIE ROSE EARLY, FIXED a three-course breakfast for Jim and the kids.

"It's French themed," she announced. "French toast, French roast, and—just to make sure you get enough carbs—French croissants."

"I could really use that coffee," Jim said. "I guess I'm not used to wine at altitude."

"Help yourself," Bonnie said.

She'd hoped for a picnic in the meadow, but the sky was overcast, so they sat in the dining room of what Rudy called the proprietor's apartment: a five-room home set off in the main lodge. The kids were still in their pajamas, still blinking sleep from their eyes. Bonnie watched them lick syrup off their forks and felt as though she were watching a memory—the memory that would carry her through their long, five-day absence. Just a few more months to go, she reminded herself. Seventy-two days, to be exact, before they'd be living here instead of visiting.

After breakfast, Jim Jr. insisted on a round of Uno.

"Why don't you kids get washed up and changed first?" Bonnie said. "I'll meet you in the living room."

Jim helped her clear the table, then said he was going out to grab some air.

"I've got a long drive ahead of me," he said. "And I'm feeling a little fuzzy."

"Better hurry," Bonnie told him. "It's going to start thundering any minute."

An hour later, Bonnie and the children were sitting on the living room floor, arguing over whether Mindy had remembered to say Uno before her last discard, when Jim came rushing in, yelling Bonnie's name.

"What is it?" Bonnie asked.

"You need to come see this," he said. "Now. Kids, you stay here."

She followed him through the lodge, asking again and again what was wrong. But as soon as they stepped outside, she saw. The windshield on her Jeep was smashed to bits. Someone had pegged it dead-center with an object large enough and hard enough to suck the whole sheet of glass inward.

"My god," she said. "Who the hell..."

"It must have happened while I was out walking," Jim said.

Bonnie stood at the edge of the porch, staring, her arms akimbo, her mouth wide open. She figured the fear would come later, once Jim was gone. Right now, she wanted to kill someone. Starting with that biker at the bar.

Jim walked over to the Jeep, opened the driver-side

door, and pulled out a red brick wrapped in a pale-blue sheet of paper.

"Let me see that," Bonnie said, running up to him. He handed it over without objecting. Bonnie tore off the rubber bands, let the brick drop to the ground as she straightened out the note.

It read: LAST WARNING, YOU RICH BITCH.

* * *

The thunder was short lived, though the rain lasted into the late afternoon. They sat by the bay window in the dining room and watched the storm while they played Chutes and Ladders, Monopoly, Go Fish. Jim was quiet and on edge, would snap at the children when they broke the rules or asked for a do-over. Bonnie chatted nonstop, laughed when nothing was funny, praised the kids for nothing in particular.

"Are you guys fighting?" Mindy asked.

"You're not supposed to ask that, stupid," her brother scolded.

"Hey, don't talk to your sister like that," Jim said.

"I think we all need snacks," Bonnie said. "I'll go heat up some cookies."

"And I'll help," Jim said.

Bonnie should have anticipated that: the last thing she wanted right now was to be alone with Jim. In the kitchen, out of earshot of the children, he launched right in.

"*Last warning?*" he quoted. "You want to tell me how many others there have been?"

"None that came with property damage."

"That doesn't answer my question."

"No, it doesn't," she said, transferring a batch of snickerdoodles from tin to tray. "You told me you don't want to be involved in lodge business. Well, this is lodge business."

"No," Jim corrected her, "business is ledgers and balance sheets. This is a death threat."

Bonnie slid the tray into the oven and set the timer for five minutes.

"Stop being so dramatic," she said. "They're just trying to scare me off. If they wanted to hurt me, I'd be hurt."

"*They?* So you know who's behind this?"

"I have an idea. No proof."

"Then why won't you go to the police?"

"You know, if you're really going to pretend to help me, you could at least pour the milk."

"Answer my question."

"I told you, I'll call once the kids are gone. I don't want to frighten them. I don't want them to be afraid of this place. And don't you say anything to them, either."

Jim punched the counter with the side of his fist.

"Fine," he said. "I'll fill them in at your funeral."

"Just pour the damn milk," Bonnie said.

* * *

The rain let up around four p.m., then stopped altogether. Bonnie hid the Jeep before seeing Jim and the kids off. Mindy cried, clutched her mother's leg, begged to stay.

"Soon, love," Bonnie said.

"I bet that makes you happy," Jim said under his breath.

Bonnie brushed him off, leaned into the car and gave Jim Jr. a kiss.

"Sleep well," she said.

* * *

That night, Bonnie sat at her desk in her office while Rudy paced the room. She unlocked a drawer, slid it open, pulled out a folder containing a half-dozen pale-blue sheets of paper. She placed the first threatening letter side-by-side with the one Jim had taken from her car.

"The writing is the same," she said.

"Of course it's the same," Rudy said. "I'm begging you to let me handle those rednecks."

Bonnie raised one eyebrow.

"You want me to sanction violence?" she asked.

"You tried the cops. They're not going to do anything until you're dead."

"That's not exactly what they said. They need proof."

"Yeah, well...I don't."

Bonnie slid both letters back into the file.

"Calm the testosterone," she said. "Why don't we try setting up some cameras first?"

Rudy grinned, walked around behind the desk, began massaging her shoulders.

"I'm worried about you," he said. "These guys run around in the dark like cowards. They are cowards. But cowards can be the most dangerous. They go too far without meaning to."

Bonnie stood, turned so she was facing him.

"The wisdom of Rudy Manuel," she said.

Their kiss was long and fiery—the kiss of new lovers who'd been kept at arm's length for days on end. Bonnie was only mildly disturbed by the fact that she felt no guilt.

Rudy pulled back, smiled.

"I swear," he said, "I never did this with the Edwards Group."

CHAPTER 7

THE NEXT MORNING WAS sunny and mild. Bonnie decided to spend the day adding markers to the section of a hiking trail where several of her guests had lost their way. The trail led from the backside of the meadow upslope through forest dense with sequoias to a waterfall fed by a winding creek. The cascade itself was so small that no one had bothered to name it, but Bonnie found the algae coloring the surrounding stone mesmerizing, and the sound of the water itself was calming even on the most stressful of days. She loaded the markers, nails, and a hammer into one compartment of her Swiss Army backpack, and a picnic lunch complete with an airline-sized bottle of red wine into the other.

She set out at a little after eight a.m., knowing full well that there were more important things she could be doing. The guests who'd complained were intoxicated at the time, and she was pretty sure the incident wouldn't repeat itself. But this was the best excuse she had to give herself the kind of day she needed after an awful, high-anxiety forty-eight hours. She needed to reconnect with the mountains, to remind herself of why she'd fallen in love with Camp Nelson in the first place.

Most important, she needed to be alone. Away from Jim and Rudy and even the kids. Away from demanding guests. Away from phones and fax machines. Someplace where she couldn't be reached and wouldn't be disturbed. It wasn't that she wanted to think—she wanted to take a break from thinking.

According to her inebriated guests, the trickiest part of the trail came in the long stretch between two granite outcroppings. The forest was thick and steep there, and the path was continually covered with a fresh layer of duff. Bonnie passed the first outcropping and had to admit that it was harder to pick the trail back up than she'd remembered. The markers were scarce, and as she hiked upslope she sometimes had the sensation that she'd gone off course and was simply standing in the middle of an untamed forest. More than once she had to backtrack, return to the first set of rocks, and start over.

In theory, it was impossible to get lost since at least one of the two outcroppings was never more than a few steps from view, but Bonnie could understand how, if you ventured here in the dark, or in an altered state, you might start to panic. And her guests had spoken the truth: there were no markers to be found anywhere. It was, Bonnie thought, simply a matter of spelling out the straightest line possible between the two clusters of granite. From there, the trail became crystal clear as it followed the creek the last mile up to the waterfall.

She chose a place to start, knelt down, and opened her

backpack. The markers she'd brought with her were oval reflectors like the ones you'd find on the back of a bicycle. Shine your flashlight around until some of that light came back at you, and you shouldn't have any difficulty at all.

Her plan for the day was succeeding. She lost herself in the sun and shade, the quiet, the thin mountain air. Sometimes she would remember where she was and think: *I'm kneeling at the base of a 140-foot tree, five thousand miles above sea level. This is my life now. This is the life I've made.* When she was done working, she would continue on to the waterfall. She knew exactly where she'd spread her blanket and eat. She could already feel the wine moving through her body, warming her from the inside. And then she would lay back, shut her eyes, and listen to the water.

She was about halfway done when she heard a birdcall she didn't recognize coming from maybe a hundred yards below. It sounded to her like the highest pitch of a tin whistle played in a long-short-short pattern. She was tempted to hike back down and see if she could identify the species, but then she heard the same call coming from roughly the same distance in the opposite direction.

They must be talking about me, she thought. *Warning the forest that there's an intruder.*

She smiled, took a sip of water, went back to work.

But then what had to be another of the same kind of bird perched somewhere to the east joined the conversation, repeating the exact same call. She stood and listened, trying to envision the bird: she guessed small, maybe the size of her fist, and yellow-breasted with black wings. She wanted very badly to see one, to know if what she pictured was accurate.

She tried to talk back to them by imitating their call, but her attempt came out breathy and uneven. Still, they responded, or seemed to, with each bird sounding off in rapid succession. Not only that, but she was sure they were inching closer. She tried her hand at their call again—tried, even though she knew it was impossible, to make her version sound friendly, nonthreatening.

But her whistling appeared to rattle the birds. Their song altered. The pitch dipped an octave lower; the long opening note dropped off. And then the call changed completely. Instead of a single pitch there were two, one high and one low, and the sound no longer resembled a tin whistle. More like a parrot imitating human speech, Bonnie thought.

And then she understood: these weren't birds closing in on her.

She concentrated until the two short syllables came into focus: *rich bitch, rich bitch, rich bitch.* From the north, the south, the east. *Rich bitch, rich bitch, rich bitch.* One at a time, and then in unison.

They were on her now, no farther than twenty feet in each direction. She could see them darting between the trees, bandanas hiding their faces as if they were grown men playing cops and robbers.

Despite herself, Bonnie screamed. And then she grabbed her backpack and ran, the voices behind her chirping *rich bitch, rich bitch, rich bitch* all the way to the meadow.

CHAPTER 8

A WEEK HAD PASSED since the incident at Camp Nelson Saloon, and Bonnie was determined to put in another appearance. She walked the access road at a little after sundown. Rudy followed close behind.

"You don't need to prove anything to anyone," he said. "Least of all that inbred trash."

"That's where you're wrong," Bonnie said. "They can't think I'm backing down."

"Then let me go alone."

"Ha! Thanks, but I don't feel like making a trip to the hospital or the morgue tonight. Besides, they need to see my face. If I send you, it looks worse than if I do nothing at all."

"And what if they decide to start something? How are you going to—"

"I'll play it by ear."

They walked the rest of the way without talking. At first glance, it seemed Bonnie had already won. Apart from Kelly and a large red-haired biker at the far end of the bar, the place was empty.

"Looks like they're trying to hit me in my wallet," Bonnie said.

"Or maybe it's just early," Rudy said.

"Let's find out."

They sat dead-center at the bar, took two of the same stools the delinquent bikers had occupied a week earlier.

"Evening ma'am," Kelly said. "Rudy. What can I get you all tonight?"

Bonnie remembered how Kelly had smirked while she wiped beer from her pants. She decided to have a little fun at her employee's expense.

"I could really go for an Old Fashioned," she said.

"That a microbrew?" Kelly asked.

"It's a cocktail. Part bitters, part... You know, never mind. I'll just take a Manhattan."

Kelly gave a blank stare. Rudy covered his grin.

"How about a Sidecar?" Bonnie asked.

"This is a beer and shots bar, ma'am," Kelly said.

"Well, I guess we'll need to fix that, won't we?" Bonnie said, smiling. "Meanwhile, pour me a Pilsner."

"I'll take a Jameson, on the rocks," Rudy said.

They carried their drinks to a nearby table. Bonnie sat down, then popped back up.

"There's something sticky on my seat," she said, reaching for a napkin. "I'm telling you, that woman really needs to go. And this jukebox needs an overhaul. Or at least a song with more than three chords."

"Country and Western sells booze," Rudy said. "More than rock or pop or jazz. That's a fact. There have been studies."

"Well, maybe we don't need a bar at all," Bonnie said.

"Let's take one thing at a time."

They were quiet for a while, Bonnie casting glances at the door, Rudy staring down into his drink, giving the ice an occasional stir.

"No family this weekend?" he asked.

Bonnie frowned. "Jim says he won't bring the kids back until it's safe. Can you believe that? He's never thought twice about anyone's safety—he just wants to drive a wedge between me and this place."

Rudy went back to poking at the ice in his glass, pushing a cube down with his straw and then watching it float back up.

"You know you're supposed to drink that, not play with it," Bonnie said.

Rudy's smile looked more like a grimace.

"I'm out of practice," he said. "To be honest, I kind of gave it up when I moved out here. I guess you could say that I moved out here in order to give it up."

"I'm sorry," Bonnie said. "I had no idea. I'll take these back and get us two Cokes."

"No, it's all right," Rudy said. "I'm ready now. I'm all grown up. I should be able to enjoy a drink like anybody else."

"You should be able to, or you are?"

"I am."

"You're sure?"

"I'm sure. I promise."

He lifted his glass in a toast.

"To growing up," he said.

They drank, then sat grinning sheepishly at one another.

"Let me ask you something," Bonnie said.

"Shoot."

"You've been living out here for a while now. Does it ever get old? Are you still happy?"

"Happier now than ever," Rudy said, winking.

"That's not what I mean," Bonnie said. "You could have met a girl anywhere. Do you miss...civilization? Do you ever feel like you made a big mistake?"

"If I felt that way, I'd leave," Rudy said. "But this is where I belong. I'm a better person now. I'm better because of this place."

"You mean because you stopped drinking?"

"That's part of it."

"What's the other part?"

Rudy tapped his glass.

"I'll need a few more before I answer that one."

"How about this? How about we have one more, then take a late-night stroll up to the lake?"

"That's why you're the boss," Rudy said. "You have all the good ideas."

Bonnie looked over her shoulder, signaled to Kelly for another round. The clock above the bar read ten p.m.

"Seems like they really are boycotting me," she said. "Honestly, it's a relief. I'm going to remake the place from top to bottom. A high-end bar for discerning guests. A bartender who knows how to make a Manhattan."

She wondered if the bikers realized they'd gone too far that morning in the woods. Maybe they'd scared themselves off. Maybe they expected the cops to come swooping down if they set foot anywhere near Camp Nelson Lodge.

"Hold that thought," Rudy said, cupping a hand to his ear.

Bonnie listened, caught the roar of approaching motorcycles. Sure enough, the bikers came filing in a short time later, the same gaggle Rudy had tossed out the week before. It looked to Bonnie like they'd been drinking already. The towering rabble-rouser in the red bandana wobbled as he walked, and his entourage was cackling like a gang of teenage girls.

"Hey, Kelly," the leader called, "line 'em up. And crank up the music while you're at it."

Rudy leaned across the table.

"What do you want to do?" he whispered.

Bonnie shrugged.

"It's a new day in a free country, right?" she said. "We sit here and enjoy our drinks."

She got ready to be stared down, called names, laughed at, even spit on. But they walked past her table without so much as acknowledging her or Rudy. Bonnie watched them gather their drinks at the bar, then huddle around a nearby table.

"You want to take that walk now?" Rudy asked.

"Uh-uh, no way," Bonnie said. "We stay right here until they leave."

"All right, as long as you don't mind being seen out and about with the help. Especially the male help."

"I don't mind at all," Bonnie said. "Anyway, it looks like they've come to their senses."

"It's a little early to make that call," Rudy said.

Two hours and four rounds later, the bikers were the last of the paying customers to leave. They mouthed an ominous "Goodnight" to Bonnie and Rudy on their way out but were otherwise well behaved.

"Maybe they really have come around," Rudy said.

Bonnie laughed.

"What's so funny?" Rudy asked.

"You're slurring your words."

"I told you, it's been a while."

"And it's been a long time since I took advantage of a drunk guy. Why don't I steer you back to my cabin?"

Rudy smiled.

"As long as you promise to take advantage of me," he said.

CHAPTER 9

"SOME PEOPLE GO TO church on Sunday mornings," Sergeant Wylie said.

"Yeah, and some people sleep past sunrise," his partner O'Dowd said.

They turned onto the access road and headed for Camp Nelson. It was a perfect California morning, clear and crisp with nothing moving or making a sound save the occasional bird dive-bombing an earthworm. O'Dowd slowed the car as they passed the saloon.

"Nothing doing there," Wylie said.

But then they emerged from the forest into the clearing and the quiet morning seemed like a distant memory. There were squad cars with their lights spinning parked at random intervals all around the property. Uniform officers moved in and out of the cabins, interviewing guests. Men and women in lab coats were unpacking the forensics van. It was hard to tell what the police tape was meant to keep in and what it was meant to keep out.

"Looks like we found the action," Wylie said.

"Yeah," O'Dowd said, "and it looks like they started without us."

He pulled up behind the last squad car and cut the engine.

"You're the primary on this one, right?" he asked.

Wylie glared at him.

"You know, for someone so young you're awfully damn lazy," he said.

"I'm forty-four."

"You've got time yet. I didn't start phoning it in till I turned fifty."

A trooper fresh from the academy handed them two pairs of latex gloves and scrub booties.

"Main scene's over there," he said, pointing to Bonnie's cabin.

"You mean the bodies?" O'Dowd asked.

"Yes sir. Or at least one body. The other vic is still breathing."

"I thought we had two DOAs," Wylie said.

"Well, by the time you walk over there you might," the trooper said. "The woman's all the way dead, but the male is touch and go."

Wylie and O'Dowd looked at each other, then turned and ran. They shouldered their way through a circle of lab coats and burst into the cabin, both of them breathing hard. A pair of EMTs were preparing Rudy for transit. They'd wrapped a thick bandage around his skull and fitted his head into a foam contraption that looked to O'Dowd like the packaging his stereo had come in.

"Can he talk?" Wylie asked.

"He's been shot in the head," the lead EMT said. "You'll be lucky if he ever talks again."

Wylie leaned over the stretcher.

"You mean to tell me this son-of-a-bitch has a bullet in his brain and he's still alive?" he asked.

"I can't say for sure if it hit the brain or not."

"Any chance he'll recover?" O'Dowd asked.

"There's always a chance," the EMT said. "But I wouldn't count on it."

Wylie and O'Dowd watched them wheel Rudy away, then turned to the bed. Bonnie lay on her back with her legs tangled beneath her. The wall behind the bed was spattered with blood and brain matter.

"She had no chance at all," O'Dowd said.

"Yeah, it was over real quick for her."

A crime scene photographer neither of them had noticed before stepped to the foot of the bed and began snapping pictures.

"Hey, take a look at this," O'Dowd said, pointing to the nightstand. "We've got a stuffed money clip, a knockoff Rolex, and a silver cross."

"Huh," Wylie said. "Definitely not a robbery."

"Nope," O'Dowd said. "Not that anyone would have come all the way out here to rob just one cabin."

"So we're looking at an intentional hit."

"One of them was the target, anyway. Could be the other one was collateral damage."

"Doesn't make our job any easier."

O'Dowd shrugged.

"Let's hope our hitman forgot to wear gloves."

* * *

Without the kids in tow, Jim managed to make the four-hour drive in just under three hours. He sped into the clearing, parked his Mercedes among the squad cars, and ran for Bonnie's cabin.

"Where is she?" he yelled. "Is she in there? Is my wife in there?"

Someone reached out and caught his arm as he ducked under the police tape. It was Wylie.

"Sir," he said, "we're still investigating. This is as far as I can let you go."

"What are you talking about? I own this place. They told me my wife is dead."

"You're Mr. Hood?"

Jim nodded.

"God," he said. "I feel like I'm going to pass out."

"Why don't we have a seat over here in my car," Wylie said. "I'll have someone bring you a bottle of water."

He snapped his fingers at a passing uniform cop, then handed him a dollar.

"Let's get this man some water," he said. "There's a vending machine in the lodge."

"Yes sir."

Jim sat on the passenger's side, Wylie behind the wheel. Jim scanned the property. So much trouble, he thought, over a backwoods dump. Even if Bonnie had made improvements.

"What happened?" he asked.

"What did they tell you?"

"Only that Bonnie was dead. That she'd been killed."

Wylie cleared his throat. He wished like hell it had been O'Dowd standing there when the husband came charging up the path.

"She was shot," he said, "late last night or early this morning."

"Jesus Christ."

"There's more," Wylie continued. "There's no easy way to say this, so I'll just come out with it: your wife wasn't alone."

Jim cocked his head like he was struggling to comprehend what Wylie had just told him.

"What do you mean? Was someone else hurt?"

"Rudy Manuel, her handyman. It looks like they were in bed together when the shooter—"

"You're telling me Bonnie was with another man? I don't believe it. Not with him. Not with that little…"

Wylie studied him out of the corner of one eye. The tears were real. The confusion seemed real, too.

The officer returned with a bottle of water. Wylie passed it to Jim, waited while he took a long swig.

"I'm sorry," he said, "but I have to ask: you really didn't know your wife was having an affair?"

Jim struck the dashboard with the palm of one hand.

"Of course I didn't," he said.

"Easy now," Wylie said. "I'm not judging. Things happen in a marriage."

"Not in my marriage. We have two kids. We built a small empire together. Bonnie wasn't going to risk all that for a fling with a glorified vagrant."

He'd said more than he meant to. He looked over at Wylie, found no hint of suspicion or blame.

"It was those bikers," Jim said.

"Bikers?"

Jim told Wylie about the brick through the Jeep window, the threatening notes, the confrontation at the Camp Nelson Saloon. He spoke quickly, his voice breaking now and again, his forehead damp with sweat.

"I see," Wylie said.

"You see what? Why didn't you people protect her? Isn't that your job?"

I could ask the same of you, Wylie thought.

"Listen, Mr. Hood," he said, "why don't you go get a cup of coffee in the lodge? I'll come talk to you again in a little bit, when I know more. If you like, I could have an officer sit with you."

"I'd rather be alone," Jim said.

He didn't bother to shut the door behind him. Wylie watched him walk across the property, then went looking for O'Dowd. He found his partner on the phone in Bonnie's cabin. O'Dowd nodded, held up one hand.

"Got it," he said into the receiver. "Thank you, that could be a big help."

He hung up, looked over at Wylie.

"Did you get anything off the husband?" he asked.

"Not really," Wylie said. "Only that he was quick to point the finger. What was that call about? You sounded almost hopeful."

"I don't know if it's good news or bad," O'Dowd said. "Our living vic has quite a rap sheet. Including a five-year stint for armed robbery."

"Well now, that's interesting. Could be he crossed the wrong people and was hiding out up here."

"Could also be a red herring."

Wylie nodded.

"Let's hope Mr. Manuel's feeling chatty when he wakes up," he said.

"*If* he wakes up," O'Dowd said.

CHAPTER 10

RUDY LAY IN A hospital bed in a private room with a bandage wrapped tight around his skull and a brace holding his head and neck still. An IV ran from one arm. A computer monitor charted his vitals. His eyes were shut and had been for the more than two hours Wylie and O'Dowd sat with him. Wylie dozed in a plastic armchair, slipping in and out of a recurring nightmare that saw him go bankrupt just months into his retirement. O'Dowd kept one eye on their witness and the other on an episode of *Three's Company*. The room smelled like menthol and rubber, and O'Dowd wondered what exactly he was breathing in.

Rudy stirred a little, his nostrils flaring and his fingers twitching, and then came to.

"Hey," O'Dowd said, snapping his fingers. "Hey, he's awake."

Wylie rubbed at his eyes, then pushed himself out of the chair.

"But is his brain working?" he asked.

"Only one way to find out."

They stood on opposite sides of the bed, watching. At first, Rudy seemed conscious but unaware, as if he didn't know where he was or what had happened to him and was too far gone to ask questions. Little by little, though, his eyes started to focus. He took in his surroundings as best he could without moving his head, then tried to speak but found his mouth too dry.

"The nurse said it would be okay to give him a sip of water," O'Dowd told Wylie.

He stuck a straw in a Styrofoam cup, transferred water from a green pitcher, and held the cup out to Rudy. The act of pursing his lips seemed to cause Rudy pain, but with a little effort he managed to drink.

"Thank you," he said, his voice strained, feeble.

O'Dowd wondered if the bruising and swelling around Rudy's eyes were caused by the surgery or the bullet itself.

"Do you know who I am?" O'Dowd asked.

Rudy raised one hand and pointed to the badge hanging from O'Dowd's jacket pocket.

"Cops," he said.

"Do you know where you are? And how you got here?" Wylie asked.

Rudy tried to nod, found himself restricted by the brace.

"Yes," he whispered.

Wylie and O'Dowd exchanged encouraging glances.

"Can you tell us who did this to you?" O'Dowd asked.

Rudy moved his jaw back and forth as though preparing to speak in full sentences.

"Bonnie?" he asked. "Is she..."

O'Dowd started to answer, but Wylie held up a hand: best not get him excited.

"We don't know yet," Wylie said. "What's important now is that we find who did this."

Rudy shut his eyes again, either with relief or with the strain of trying to remember.

"I don't know," he said.

"You didn't see him before he fired?" O'Dowd asked.

"It was dark. He was in the shadows."

"So there was just one assailant?" Wylie asked.

"Yes."

"Did you notice anything about him at all?"

"He was tall," Rudy said. "Maybe six four. And big. Very big."

"Fat big, or scary big?" O'Dowd asked.

"Scary big."

"Any big, shadowy men in your past?" Wylie asked.

"What do you mean?"

Words seemed to be coming a bit more easily. He seemed to want to cooperate.

"We've had a look at your rap sheet, Mr. Manuel," Wylie said. "You're more or less a career criminal."

"Uh-uh. I've been clean a long time now."

"So you switched careers. Still, sometimes a criminal's past will only stay buried for so long. Maybe someone you double-crossed just got out. Maybe someone you robbed had trouble tracking you down."

Rudy attempted to clench his fists but couldn't find the strength.

"No," he said. "There's no one."

"You're sure?" O'Dowd asked. "You can't think of a single soul who would want to hurt you?"

"Not like that."

"What do you mean?"

"Anyone who'd want to do me would come straight at me. They'd have something to say. They'd want something from me first. This guy just started firing."

"Your blood alcohol was sky high," Wylie said. "Could be you're blanking on the conversation."

"No. I remember."

"You remember anything else?" O'Dowd asked. "Anything at all."

Rudy took a minute to think.

"His hair was long and curly. I saw it in his shadow against the wall."

"Any chance you could give us a color?"

"No."

"All right, Mr. Manuel," Wylie said. "We'll let you get some rest. But chances are we'll be back with more questions."

Rudy shut his eyes, already drifting back into sleep.

* * *

The detectives sat on a bench in the hall outside Rudy's room and compared notes.

"I wish it didn't, but his story makes sense," Wylie said.

"How so?"

"If the shooter was one of his old running bunnies, the cash and jewelry wouldn't have been sitting there for us to find. A career thief doesn't take a pass just because robbery wasn't on the agenda that day."

"So you believe him when he says he didn't get a good look at the guy?" O'Dowd asked.

"I do."

"Where does that leave us?"

Wylie rubbed at his eyes like he was still half dozing.

"You know," he said, "some witnesses reported seeing a tall biker type at the saloon on Saturday night. They thought he had to be waiting for someone, but he just sat there by himself drinking bottles of Heineken all night. It isn't the kind of place people just stumble on."

"Maybe he was a guest," O'Dowd offered.

"Maybe, but his description doesn't fit the bill. Bonnie was turning the lodge into a yuppie getaway. The registry shows all families that weekend. There were more kids on the property than adults."

They were quiet for a minute, each trying to figure their next move.

"It's a long shot," O'Dowd said, "but let's have forensics go over Saturday night's beer bottles with a fine-tooth comb. Maybe our guy's in the system. If he is our guy."

"Can't hurt," Wylie said. "Meanwhile, let's make sure we know everything there is to know about Mr. Jim Hood."

CHAPTER 11

THE FUNERAL AND VIEWING were finally over. Everything about the day felt wrong to Jim, like it had been meant for someone other than Bonnie. She'd never been a churchgoer. The cross and the stained glass and the pews and the strange attire of the man addressing the crowd all seemed to confuse his children. Mindy in particular couldn't wrap her brain around the fact that her mother was lying a few feet away in that closed box. Jim Jr. let out a tremendous sneeze every time the altar boy waved his incense.

It was Bonnie's parents who'd demanded a traditional service. They had never approved of Jim beyond his finances, especially not his mother-in-law, whose previously snide comments turned downright hostile after her daughter's death. "You should have been there with her, you know," she'd said at church that morning. "But then I suppose Bonnie went up there to get away from you." She wasn't being malicious: she was simply too devastated to worry about Jim's feelings.

Family, friends, colleagues, and neighbors were gathered now at the Hood home. The children appeared more at ease with so many familiar faces joined in a familiar setting. Jim Jr. sat on his grandfather's lap and played with a Rubik's Cube. Mindy, without asking permission, changed out of her dress and into her favored jeans and a T-shirt. Jim had the event catered, but Bonnie's mother insisted on making ambrosia, which she claimed was Bonnie's favorite childhood dessert though Jim had never seen his wife eat so much as a spoonful.

He'd hoped to open the backyard to guests, but it was a rare overcast night in SoCal. Even the Hoods' sprawling and well-furnished living room couldn't quite accommodate upwards of fifty people. Guests spilled into the family room, the kitchen, even the master bedroom. Jim mingled, listening to condolences and fond memories, nodding and smiling where appropriate, saying little, keeping each conversation brief. The facts of Bonnie's death — in particular the fact of Rudy — had made the papers. Jim felt people looking at him with two expressions at once, as though attempting to mirror the mix of shame and grief they believed he must be feeling.

As the night wore on and people continued drinking, Jim seemed to become more and more invisible. He overheard things, the kind of things no one would have said to his face, though he wondered if deep down they wanted him to hear.

"You can't blame her," a friend of Bonnie's told someone Jim didn't recognize. "She was faithful to him for all those years, and he barely paid any attention to her outside of the business."

"Maybe it wasn't Jim who pulled the trigger, but it might as well have been," said a cousin Jim had seen maybe a half-dozen times in his life.

Bonnie's mother, after a few glasses of sherry, went even further: "Someone paid to have my daughter killed, and I know damn well who that someone is."

It was the same wherever Jim went in the house. He needed to calm down. He needed a stiff drink. He was standing in the kitchen, filling his glass with ice, when the worst possible thought occurred to him: What if the children were overhearing these conversations, too? He tossed his glass in the sink, looked around frantically, then ran down the hall and burst into the living room. He found Mindy and Jim Jr. sitting on the floor with Bonnie's brother, playing a game of Chinese Checkers, Jim Jr.'s latest obsession.

"Kids, kids," Jim called, louder than he meant to. "It's getting late. I think we need to start saying goodbye to our guests."

"Just let us finish this game," Jim Jr. said.

Jim felt panicked, like the boy's failure to act quickly might somehow cost another life.

"Now," he said.

Despite himself, he could feel his face turning red and his jaws flexing.

"Your mother's dead, and you're sitting there playing a game," he shouted. "What the hell's wrong with you?"

He scanned the faces in the room, saw the makings of an angry mob staring back at him.

CHAPTER 12

THE TULARE COUNTY HOMICIDE Bureau, with its fake wood paneling and softball league pennants, looked like a semifinished basement though it sat on the second floor of Camp Nelson's municipal building. O'Dowd had to turn sideways in order to shuffle through a hallway jammed with mismatched filing cabinets. He entered a room full of cluttered desks and disgruntled detectives and shouted Wylie's name from the opposite side of the floor.

"I'm trying to work here," Sergeant Sandercoe protested from across the room.

"Oh please," O'Dowd said. "Like you know how to do anything on that computer besides play solitaire."

O'Dowd reached Wylie's desk and took a moment to catch his breath.

"You all right there?" Wylie asked.

"You aren't going to believe this," O'Dowd said. "We got a hit. Off those bottles."

"The Heineken bottles?"

"Yeah. A guy named Bruce Beauchamp from Fontana. Construction worker by day, drug dealer by night. He has a page and a half worth of priors. And get this: he's six four, 240 pounds, and has curly hair."

"Not bad," Wylie said. "Any connection to Rudy Manuel?"

"Too early to say, but I doubt it. They did their stints at different facilities, and they went away for different crimes."

"We have an address for Mr. Beauchamp?"

"A trailer park halfway down the coast to LA."

"All right, then," Wylie said. "Let's get the cavalry lined up."

* * *

They met the local task force at five the next morning, in the parking lot of an abandoned strip mall three miles from Beauchamp's trailer camp. The sheriff's office sent three squad cars and a SWAT van.

"Seems like a lot for just one guy," O'Dowd told Sergeant Sandercoe, the SWAT team leader.

"These trailer parks can turn into combat zones real quick," Sandercoe said. "Our incident commander doesn't like us taking chances."

Wylie guzzled his coffee.

"Fine by me," he said. "I gave up on guts and glory a long time ago."

The sergeant spread out a map of the trailer park on the hood of O'Dowd's sedan and drew a circle around Beauchamp's home with a red marker.

"We'll serve the warrant," he said. "You hang back here, at the park's entrance. Once we've got him in cuffs, he's all yours."

O'Dowd yawned.

"He boring you?" Wylie asked.

"I'm a night owl by nature," O'Dowd said. "Coffee doesn't work for me before the sun's up."

O'Dowd and Wylie made the short drive sandwiched between SWAT's unmarked van and the three squad cars. They peeled off at the entrance, cut the sedan's headlights, and sat waiting for the go-ahead to come over the radio.

They didn't have to wait long. By the time Wylie tore the cellophane off a fresh pack of cigarettes and lit one, the sergeant's voice was already summoning them through a haze of static.

"Beauchamp must not be a fighter," O'Dowd said.

"Let's hope he coughs up his confession that quick."

They found him sitting on the makeshift stoop in front of his broken-down trailer, hands cuffed behind his back. He wore a stained tank top and an old pair of jeans, and his curly red hair was clearly fresh off the pillow. Sergeant Sandercoe stood over him like he was the prize at the end of a big-game hunt.

"He give you any trouble?" O'Dowd asked.

"No sir," Sandercoe said. "Had a Glock on the nightstand, but he slept right through us kicking the door in."

"I thought felons weren't allowed to have guns," Wylie said, for Beauchamp's benefit.

"You know, I don't believe they are," O'Dowd said. "I believe that's what you call a violation."

"I got no clue what you guys are doing here," Beauchamp said, without much conviction.

"We'll tell you all about it in the car," Wylie said. "Right after we read you your rights."

"I know my rights."

"I guess you would by now," O'Dowd said. "Come on, let's go."

Beauchamp stood, seeming to keep rising well past the six foot four Rudy had described. Wylie had to slide the passenger seat forward in order to fit him in the back of the sedan. Neighbors stepped outside to watch, the men bare-chested and the women in curlers. Their expressions were none too friendly.

"Sandercoe wasn't kidding," O'Dowd said under his breath.

"Yeah, let's scat," Wylie said.

The sun was starting to show by the time they hit the highway. Wylie and O'Dowd had planned to say as little as possible until they got back to the station, but Beauchamp wouldn't have it.

"I'm hungry and I gotta piss," he complained. "This is cruel and unusual."

"Pipe down," Wylie said.

"Where are you taking me? At least tell me that much."

"Someplace you've been before."

"I've been a lot of places. And I didn't break any laws. What you're doing right now is called kidnapping. State-sanctioned kidnapping."

"We're going to have a nice, civilized conversation," O'Dowd said. "That's all."

"Then let's have it here. Go ahead and ask your questions. I got nothing to hide."

"All right," Wylie said, pivoting in his seat. "Why don't you tell us what you were doing up at Camp Nelson two Saturdays ago?"

"That what this is about? A working man can't take a weekend to himself without getting dragged to the precinct house?"

"No offense, Mr. Beauchamp, but you don't strike me as the kind of guy who has the luxury of weekend R&R," Wylie said.

"Why? 'Cause I live in a trailer? I make more in a month than you two put together."

"Like I said, Mr. Beauchamp..."

"So I guess you're Tulare County cops? That where we're headed? Camp Nelson?"

"See, now you've ruined the surprise," Wylie said.

Beauchamp perked up a little, like he saw an advantage in dealing with backwoods cops.

"What is you think I did up there?"

"I got a better idea," O'Dowd said. "Why don't you tell us what you did up there?"

"All right. A friend from the job site told me about the place. I'd been having trouble with my girl and needed to clear my head. A weekend of fishing and hiking seemed like just the thing."

"No drinking?"

"Yeah, some of that, too."

"Where?"

"I don't know if the place even had a name. It was down a country road, way off the beaten path."

"How'd you find it?"

"Desk clerk where I was staying suggested I check it out. He drew me a map."

"Where were you staying?"

"Motel Six. Go ahead and check their records."

"We will," Wylie said. "Meanwhile, what's your friend's name? The one who recommended Camp Nelson."

"John."

"What's John's last name?"

"I don't know."

"You don't know?"

"We're work friends. We talk on our lunch break, that's all."

"So if we show up at the site on Monday morning we'll be able to find this John?" O'Dowd asked.

"Maybe."

"Maybe?"

"He's a day worker. He goes wherever they send him."

"But your foreman would know how to reach him, right?" O'Dowd followed up.

"I guess."

"What about your girl?" Wylie asked. "She have a name? A number?"

Beauchamp sunk down, pushed his knees against the back of Wylie's seat. They'd made it clear that he was in for the long haul.

"You know what?" he said. "Why don't you guys call and get me a lawyer. I'm gonna rest up now. Make sure I got my wits about me."

"That's a good idea, Mr. Beauchamp," Wylie said. "The best one I've heard in a while."

CHAPTER 13

JIM JR. AND MINDY sat finishing their breakfast at the kitchen table while their father talked on the phone with a Camp Nelson detective. They watched him pace the floor, wandering as far away as the phone cord would allow, then retracing his steps. Now and again he would ask a question—*So he's not local? How long has he been out? But he hasn't confessed?*—then nod intently while he listened to the answers.

"Sounds like they caught the guy who shot Mommy," Jim Jr. said.

"Shush," Mindy told him.

She walked over to her father and whispered, "Daddy, what is it?"

"Can you hold on a second?" Jim said into the receiver.

"Why don't you kids wait for me in the living room?" he said. "The cartoons should be on now."

"But Daddy—"

"I'll be right there."

Mindy stayed put. Jim Jr. pretended not to hear.

"Now!" Jim said.

The children walked away at a snail's pace. Jim returned to his call.

"Just so I'm clear," he said, "you *have* made a formal arrest?"

"Yes sir, we have," Wylie confirmed.

"So you're confident it was this Beauchamp who killed Bonnie?"

"He wouldn't be in jail otherwise. Still, I'm not the judge or jury."

"And all you've got is a fingerprint?"

"We also have an eyewitness, Mr. Hood. One who seems to be getting stronger and remembering more every day."

"You mean the man who was sleeping with my wife?"

Wylie let the question pass.

"I'll be in touch when we know more," he said. "Meanwhile, feel free to call me any time."

Jim found Mindy and Jim Jr. sitting at attention on the couch, both of them too eager to speak or move. He crouched on the floor in front of them, put one hand on Mindy's arm and the other on Jim Jr.'s knee.

"I've got big news," he said. "They've arrested the man who killed your mother," he said.

"Told you!" Jim Jr. said.

Mindy ignored her brother.

"Who?" she asked. "Who is he?"

"Yeah, who is he?" Jim Jr. echoed.

Jim hesitated, not sure how much he should share or withhold.

"A man named Bruce Beauchamp," he said.

"Yeah, but who *is* he?" Mindy insisted.

"I don't really know," Jim said. "At least I don't know much. He's a construction worker. He's been in prison before."

"Are you going to kill him?" Jim Jr. asked, his voice full of hope.

"Ask a real question," Mindy said.

"That is a real question."

"No it isn't. The man's in jail already. You know Daddy can't kill him in jail."

"He could if—"

"Kids, kids," Jim interrupted. "No arguing, please."

They were quiet for a moment, as though arguing were their only means of communication, and then, to Jim's surprise, they began asking many of the same questions he'd asked Wylie.

"Why?" Jim Jr. wanted to know. "Why did he do it?"

"Did he know Mommy?" Mindy asked.

"Was he mad at her?"

Jim shook his head.

"I wish I had answers for you," he said. "I never heard of this man before."

"But he must have had a reason," Jim Jr. insisted.

"Bad guys have all kinds of reasons," Jim said. "They aren't always personal. Maybe he wanted to rob Mommy, and she wouldn't let him."

The explanation sounded lame to him, but he had nothing better to offer.

"How do the police know it was him?" Jim Jr. asked.

"Because of his fingerprints," Jim said. "They found them nearby."

"But did he say he did it?" Mindy asked.

"No. At least not yet."

"So there's just fingerprints?" Mindy pressed. "What if they have to let him go?"

Her eyes were welling up, and her voice sounded panicked. Jim Jr. seemed to catch her fear.

"No, no, no, sweetie," Jim said. "Fingerprints are—"

"What if they let him go and he gets in his car and comes looking for us?" Mindy asked.

"He wouldn't do that."

"Why not? If he wanted to kill Mommy, he must want to kill us, too."

Jim sucked in a long breath. He couldn't remember ever feeling so powerless to calm his own children.

"That's not how it works," he said. "Besides, the police won't let him go. They have more than fingerprints. They have an eyewitness. Someone who saw the man do it."

"Why didn't the witness stop him?" Jim Jr. asked.

"He tried," Jim said. "I have to give him that much. He tried."

CHAPTER 14

Six Months Later

RUDY TOOK THE STAND wearing a V-neck sweater and a collared shirt. The tip of a long and jagged surgical scar crept out from beneath his hairline, but otherwise he appeared fully recovered. Beauchamp sat beside his lawyer at the defendant's table, doodling in a legal pad. Jim couldn't say what made him more uncomfortable: having to keep his gaze on Rudy, the man who'd slept with his wife, for however long this cross examination would take; sitting just a few yards away from Beauchamp, the man who'd murdered his wife; or spending day after day sandwiched between his in-laws, who barely spoke to him.

The prosecutor had finished tossing softball questions at Rudy, and now it was the defense's turn. John Cotzee, Beauchamp's public defender, stood and scanned the jury, then stepped forward. He and his client were a study in contrasts. Beauchamp looked like Paul Bunyan stuffed into a double-breasted suit, while Cotzee was maybe five nine and weighed no more than 150 pounds. Beauchamp, in his late forties, still had a full head of wiry red hair; Cotzee, barely thirty, shaved his head to the bone. Beauchamp struggled to make eye contact and always appeared on the verge of blushing; Cotzee looked like the kid who was picked last for every team sport, but he had a sharp tongue and had already made several of the state's expert witnesses seem like stammering amateurs. Rudy was visibly rattled.

"Mr. Manuel," Cotzee started, "let's cut straight to the chase: you'd been drinking on the night you were shot and Mrs. Hood was killed, isn't that right?"

"I'd had a nightcap," Rudy said.

Cotzee gave a theatrical double-take.

"A nightcap?" he repeated. "I've read your medical records, Mr. Manuel. You had several DUIs worth of alcohol in your blood when the paramedics found you."

"Maybe it was more than one."

"You see, that worries me, Mr. Manuel. If you can't remember that much, how can we expect you to remember anything at all?"

"I remember just fine," Rudy said.

"We'll see. Why don't you start by walking us through that evening. What had you been drinking? And where? And with whom?"

Rudy cleared his throat, wiped a line of sweat from his upper lip.

"Whiskey," he said. "I'd been drinking whiskey at the Camp Nelson Saloon."

"With?"

"Bonn...Mrs. Hood."

Cotzee turned and pointed at Jim.

"In other words," he said, "you were on a date with this man's wife."

Jim did his best not to react.

"No," Rudy said. "It wasn't like that."

Cotzee raised one eyebrow.

"What was it like then?" he asked.

"I worked for Mrs. Hood. I was the property's caretaker. We'd been having trouble at the bar."

"Trouble?"

Rudy described the small gang of unruly bikers, focusing in particular on the beer their leader had dropped at Bonnie's feet.

"Was that the only incident with these bikers?" Cotzee asked.

"No," Rudy said. "There were others."

"In fact, Mrs. Hood had been receiving death threats for some time, all delivered on identical sheets of pale-blue paper. Isn't that right?"

Rudy nodded.

"One of these threats was wrapped around a brick and thrown through the windshield of her Jeep, isn't that also correct?"

"It is."

"And up until her death, you'd assumed it was this band of disgruntled bikers who'd been sending the threats?"

"Yes."

"A reasonable assumption. Mrs. Hood, in their view, was an outsider who sought to disrupt, if not outright destroy, their social hub. Camp Nelson Saloon had been their watering hole for a long, long time. Mrs. Hood wanted them gone. She wanted to replace them with

Silicon Valley types. People with better manners and deeper pockets. Am I wrong?"

Rudy hesitated. There was more to the story, and the yes-or-no question left him flustered.

"She wanted to make the saloon part of the lodge," he said. "She wanted it to be for the guests."

"So she did want the locals gone?" Cotzee asked.

"Maybe, but—"

"Let's revisit your relationship with Mrs. Hood," Cotzee interrupted. "She was more than your employer, wasn't she?"

Rudy looked around the courtroom as though he'd written the answer somewhere on the walls.

"It's not a trick question, Mr. Manuel."

"We were friendly," Rudy said. "We liked each other."

"A little more than friendly," Cotzee sniggered. "You were sleeping with her, weren't you? In fact, the two of you had sex less than an hour before she was killed."

Murmurs broke out all around the courtroom. Rudy turned crimson.

"No," he said. "That's not right."

"So the police reports are wrong? You weren't found lying in your underpants on Mrs. Hood's bedroom floor?"

"Yes, but..." He sputtered out. Beauchamp lifted his head from the legal pad, looked surprised for the first time since the trial began. Jim didn't know who to root for.

"But what, Mr. Manuel?" Cotzee pressed.

Rudy looked down at his hands.

"I heard a noise. I came running."

"From where?"

"I was staying in the cabin next door. In case something happened."

Cotzee's eyebrows shot halfway up his forehead. There was more rumbling across the room. The judge issued a stern warning.

"So you *weren't* having an affair with Mrs. Hood?" Cotzee continued. "Is that what you're saying?"

Rudy squared his shoulders, leaned closer to the small microphone.

"We were friends. We both cared about the property. That's all."

"But that isn't what you told police," Cotzee said.

"I'd just been shot. Everything was fuzzy. I was confused."

"About whether or not you were sleeping with your very attractive and very wealthy boss?"

"I don't know. Maybe I wanted it to be true. Maybe my mind was playing tricks."

"Because you'd been shot in the head?"

"Yes. But now—"

"Let's recap, Mr. Manuel," Cotzee said. "You came here today to testify against Mr. Beauchamp, correct?"

"Yes."

"And how do you think your testimony is going so far?"

The prosecutor objected. The judge sustained.

"Withdrawn," Cotzee said. "But the fact remains, Mr. Manuel, that you've reversed your story on more than one key point, and there's more than ample reason to doubt your memory. First, you told the police it was dark that night and you couldn't see more than the assailant's silhouette. Earlier today, you told this court that you have no doubt it was Mr. Beauchamp standing in that room with the gun in his hand. Which is it?"

"It was him," Rudy said. "I'm sure it was him."

"Because you're one of those rare people whose memory improves with time and trauma?"

"I'm healed now. It all came back to me."

"I see. Still, it was dark that night, you were drunk, and then you were shot in the head. Isn't it at least possible that your memory of the shooting remains faulty?"

"I know what happened," Rudy said.

"Maybe. Do me a favor, would you? Give us a physical description of Mr. Beauchamp."

Rudy looked confused.

"That's him sitting right there," he said, pointing.

"Yes I know, but pretend he isn't there. Pretend I'm a sketch artist. What words would you use to describe Mr. Beauchamp?"

"Well, he's tall."

"Taller than six feet?"

"Yes."

"What else? What about his physique?"

"I'd say he's stocky. Big boned."

"Excellent. And how old would you say he is?"

"Between forty-five and fifty."

"Now, Mr. Manuel, how would you describe the customer who dropped his beer at Mrs. Hood's feet? A suspect you yourself introduced to this court."

Cotzee had done his homework. Rudy felt himself shrinking on the stand.

"I didn't say he was—"

"Please just answer the question. Was this man also taller than six feet?"

"Yes."

"Was he also big boned and stocky?"

"Yes."

"And would you say that he was also somewhere between forty-five and fifty?"

"Could be."

"Late at night, in the pitch dark and under the influence of a great deal of alcohol, mightn't it be difficult to tell them apart?"

"I guess, but—"

"At least as difficult as determining whether or not you'd been sleeping with the woman he murdered?"

"You're twisting my words. I—"

"Just be glad that I'm not allowed to discuss your own extensive arrest record, Mr. Manuel."

This time the prosecutor jumped to his feet.

"Withdrawn," Cotzee said. "I have nothing further for this witness."

Jim looked over at Beauchamp, caught the faintest hint of a grin.

CHAPTER 15

"WHAT EXACTLY LED YOU to my client, Detective O'Dowd?" Cotzee asked.

O'Dowd, who'd stayed up all night rehearsing his testimony, then compensated for the lack of sleep by drinking a pot of coffee and three shots of espresso, explained in a jittery voice how witnesses from the saloon had led them to Beauchamp's fingerprint.

"And what was it witnesses noticed about my client?" Cotzee followed up.

"They thought his behavior was unusual."

"Unusual how?"

"He sat at the end of the bar, drinking alone. At first people thought he must be waiting for someone, but nobody came, and he didn't budge from his stool the whole night."

"Anything else?" Cotzee asked.

O'Dowd understood from Cotzee's tone how thin their path to Beauchamp must seem.

"Just that it isn't the kind of place people wander into," he said quickly. "It's off a small country road. Only locals know about it."

"And my client told you that a local recommended the place to him. Isn't that right?"

"Yes, but—"

"Have you ever had a drink alone in a bar, Detective O'Dowd?"

"I guess so."

"And you weren't breaking the law, were you?"

"Of course not. That's not what—"

"Did any of your witnesses place Mr. Beauchamp at Mrs. Hood's cabin later that night?"

"No, they didn't."

"How about in the vicinity of the cabin?"

"No."

"Anywhere on the property other than the saloon?"

"No."

"Were you able to establish any connection whatsoever between Mr. Beauchamp and Mrs. Hood?"

"Only that they spent most of that night in the same place."

"As did any number of people. Tell me, what was my client's motive for killing Mrs. Hood and shooting her lover? In your opinion."

"We think Mr. Beauchamp went to the saloon looking for a mark—someone to rob. He followed Mrs. Hood back to her cabin. He didn't expect to find Mr. Manuel there. Things went bad, and he panicked."

"You think? That all sounds awfully murky to me. I hate to use the term 'witch hunt,' but it fits here. Wouldn't you agree?"

"No," O'Dowd said. "I wouldn't."

"Really? You couldn't find a viable suspect, so you went after the one person the locals called strange, though really there was nothing at all strange about his behavior. It happens all the time: *He doesn't fit in, so he must have done it.* That kind of logic has landed more than one innocent man in prison, and of course it's the taxpayers who foot the bill."

"Mr. Beauchamp had a history of—"

"Of robbery, Detective O'Dowd. Mrs. Hood and Mr. Manuel weren't robbed, though their valuables, including a sizeable wad of cash, were lying in plain sight. So I'll ask again: do you have any physical evidence whatsoever linking my client to Mrs. Hood's murder? I mean apart from a fingerprint found a half-mile away from the crime scene."

O'Dowd hoped he didn't look as beaten as he felt. He hadn't expected to be put through the wringer by a public defender.

"Please answer the question, Detective O'Dowd," Cotzee said.

O'Dowd cleared his throat.

"We also had an eyewitness," he said.

"Ah, yes," Cotzee said. "An eyewitness who saw a 'tall, shadowy figure.' An eyewitness who offered police no description of his assailant until *after* you'd made an arrest. We're all very familiar with Mr. Manuel. Like I said, what we have here is more witch hunt than investigation."

Jim watched O'Dowd leave the stand and exit the courtroom. As he turned back toward the judge, he locked eyes with Beauchamp. Neither man blinked or looked away until the next witness was called.

* * *

A few days later, it was all over. The jury deliberated for just an hour. When it was time for the verdict to be announced, Jim sat in his habitual front-row seat, flanked by his in-laws. The jury foreman, a retired postal worker in her mid-sixties, held up a piece of paper and took as long as humanly possible to read the phrase: "We the jury find the defendant..." After an equally lengthy pause, she added the phrase: "Not guilty."

Bonnie's mother let out a long wail that seemed to silence all other grumblings in the courtroom. Jim put his hand on her shoulder; she swiped it away and recoiled into her husband's arms.

Jim turned to watch Beauchamp's reaction. He had Cotzee in a bear hug and was crying and smiling at once. Beauchamp spotted Jim watching and turned to face him. His smile dropped away. He had the look of a school bully who's spotted his prey from across the cafeteria. Jim locked eyes with his wife's killer for a second time. To his surprise, he felt more anger than fear.

CHAPTER 16

JIM AND THE KIDS made their final trip to Camp Nelson on a chilly Thursday in late October. Jim thought the occasion would mean more to the children if they were allowed to take off from school, and of course the trails would be less crowded on a weekday. He booked a suite in a nearby luxury hotel. They skirted the lodge, headed straight into the mountains, and parked at a small trailhead. Mindy was out of the car before he'd cut the ignition. He leaned over and shook his son gently awake.

"Come on, buddy," he said.

Mindy wandered over to the nearest sequoia and placed both hands on the trunk as though the tree needed her support. Jim fetched his wife's urn from the trunk.

"Can I carry it?" Mindy called. "I want to be the one to carry it."

She came running over. Jim smiled. Mindy was like her mother: eager to tackle the most difficult part of any new task.

"Button up your jacket first," he said.

"Okay."

"And be very careful."

"I will," she said. "I promise."

They made the short hike up to an alpine lake Bonnie had called one of her greatest loves. The air was thin at this altitude, and Jim made an effort not to appear winded. When they reached the water, Mindy handed over the urn without his having to ask.

"There's no place she'd rather be," he said. "Especially on such a beautiful day."

Mindy began crying, softly; Jim Jr. put a hand on her back, then started bawling himself. Jim took off his shoes, waded out into the lake, unscrewed the top of the urn, and let his wife's ashes fall. Then they walked back to the car without saying a word.

* * *

Mindy sat in the back, staring out the window at the gorge below. Jim Jr. lasted just a few miles before he fell asleep. Jim focused his attention on a radio show about home repairs.

"Where are we going now?" Mindy asked.

"The hotel," Jim said.

"Why can't we stay at Mommy's lodge?"

"Because it isn't Mommy's lodge anymore."

"But why can't we keep it?" she asked.

Jim switched off the radio, looked over his shoulder.

"We talked about this," he said.

"I know," Mindy said. "I know it was Mommy's job. I know we can't keep it as a business. But we could go there on weekends, like before. It could be our summer house."

"Do you remember what it looked like the first time we visited? How it was all rundown and broken?"

"Yes," Mindy said, though really she'd fallen for the place at first sight, like her mother.

"Well, that's what happens when there isn't somebody to take care of it all the time. A place that big needs attention every day. It needs somebody to clean the rooms and fix things when they break. Somebody to water the flowers in the summer and clear the snow in the winter."

Mindy flashed on an idea, an idea that had been building since her mother's death.

"I could do it," she said.

"Do what?" Jim asked.

"Run the lodge. Water the flowers and clear the snow and clean the rooms."

Jim hid his grin.

"What about school?" he asked.

"I don't mean now," she said. "When I'm eighteen. It could be my job."

"With a brain like yours, you'll be headed to college when you're eighteen. You can be anything you want. A doctor. A lawyer. A professor."

"But I hate school. And I want to run the lodge."

"Honey, even if I agreed to hand the place over to you on your eighteenth birthday, who's going to look after it in the meantime? It will go right back to the way it was before Mommy fixed it up."

He was growing tense. He heard his voice begin to strain.

"So I'll fix it back up," Mindy said.

Jim knew he should stop. There was no point in reasoning with an eleven-year-old who would likely have a new obsession in a week's time, but he felt inexplicably determined to close the subject, to know that he wouldn't have to dodge her pleas tomorrow at breakfast, and then again the day after, and the day after that.

"With what money?" he asked. "Repairs on a place like that cost a fortune."

Mindy thought it over.

"I'd pay you back," she said. "Once the lodge was making money again. It wouldn't take long at all."

Jim's patience cracked.

"Why?" he said. "Why in the world would you want to spend your life in the place that killed your mother?"

Mindy glared out from the backseat.

"This place didn't kill Mommy," she said. "Bruce Beauchamp did."

Jim gathered himself.

"I know, honey," he said. "It's hard to explain. If she hadn't been up here, if she'd stayed at home, then I would have been able to protect her. He wouldn't have been able to—"

"But he did and you didn't," Mindy shouted. "And now he's free and he's going to come after us, and you can't do anything about it."

Jim Jr. startled awake. He sat staring at his father. Jim switched off the radio, slowed to just below the speed limit.

"Listen," he said, "Bruce Beauchamp is a coward. Only a coward would hurt a woman. He won't come anywhere near us. It's over, you understand?"

Mindy crossed her arms and threw herself back against her seat.

"I understand," her brother said.

"Good," Jim said.

He switched the radio back on. He hated to admit it, but Mindy had spooked him. He glanced in the rearview mirror as though Beauchamp might be tailing them, then patted his jacket to make sure the .9mm handgun he'd purchased after the trial was still tucked in its holster.

CHAPTER 17

WHEN THEY GOT HOME on Friday night, the phone was ringing.

"I'll get it," Mindy said, sprinting into the kitchen.

Jim dragged their bags through the living room, then plopped down on the couch and switched on the television. Jim Jr. sat in the armchair and took up a handheld baseball game. Jim started to drift off when he heard the phone ring again.

"Mindy," he yelled, "I thought you were going to get it?"

He muted the television, heard Mindy speaking in her grown-up telephone voice.

"Hello, Hood residence," she said.

"Hello," she said again. "Hello?"

She came running into the living room as though someone were chasing her.

"Who was it?" Jim asked.

"I don't know," she said. "They hung up. Both times."

"Huh," Jim said.

"Daddy, I'm scared," Mindy said, climbing into his lap.

"Why, honey? It was probably just a wrong number."

"What if it was him?"

"If he was going to kill us, he wouldn't call first," Jim Jr. said, looking up from his game. "Unless maybe he wanted to make sure we were home."

Mindy stifled a little scream. Jim started to reprimand his son but stopped when he heard the phone ringing again.

"Let me go this time," he said, lifting Mindy off his lap.

But when he got to the kitchen, instead of answering, he pulled the cord from the phone and took the receiver off the hook. Then he lowered the volume on the answering machine, hit play, and listened to a long string of hang ups.

Maybe Jim Jr. was right, he thought. *Maybe Beauchamp wants to make sure I'm home.*

He toured the house, checking that the windows and doors were all double locked.

Back in the living room, he found his children sitting exactly as he'd left them, looking anxious and expectant.

"Let's have some fun this weekend," he said. "They're going to hold a fair at the beach tomorrow. Ferris wheels and game booths and cotton candy. How'd you like that?"

* * *

The boardwalk was crowded with people queuing up at the game booths and food booths and fortune-telling booths. Beyond the boardwalk, families spread out on the sand, the children building castles and forts, the adults scouting for shells.

Jim Jr. tugged on his father's sleeve and pointed to a shooting gallery.

"Can I, Dad? Please? I promise I'll give Mindy my prize."

"I can win my own prize," Mindy said.

"Sure," Jim said. "We're here to have fun, aren't we?"

"Me too?" Mindy asked. "I want to play, too."

"Both of you," Jim said. "When you're done, we'll find something to eat."

The game involved shooting duck cutouts with an air gun. Jim always marveled at how his son, whose grades demonstrated no great ability to focus, could lose himself instantly in the most trivial competition. Mindy eyed her brother, let him go first, tried to best him with every shot. Jim watched them, thinking this was the first real family day they'd had since Bonnie died. It was the first day they had nothing to do but be a family. No errands to run. No people to visit or entertain. Life would be good again, he thought. It would just take time.

In the end, Jim Jr. won a rubber whale and Mindy a stuffed porcupine.

They continued farther down the boardwalk and found a booth that sold pizza cones and funnel cakes. Jim bought three of each. They were eating and leaning against a railing when he spotted Beauchamp, or someone who could easily pass for Beauchamp, watching them from a distance. Jim nearly choked on his food. He stood up straight to get a better view, felt his gun pressing against his side.

He managed to stay calm while they finished their meal, talking in a cheery voice about nothing in particular and stealing the occasional glance, trying to determine if the person in question really was Beauchamp. The man was the right size and shape, and he seemed to return Jim's interest, but he was too far off to be sure; he might just be a stranger who wondered why Jim kept looking his way.

"Let's keep walking to the end," he told Mindy and Jim Jr. "You kids can run ahead if you want. Just don't run so far that you can't see me."

He watched them go, then pivoted with the intention of staring down Beauchamp, if it was Beauchamp. But the man was gone. He'd vanished, like the villain in a movie. Jim stood on his tiptoes and searched as far as he could see, but there was no trace. How could a man that tall and broad just disappear? At the very least, Jim should have been able to spot the hunting cap bobbing above the crowd. He wondered if his mind had been playing tricks, if all the sleepless nights since Bonnie died were catching up with him.

* * *

Back home, Jim checked the answering machine. This time there was a message. He looked around to make sure the children were out of earshot, then pressed play. He recognized Beauchamp's voice immediately:

"I'll be at your office on Monday morning, and don't think you can brush me off 'cause I will sink you."

Jim listened to the message a second time before he erased it. His mind wasn't playing tricks: Beauchamp was coming for him.

CHAPTER 18

BRUCE BEAUCHAMP PARKED HIS rusty Nissan pickup among the BMWs and Mercedes-Benzes in the lot outside a four-story glass and steel building. This was a part of town he didn't know well, a part he associated with fat cats and corporate crime.

He set his sunglasses on the dashboard, looked at himself in the rearview mirror, then licked his palm and tamped down a cowlick sticking straight up from the center of his head.

He spotted four security cameras before he'd reached the automatic revolving door. The marble lobby featured a fountain and a half-dozen ficus trees.

A Muzak version of the Eagles' "Hotel California" played through hidden speakers.

Hood Realty was located on the third floor. Beauchamp pressed the elevator button, then decided to burn off some energy by taking the stairs.

At first glance, Jim Hood's office looked and smelled

like a doctor's waiting room. There were potted plants in every corner, silver-framed photos of luxury properties hanging on the walls, a mild odor of potpourri. It was the kind of place that tried hard not to offend and ultimately made no impression at all. The middle-aged receptionist in her beige pantsuit fit right in. She was working on a crossword puzzle and didn't seem to notice Beauchamp enter. He wished he'd worn something fancier—not a suit, necessarily, but maybe a V-neck sweater instead of his plaid button-down. Maybe she would have noticed him then. He walked over to her desk, cleared his throat.

"My name is Bruce Beauchamp," he said. "I have an appointment with Mr. Hood."

She smiled without looking up, pointed to a door on the opposite side of the waiting area.

"He's expecting you," she said.

"Thanks."

He felt off his game, out of his element. He turned his back to her, took a moment to gather himself, then marched into Jim's office and shut the door behind him. Jim was sitting at a large oak desk, studying some kind of spreadsheet. *A pencil pusher*, Beauchamp thought. *He doesn't stand a chance.* Jim moved back in his chair, gestured for Beauchamp to sit. Beauchamp shook him off.

"This won't take long," he said, leaning forward with both palms on the desk. "I delivered on my end, but you—"

Jim held up a hand and smiled.

"I understand," he said. "I had some cash flow problems, but I'm delivering now."

He opened the center drawer of his desk, still smiling. Beauchamp stood up straight and seemed to relax.

Without saying another word, Jim pulled out his .9mm handgun and fired twice into Beauchamp's forehead. Beauchamp fell straight back, landing with an impact that shook every object in the room. Jim walked around the desk, stood over Beauchamp, and fired five more times into his chest. He heard a scurrying in the waiting area. He rushed over to his filing cabinet and took out a second handgun wrapped in a towel. Careful not to touch the weapon directly, he placed it in Beauchamp's right hand and folded the large man's fingers around the handle and trigger.

Outside, he found the receptionist gone and the front door wide open. He drew a few deep breaths, then picked up the phone.

"911, what's your—"

"Help me," Jim cut her off, his voice booming and hysterical. "The man who killed my wife came to my office. He pulled a gun. I shot him. He isn't moving. Hurry. I'm begging you."

He hung up, pleased with his performance, and stood watching the blood pool around Beauchamp's head.

CHAPTER 19

KRISTINA HARING, JIM'S receptionist, sat on the edge of the lobby's fountain, too distraught to feel the cold spray hitting the back of her neck.

"I'm dizzy," she told the plainclothes officer. "It's like I'm fighting for every breath."

"Just take it nice and easy, ma'am," the officer instructed. "The incident is over. You're safe now."

"The incident?" she repeated. "Forgetting your wallet at the supermarket is an incident. A shootout at work is...I don't know what it is."

The officer pressed on.

"How many shots did you hear?" he asked.

She shut her eyes, tried again to suck in a deep breath.

"First there were two," she said. "I ducked down behind my desk. Then I don't know how many I heard. They came one on top of the other. I must have run. I don't even remember how I got down here."

"Have you talked to Mr. Hood since?"

"No. I assumed...I figured he was..."

"Did you know he kept a gun in his office?"

"I had no idea. This is the last thing I ever expected. Jim's clients are all..."

"Rich?"

"Upstanding. And it's not like this is a cash business. I just can't imagine why anyone would target Jim. The man's been through so much."

"How would you describe Mr. Hood?" the officer asked.

"What do you mean?"

"Does he have a temper? Have you ever seen him blow up at someone? At you?"

"My god, no. I can't even imagine it. He's the most even-keeled person I've ever met. There are times I wish he'd show a little more emotion."

"Are you saying he's cold?"

"No, I'm not saying that. But he's always in control of himself. At least at work he is."

"And you weren't able to hear any of their conversation before the shooting started?"

"No, but there couldn't have been much talk. He'd only been in there a minute. Maybe not even."

* * *

"Have you had any other contact with Mr. Beauchamp since the trial?" Detective Kyle Davis, a fifteen-year veteran of Homicide, asked Jim.

"No, none," Jim said.

"Not even by phone?" Detective Paul Greene, Davis's rookie partner, asked.

Jim shook his head. They were standing in the hall

outside his office while forensics pored over the crime scene. Jim's eyes were red around the rims, and he seemed to be marching in place, as though his body had become one long twitch.

"And he had no feud with your family?" Davis asked.

"I'm telling you, I never saw him before today."

"So he just showed up here with a gun after he'd been acquitted of murdering your wife?" Greene asked.

"My god," Jim said, as though he hadn't heard the question, "I killed a man."

He pressed his back against a wall, struck himself hard in the forehead with an open palm, and kept hitting himself until Davis grabbed his wrists.

"Why don't you take time to gather yourself?" Davis said. "Go home and lie down for a bit. We'll talk later."

"All right," Jim said, blinking furiously and staring at the floor. "I guess I'll do that."

"I can have someone drive you if you want," Davis offered.

"No, I'll be okay," Jim said.

The detectives watched him scuffle off toward the elevator. Greene, puzzled, turned to Davis.

"You bought that performance?" he asked.

"I'm not sure," Davis said.

"Shouldn't we keep pressing him? Isn't he more likely to slip up now, before he's had time to think?"

"Maybe, but you can't catch someone in a lie if you don't know the truth. Let's gather the facts before we do anything else."

Greene followed Davis into Jim's office. There were lab techs bustling about, dusting the walls and furniture, gathering fibers from the carpet. The detectives stood over Beauchamp, examining his wounds, taking notes on the position of his body.

"I guess it could be self-defense," Greene said.

"How do you figure?" Davis asked.

"Beauchamp pulls a gun, but Hood is faster," Greene began. "He fires twice from behind his desk. Beauchamp staggers but doesn't go down. He's a big guy. He raises his gun again. Hood fires and keeps firing until Beauchamp falls."

"It's a possibility," Davis said. "Just not a very likely one."

"Why not?"

"Two reasons. First, Beauchamp, the career criminal who's almost definitely killed before, is the one who walks into the room and pulls a gun, but he doesn't get off a single shot? While Hood, the real estate geek with no priors, manages to empty his weapon? Doesn't smell right."

"Doesn't mean it's impossible."

"No, it doesn't."

"What's your second reason?"

"In all the years I've been doing this, I've never seen a gunshot victim fall straight back without having his weapon knocked from his hand."

"Beauchamp is a big man."

"I've seen them all sizes. Beauchamp would be the first, and I'm suspicious of firsts."

Greene thought it over.

"Okay," he said, "so maybe self-defense is a reach."

"A pretty far reach," Davis agreed. "But that doesn't make the case a slam dunk. There were two people in this room, and only one knows what really happened. And he's about to hire some very expensive lawyers."

CHAPTER 20

DAVIS AND GREENE DROVE north to break the news to Sharon Beauchamp, the victim's widow. Neither detective was surprised to find her at home in the middle of the afternoon. Sharon was only forty-five, but drug use and decades of hard living and poor nutrition had yellowed her teeth and shriveled her skin. She came to the door wearing ripped leggings and a long gray sweatshirt. The cigarette in her mouth was mostly ash.

Davis held up his badge.

"We're here about your husband," he said.

"Who else would you be here about?"

She waved them in, cleared coupon flyers and magazines and a dirty breakfast bowl from the couch, then gestured for them to sit. She dropped into a hard-backed chair, took one look at their faces and said: "He's dead, ain't he?"

Greene, caught off-guard by her matter-of-fact tone, let Davis take the lead.

"If you mean your husband," the senior detective said, "then yes, he is."

Sharon lit a new cigarette with the butt of the old one. Any object left lying around served as an ashtray: empty cans, the sole of a worn-out shoe, a cereal bowl, a coffee mug. The trailer smelled like its windows hadn't been opened in months. Greene wanted to take the conversation outside, but he knew Sharon would be less likely to cooperate with neighbors watching.

"That's who I mean," she said. "I had a bad feeling this morning. I told him not to go."

"Told him not to go where?" Davis asked, curious to see how much he could tease out of her before she started asking questions of her own.

"Where I'm guessing you found him," she said. "In that prick's office. Or somewhere nearby."

"Which prick would that be, ma'am?"

"Call me Sharon. I was already feelin' old. Now I'm a widow to boot."

"Sharon," Davis corrected. "Who was it your husband had gone to see?"

"I'm guessing you know that already, but I understand why you gotta ask. His name's Hood. Jim Hood. And he played my husband for a big fat fool."

"How's that?"

Davis kept his questions deliberately short: Sharon was off and running on her own, and he didn't want to slow her down. Greene took mental notes.

"Look, I know what it is you want to know, so I'll just come out and give you everything I got. Hood said he'd pay Bruce to kill his wife. Twenty-five grand up front, plus another twenty-five once it was done. Well, it was done. Bruce nearly went away for it, and he kept his mouth shut about Hood all through the trial. That deserves a bonus if you ask me, but Bruce never even saw that second payment. He went there today to get it. I told him to shoot first and haggle later, but he never did listen to me."

Greene fought to keep his jaw from dropping. Sharon didn't seem to realize she'd confessed to multiple felonies, from withholding information about a crime to aiding and abetting a murderer, though it would be nearly impossible to make any charge stick since her husband had been acquitted.

"Your husband told you all of this?" Davis asked.

"He more than told me: I saw that first twenty-five. Of course it's all gone now, and I don't got a thing to show for it. Hell, I still got two payments to make on this sorry-ass trailer. We were supposed to put that money towards a real house. Not that I believed it would ever happen. This sardine can'll be my tomb."

Her voice was nonchalant, as though she were complaining about a slight hike in the price of gasoline.

"How did your husband come to know Hood?" Davis asked.

"Bruce did some work for him a while back. Legit work, on one of his properties."

"How long ago was this?"

"Maybe ten years back. Bruce had just gotten out. Again. Jim looked like a real hero then, giving an ex-con a second chance when no one else would. He probably hired Bruce *because* he was an ex-con."

"Do you know if your husband ever did any other side jobs for Hood?" Davis asked.

"He did some moving-man work for a couple of Jim's clients. Nothing against the law."

Davis looked around at the duct-taped furniture and the stacks of trash. He knew the answer to his next question before he asked it.

"You wouldn't happen to have any paperwork showing that your husband worked for Jim Hood? Pay stubs, maybe?"

"He paid Bruce under the table. A blank envelope filled with cash every Friday. Maybe you can get the son-of-a-bitch on tax evasion, the way they did with Al Capone."

"We'll look into it," Davis said. "Do you know if Bruce had any friends who also worked for Hood?"

"You mean like to corroborate?"

Davis nodded.

"Bruce was a loner. Kept to himself on legit jobs and was strictly solo in the criminal world."

"Do you know if he did any other contract work?"

"You mean killings?"

Davis nodded again. Sharon blew out a deep lungful of smoke.

"Ha!" she said. "If he did, I'd be sampling cocktails on a beach somewhere. He did plenty of strong-arm stuff, though. Broke more bones than a schoolyard swing set. Usually for pocket change."

Davis leaned forward, made his voice soft and gentle.

"I hope this isn't indelicate," he said, "but you don't seem very broken up."

She shrugged.

"I guess I could sense the end coming. For both of us. Thirty years of chasing a high'll do that. I won't be far behind now. I just hope I make it to testify against Hood."

* * *

"Doesn't seem like she's hiding anything," Greene said, sliding behind the wheel.

"Yeah," Davis said, "but what kind of a witness will she make? She's an aging junkie who married a killer and probably has a rap sheet as long as his."

Greene turned the ignition, tapped his horn to scare off a flock of pigeons who were pecking at breadcrumbs in the gravel behind their car.

"So what's our next move?" he asked.

"We use what she gave us against Hood. Invite him down to the station as a witness and then hit him with what we know."

"Won't he just demand a lawyer?"

"Maybe. But a guy like that probably thinks he's about a thousand times smarter than a couple of glorified civil servants. We might get lucky."

"I'll make the call," Greene said.

CHAPTER 21

DAVIS SAT ALONE WITH Jim in an interrogation room while Greene watched through the two-way mirror.

"You see," Davis said, "we know that Beauchamp used to work for you. He was fresh out of prison when you hired him on one of your construction sites."

"So?" Jim asked.

Davis flashed a quizzical look.

"So you never mentioned that before. Not to us. Not when he was on trial for killing your wife. You claimed you'd never laid eyes on him."

"I hire a lot of people. Most of them are day workers. If Beauchamp did work for me, I have no memory of it."

Davis leaned back, folded his hands behind his head and smiled.

"You know," he said, "my hardest day as a parent came when my son learned the word 'coincidence.' He was seven, maybe eight. He thought he'd discovered the world's secret free pass. Suddenly everything was a coincidence. When the dog vomited all over our carpet and we found an empty box of dog treats under my son's bed, that was a coincidence. When a trash can in our backyard caught fire the day my silver lighter went missing, that was a coincidence."

"Fascinating," Jim said. "Look, I've been here going on three hours. If you have a question to ask me, then—"

"My question is this," Davis said. "Was I wrong to punish my son for overfeeding our dog? For setting a fire in our yard? I mean, all I had to go on were a couple of coincidences."

Jim saw where the detective was headed.

"No," he said, "you weren't wrong."

"So I shouldn't have taken my son at his word?"

"Are you comparing me to an eight-year-old child?"

"If I were, I'd have to say his lies were more convincing."

Jim wouldn't rattle.

"There are some key differences," he said. "First, if Bruce Beauchamp worked for me and then killed my wife, I wouldn't call that a coincidence. Maybe he saw her at one of the job sites. Maybe he developed an obsession. Or maybe his obsession was with me. Beauchamp had nothing. It must have seemed to him like I had everything. Maybe he couldn't let that stand."

"Interesting theory," Davis said.

"And then, even if Beauchamp did work for me, it's not like we kept in touch. I wouldn't have seen him in over a decade. That's longer than your kid had been alive when the dog got sick. Do you know how many people have come and gone on my job sites over the last ten years? Why *would* I remember him?"

Davis started to giggle.

"That's funny?" Jim asked.

"I guess you're just too damn clever for your own good," Davis said. "I never mentioned how long ago Beauchamp worked for you. But you're right—it's been just over a decade. Is that another coincidence?"

Jim squirmed a little despite himself. Davis pressed on before his suspect had a chance to regroup.

"You know what I think," he said. "I think you hired Beauchamp to kill your wife."

"You've got an active imagination."

"Oh no, I don't have any imagination at all," Davis said. "What I have is a witness."

"A witness to what?"

"To an envelope stuffed with twenty-five thousand dollars. You were supposed to pay Beauchamp fifty grand, but you stiffed him on the second installment. I guess that could help your self-defense argument. He came to your office to demand his full payment. He had a gun, but you drew first. Of course, for that to work in court you'd have to admit to murdering your wife."

Jim gripped the edges of the table, raised up in his seat.

"I didn't kill Bonnie," he said. "You're going to take a drug addict's word—"

"I don't know what drug addict you're talking about," Davis interrupted. "What I do know is that Beauchamp earned that second twenty-five grand. He was facing life, and he didn't let out a peep about you. From where I sit, you're looking awfully ungrateful."

The last bit of Jim's patience snapped.

"Let's talk about where you sit," he said. "Let's talk about that bargain-rack suit you're wearing. Let's talk about the sad little middle-class upbringing I bet you gave that son of yours. You're right: you have no imagination. You carry a gun and send people to jail, but at the end of the day you're just another sad working stiff who couldn't think of anything better to do with his life."

Davis smiled.

"I hope you get a lot of self-made rich folk on your jury, because us working stiffs may not find you so sympathetic."

"Does that mean you're charging me?"

"I might as well. A confession would be nice, but I don't really need one. The DA's got a clear enough story to tell. You killed the killer to cover your tracks and save a few bucks."

"That's insane. I loved Bonnie."

"Once, maybe," Davis said. "But you were tired of her little mountain adventure. It was costing you money, and you had no intention of living up there, away from the action."

"That place wasn't costing me a thing," Jim said. "Bonnie was making a go of it."

"Please, Mr. Hood," Davis said. "We've been over the receipts. I believe 'hemorrhage' was the accountant's word. Then there's the fact that your marriage wasn't so strong to begin with. I mean, your wife was cheating on you with the handyman."

"Shut your—"

"Then there's the Widow Beauchamp, who, hard living aside, is about the most compelling witness I've come across. I'm a skeptic at heart, but she sold me within five minutes. You lured Beauchamp to your office thinking you could get rid of the last of the evidence and save a few bucks in the process. You should have just paid the man, Mr. Hood."

"All you've got is speculation," Jim said.

"Not true, Mr. Hood. There's physical evidence, too."

"What physical evidence?"

Davis considered whether or not to share. It was risky, but the more he piled on, the more likely Hood would be to panic.

"Bruce Beauchamp was left-handed," he said.

Jim looked confused.

"So?" he asked.

"So we found the gun in his right hand. And there wasn't a speck of blood on that gun."

"You could explain that a thousand different ways," Jim said.

"No, Mr. Hood, you couldn't," Davis said. "There's no way Beauchamp was holding a gun on you when you pumped five bullets into his chest. It's just not possible. I'll give you this, though: you put on a hell of a show for the 911 operator. You sure you don't want to do some more acting? Say how sorry you are? Shed a few tears? That kind of thing goes over big at sentencing."

Jim held up his hands.

"I want my lawyer," he said. "Now."

CHAPTER 22

JIM'S IN-LAWS WERE back in court for the trial, dressed to the nines and sitting in the front row. Jim could feel their eyes boring into the back of his skull; he imagined Bonnie's mother smiling each time the DA scored a victory. And for the prosecution, the victories kept coming.

Forensic experts supported Davis's theory of the crime scene: whether or not Beauchamp was left-handed, the impact of his fall would have knocked the gun from his hand, and the gun itself would have been spattered with blood.

A forensic accountant testified that Camp Nelson was a "money pit," costing the Hoods hundreds of thousands of dollars, a loss Jim would have recuperated through his wife's $500,000 insurance policy. He further testified that Jim's own real-estate holdings were spread so thin that he was more paper tiger than tycoon: "If things were to continue as they are now," the accountant told the DA, "he'd be bankrupt in a year."

Jim's team of celebrity attorneys couldn't stem the tide: it took the jury just under three hours to convict.

* * *

At sentencing, Jim was led into the courtroom in shackles and an orange jumpsuit. He scanned the front row and found Bonnie's parents in their usual place.

They'd left Mindy and Jim Jr. at home, just as they always did: why risk painting Jim as the single father of two bereft children when there was a good chance he'd go away for life?

The judge, a sixty-something man with slicked-back hair and glasses that looked more like goggles, called the session to order, then read a few preliminary remarks before asking Jim if he'd like to address the court. Jim stood and looked around the room. He forced himself to make eye contact with Bonnie's mother, then turned to face the judge.

"I just want to say how truly sorry I am," he began.

He'd rehearsed the speech in his cell, the way he'd rehearsed his 911 call in front of the bathroom mirror at home. But he hadn't made that call in front of an audience. Here, in the courtroom, he was keenly aware of all the people staring at him, rooting for him to fail.

"I shot Mr. Beauchamp in self-defense," he continued, "but if I could take it back, I would. Whatever the circumstances, I killed a man, and I'll have to live with that for the rest of my life."

It was like he was standing outside of himself, watching and critiquing his own performance. He was wooden, unconvincing. His voice rose and fell in all the wrong places. He'd practiced crying, but now the tears wouldn't come. And now that he'd stopped talking, he couldn't seem to start up again. He'd planned to give an outpouring of remorse, to throw himself at the judge's mercy, to beg for the Widow Beauchamp's forgiveness, but instead of pushing on he simply sat back down and hung his head.

The judge, unimpressed, sentenced him to twenty-nine years. The courtroom erupted in tears and applause. Jim kept his eyes on the ground as the bailiff led him away.

* * *

It was a long three months before Bonnie's father brought Mindy and Jim Jr. for a visit. Jim sat on one side of a thick glass wall, the kids on the other. They spoke through headsets. Mindy, Jim's tomboy, now wore a bright pink dress with a matching ribbon in her hair. Jim Jr. was suffering his first outbreak of acne. Both children put their hands up to the glass. Jim's father-in-law stood back beside one of the correctional officers. He hadn't so much as nodded to Jim.

"I wish I could bring you real clothes," Mindy told her father.

"This outfit is plenty comfortable," Jim said. "It's like wearing pajamas all the time."

Looking at them now, he regretted every harsh word, every instance when he'd lost his temper or refused to play one of Jim Jr.'s board games. More and more he wondered why he'd fought so hard against Bonnie's version of the future. A quiet country life spent watching his kids grow up ... what else had he wanted?

"You look bigger, Daddy," Jim Jr. said. "I bet everyone here is afraid of you."

Jim smiled.

"It's not muscle," he said. "It's all the delicious meals they've been feeding me."

In fact, prison food had put a good twenty pounds on him. His face was bloated, and for the first time in his life his gut jutted out over his waistband.

"We saw you on the news," Mindy said.

Jim winced. He'd hoped his in-laws would shield the kids from media coverage. There was a difference between knowing the truth and being slapped with it day in and day out.

"I guess I'm famous now," he smiled.

"It isn't true, is it?" Mindy asked.

"What isn't true, honey?"

He regretted the question almost before he'd finished asking it. Better, he thought, to issue a blanket denial: *No sweetie, none of it is true. Even the police make mistakes.*

"They said that you didn't really have any money and that you hired that man to shoot Mommy and then you shot him because you couldn't afford to pay him," Jim Jr. blurted out.

Jim fought off a sharp pang in his gut.

"No," he said. "I didn't do any of those things. Your father's innocent."

But looking through the glass at his children, he accepted for the first time that he wasn't innocent. He'd spent his months in prison scheming, denying, searching for a way out. But there was no point in struggling: he was exactly where he belonged. His children would have better lives without him.

EPILOGUE

Two Years Later

"IT WILL TAKE AS much money to fix this place up as it will to buy it," Louise said.

"More, probably," Dan told her. "And a whole lot of labor."

"Still, it's a beautiful spot," she said.

"Can't argue that," he agreed.

They stood outside the boarded-up lodge, turning in slow circles as they studied the property. The balconies lining the second floor of the motel appeared to be hanging on by a thread, and the small cabins, also boarded up, were tagged with graffiti. Even the FOR SALE sign was in disrepair. Still, on a clear-blue day in autumn, with the sequoias towering above, there really was no denying the majesty of the place.

"Wasn't somebody murdered here?" Louise asked.

"I think so. I don't remember who or how, though," Dan said.

Louise shrugged.

"Well, I guess we might as well see the rest of it," she said. "There's supposed to be a stunning trail on the other side of that meadow."

They started across. The grass was thigh-high, and now and again one of them would stumble over an old car part or a discarded piece of furniture. When they reached the tree line, Louise turned back around for one more look.

"It's like a ghost town," she said. "Like something out of the Wild West."

And just as she said it, a shriveled little man wearing a torn plaid shirt and faded jeans emerged from the forest just a few yards away. He held a fishing pole in one hand and a tackle box in the other. His mostly gray hair, thinning up top, hung below his shoulders in the back. He wasn't old, but his shoulders were stooped and he seemed to have trouble walking.

"Howdy," he said, his expression none too friendly.

"Hi there," Dan answered.

"We aren't trespassing," Louise said, as though she anticipated a scolding. "We talked to the realtor, and—"

"Ah, you're investors," the man said.

"Something like that," Dan said.

Rudy looked the couple over. They were young, attractive. They had most of their adult lives ahead of them. He felt a wave of resentment that bordered on hatred.

"Well, you won't find anything better to do with your money," he said, forcing a grin.

"You think so?" Louise asked.

"I'm sure of it," Rudy said. "If I had the money, I'd buy the lodge myself. There's nowhere in the world like it."

Louise took another look over her shoulder.

"I think you're right," she said, locking arms with her husband. "I think this place has real potential."

"It does," Rudy said. "You couldn't ask for better bones."

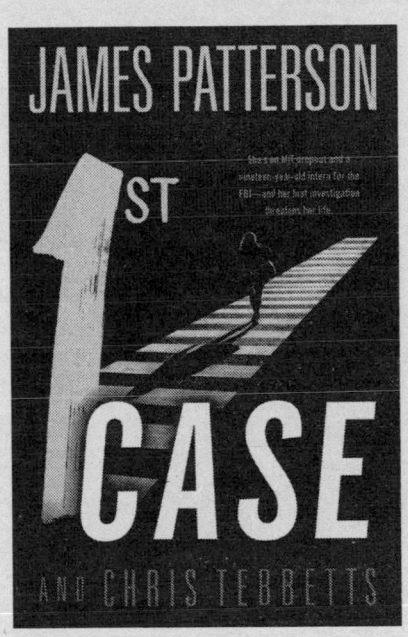

CHAPTER 1

Forensic Media Analysis Report

Case agent: William Keats, ASAC, FBI Field Office, Boston, MA

Evidence marker #43BX992

Media: iPhone 11, serial 0D45-34RR-8901-TS26, registered to victim, Gwen Petty

Recovered file: Unknown source mixed-media electronic message transcript. Source investigation pending.

I want to touch you. Your face, your skin, your thighs, your eyes. I want to feel you shiver as my hands explore every part of you.

I want to hear you. Your voice, whispering my name. Your breath in my ear. Your soft moan as I give you everything you want, and so much more.

I want to taste you. Your lips. Your kisses. Your beautiful flower, opening to my touch, my mouth, my tongue.

I want to take in the scent of you. I want to smell the perfume of your hair. The musk of your desire, bringing us closer, always closer.

More than anything, Gwen, I want to see you. Face to face. Body to body. I could pour my heart out with words forever, but words will never be enough.

It's time we finally met, don't you think?

Please say yes.

CHAPTER 2

THEY TOLD ME ahead of time to prepare myself for the dead bodies. But nobody told me how.

When I pulled up outside of 95 Geary Lane in Lincoln, all I knew was that a family of five had been killed and that I was supposed to report to Agent Keats for further instruction. Talk about jumping into the deep end, but hey, this was exactly the kind of assignment I'd been jonesing for. On paper, anyway. Real life, as it turns out, is a little more complicated than that.

"Can I help you?" a cop at the tape line on the sidewalk asked.

"I'm Angela Hoot," I said.

"Good for you," he said.

"Oh." I'd forgotten to show him my new temporary credential. I held it up. "I'm with the FBI," I said.

I could hardly believe the words coming out of my mouth. Me? With the FBI? Not something I ever saw coming, that was for sure. I certainly didn't look the part, and I didn't feel like I belonged there for a second.

Neither could the cop, apparently. He eyeballed me twice, once before he even looked at the ID, and once after. But that seemed to take care of it. He handed back my card, gave me an if-you-say-so kind of shrug, and lifted up the yellow tape to let me into the crime scene.

"Watch out for the smell," he said. "It's pretty bad in there."

"Smell?" I said.

"You'll see."

It hit me on the porch steps, before I was even through the front door. I'd never been anywhere near a dead body, much less smelled one, but what else could that acrid nastiness be? A gag reflex pulsed in my throat. I switched to mouth breathing and fought the urge to run back to my safe little cubicle in Boston.

What was I doing here? I was a computer jockey, not some *CSI* wannabe.

Up until two hours ago, I'd been a lowly honors intern at the Bureau field office, focusing on cyberforensics. Clearly, I was here to look at some kind of digital evidence, but knowing that didn't make it any less bizarre to walk into my first real crime scene.

The house was almost painfully ordinary, considering what I knew had gone down here just a few hours earlier. The living room was mostly empty. I saw all the expected furniture, the art on the walls, the fan of cooking magazines on a glass coffee table. Nothing at all looked out of place.

Most of the action was centered around the kitchen straight ahead. I'd noticed police officers stationed outside the house, but inside, it was all FBI. I saw blue ERT polo shirts for the Evidence Response Team, techs in white coveralls, and a handful of agents in business attire. Voices mingled in the air while I tried to get my bearings.

"No signs of a struggle," someone said. "We've got some scuff marks here on the sill, and over by the table..."

"Looks like the back door was the point of entry. Must have shot this poor guy right through the window."

"Yup."

They all sounded like they were discussing the score of last night's game, not a multiple homicide. It just added another dreamlike layer to the whole thing.

The lights were off in the kitchen, and one of the techs was using some kind of black light to illuminate spatters on the linoleum floor. It was blood, I realized, fluorescing in the dark. I could just make out a half empty glass of milk on the table, and a sheet-covered body on the floor, next to a tipped-over chair.

I was still standing in the doorway, silent until one of the bunny-suited techs brushed against me on his way out. I started to speak and had to clear my throat and try again, just to get the words out.

"Excuse me. I'm looking for Agent Keats?" I said to him. Even then, my voice sounded so small, so unlike me. I wasn't used to feeling this way, and I didn't like it one bit.

"Sorry, don't know who that is," the guy said, and kept moving. Somehow, I'd expected for everything to make sense here, and that I would know what to do as I went along. Instead, I was left standing there with a growing sense that I'd been dropped off in the wrong nightmare.

"Hoot, up here!" I heard, and turned to see one of my supervisors, Billy Keats, at the top of the stairs. Thank God.

He hurried down to meet me. "You ready for this?" he

said, handing me a pair of latex gloves matching the ones he was already wearing. I put them on. His demeanor was all business, and his face was grim.

"I'm okay," I said.

"You don't look it."

"I'm okay," I repeated, as much for myself as for him. If I said it enough, maybe it would come true. And maybe my stomach would stop folding in on itself, over and over, the way it had been doing since I'd arrived. "Where do you need me?"

"This way." He led me up the carpeted stairs, briefing as we went. "We've got one of the victims' cell phones in a Faraday bag. They're just clearing the body now."

The body. Some person who had been alive yesterday, now just "the body."

But that other phrase—*Faraday bag*—was like a piece of driftwood, something I could latch on to in the middle of all this unfamiliarity. At least I knew what I was supposed to do with *that*. A Faraday bag blocks out any digital signals and preserves the device in question exactly as it was found until it can be forensically examined.

"Eventually, I'm going to want you to cover every machine in the house, but this phone is going to be your primary concern."

We passed two open bedroom doors along the upstairs hall. I told myself to keep my eyes straight ahead, but they didn't obey the impulse. Instead, I stole a glance into each room as we passed.

Through the first door, I saw something truly horrendous. A woman lay on her back on the king-size bed, eyes wide-open, with a small but unmistakable dark hole in her forehead. A halo of blood stained the pale-blue pillow-case under her hair. Outside of the few family wakes I'd been to, this was the first corpse I'd ever laid eyes on. The sight of it seemed to jump right into my long-term memory. No way I'd ever forget that moment, I knew right away.

As awful as that tiny moment had already been, it was the bunk beds in the next room that really split my heart down the middle. Each bunk held a covered body, draped with a white sheet. On the lower bunk, I could see one small hand sticking out, spiderwebbed with dark lines of dried blood, which had also pooled on the rug.

Jesus. This just got worse as it went along. The tightness from my stomach crawled up into my chest. I didn't want to throw up anymore: now I wanted to cry. These poor, poor people.

"Hoot? We're in here." I looked over to see Keats already standing outside the last door on the hall. He stepped back to make way for two EMTs rolling out a gurney with a black zippered body bag on top. Beyond them, I could see what looked like a teenage girl's room, with a floral comforter and an LSHS Warriors banner.

As I came closer and got a full look, one thing jumped out at me right away. I didn't see any blood. Not like with the others.

"What's her name?" I asked Keats, looking back at the gurney as they moved it down the hall. Somehow, I needed to know who she was.

"Gwen Petty," Keats said. "Mother Elaine, father Royce, and twin brothers Jake and Michael. But if anyone in this family had information we can use, it's going to be this girl."

I only nodded. There were no words. Or maybe there were too many, racing around inside my head. It was hard to know anything right now.

"Come on, then," Keats said. "Let's get you to work."

CHAPTER 3

"WHY ISN'T THERE any blood in here?" I asked as soon as we stepped into Gwen Petty's bedroom.

I always ask a lot of questions, especially if I'm nervous. Facts are always reassuring. And if I didn't know what I was doing, well, at least I could ask questions. Always that.

Keats ran a hand over his jaw like he was trying to decide how much to say.

"It looks like he shot the others, but our best guess in here is asphyxiation," he said.

"Jesus."

"Yeah. Whoever did this had strong feelings about Gwen, one way or another."

I could feel some kind of empathetic tightness in my chest. Did that mean Gwen Petty had been strangled? Something else? What were her last moments like?

I couldn't help the morbid thoughts cascading like lines of code through my mind. It was force of habit, in the worst possible way. So I tried to focus on the room instead—on what I could actually do.

I walked over to a built-in desk in the corner. A whole collage of photos was tucked into a crisscross of yellow ribbon on a gray fabric pin board. Another photo, framed on the desk, showed a family of five, smiling on the edge of what I guessed was the Grand Canyon. They all looked so happy.

"Is this them?" I asked.

"Yeah," Keats said.

"How recent?"

"Not important," he told me, and pointed at the Faraday bag on the floor by the bed. That meant Gwen's phone had already been physically fingerprinted and sequestered. Now it was time for the geek squad, a.k.a. me. All things considered, I was grateful for the distraction and listened carefully as Agent Keats went over my instructions.

"I want to know who she's been in contact with, what she's deleted, what someone else might have deleted—everything," Keats told me. "Specifically, I'm looking for texts or images that are romantic or sexual."

I stuck my hands through the mesh sleeves that would give me access to the phone inside.

"What is it, do you know?" I asked. "iPhone? Android?"

"iPhone 11," he said. "It was powered up when we got here."

That told me where the port would be and what kind of cable I'd need to run a copy of the whole thing without altering any files. I dropped a connector cable into the bag, ran it through the exit port, and plugged it into the field kit I'd brought from the office.

One thing I'll say for the FBI: they've got the best toys.

"Soon as you finish that, I want you in the mobile unit outside. Any other devices we find, we'll bring to you. But this phone is your priority."

"What's the hurry on the phone?" I asked. I assumed it had something to do with the fact that Gwen Petty had died so differently than the rest of her family.

Instead of an answer, though, Keats only gave me a tight smile. "Listen, Angela. I know this is new for you, and I'm going to do my best to help you through," he said. "Part of that is knowing your role and sticking to it. These questions are only wasting time, and from an investigative standpoint, the clock is *always* ticking. Got it?"

I got it, all right. I really did. This wasn't about me, and I didn't need Keats treating me with kid gloves, either. If anything, I appreciated that he didn't.

I'd deal with the inhumanly sad thing that had happened here on my own time. Right now, the best thing I could do for Gwen Petty—and for that whole family— was to tighten my focus and IT the shit out of this assignment.

CHAPTER 4

IF ANYONE HAD told me five months earlier that I'd be collecting evidence at this hideous scene, I never would have believed them. But five months earlier, almost to the day, was when it all got set in motion.

The day I was kicked out of MIT.

There we were—me, my mom, and my two little sisters, packing me out of the graduate apartments in Ashdown House on Albany Street, where I was no longer a registered student, and therefore no longer welcome.

"Is this yours?" Mom asked, holding up a ratty old MIT crew T-shirt.

"No," I said. "Leave it."

I jammed shoes into a box alongside an algorithm design textbook, the world's ugliest teddy bear, and a huge tangle of miscellaneous cables. I'm not the most organized person under the best of circumstances, much less as I was hurrying to get out from under the dark cloud that MIT—not to mention my mother—had hung over my head. I wanted to get away from there ASAP. I'd get myself organized when I unpacked later, at home.

"I don't understand, Angela," Mom said. "We've gone over it five times and I *still* don't know what happened here. How is that even possible?"

"Because Angela's being *evasive*," my youngest sister, Hannah, chimed in while I kept my head down and kept on stuffing things randomly into boxes.

"Good word," Mom said to Hannah, but with her eyes still on me. "And a good observation, too."

My other sister, Sylvie, was too busy trying on my roommate's perfume to get involved. Hannah was more like me, sticking her nose in whenever things got tense.

Mom pressed on. "What exactly did the disciplinary board charge you with? Can you at least tell me that much? I mean, seriously, sweetheart. What's with the cloak-and-dagger act?"

"Please don't worry about it," I said. "It's going to be fine."

"How can you be so calm? You got kicked out of MIT halfway through your first year, for God's sake."

I was actually only two months into a graduate master's program in Computation for Design and Optimization. But I thought it better not to point that out. The less we talked about it, the sooner I'd be out of there.

Then again, my mother doesn't tolerate being ignored any better than I do. I had to say *something*.

"I don't think this program was right for me," I told her.

"That's bull crap," Hannah blurted out. "You said this program was *made* for you."

"Yeah, exactly," I said. "As in, I could teach this stuff."

That part was true. I'm not an egotist, but I'm not afraid of facts, either.

The facts were that I'd been one of the three youngest people admitted to the Boston Mensa chapter when I was four years old. I'd graduated high school with a 4.5 GPA, and I'd sailed through my undergrad years at Carnegie Mellon. I hadn't been retested for IQ since I was twelve, but the number back then was 180 on the nose. That doesn't make me a better person, but it's not something I try to hide, either.

"So you get yourself thrown out?" Mom said. "This is the solution?"

I just looked at her. She knew it was more complicated than that, even if I wasn't sharing the particulars. I hated leaving Mom so far out of the loop. It was just that the alternative—going into all the gory details of my academic demise—was an even more embarrassing prospect. Maybe I could come a little cleaner after the smoke had been clear for a few days. But in the meantime, I was all about making the quickest possible exit.

And before I had to manufacture anything else to fill that increasingly uncomfortable silence, the door to the hall banged open. My suite mate, A.A. Wang, was standing there now, heaving for breath like she'd sprinted the length of MIT's famous Infinite Corridor.

"I just heard," she said. "What the f…" She trailed off with a flick of her eyes in Sylvie and Hannah's direction. "Hi, girls. Hi, Mrs. Hoot."

"A.A., thank God you're here," Mom said. "Could you please shed some light? My charming daughter seems to be suffering from some kind of selective amnesia."

"She doesn't know any more than you do," I lied. "Leave A.A. alone."

A.A.'s birth name is Melanie, but she's a gigantic Winnie-the-Pooh fan, which is also to say an A.A. Milne fan. She took the name for her own in second grade, and it just stuck. My sisters absolutely idolized her, from the tips of her tattooed eyeliner to the toes of her fabulous shoe collection. Truth be told, I idolized her a little myself.

"Why are you just standing in the hall?" Sylvie asked.

Which is when I got the signal that A.A. had been not so subtly sending my way.

"Mom?" I said. "Can you and the girls take these last boxes down? I'll bring my bike and meet you at the car."

Mom begrudgingly accepted the box I held out, but her eyes were still on A.A. "She tells you *anything,* you call me," she said.

"Yes, ma'am," A.A. answered. She and my mother were practically friends on their own, for better or worse. I loved them both to pieces. Just not always in the same room at the same time, when they could gang up on me.

"See you downstairs, *Lisa,*" I tried, and hip-checked her toward the door.

"A mother cares," Mom said. "That's all I'm saying."

A.A. said her own good-byes then, but the smile she gave the girls never quite reached her eyes. She just waited until Mom, Sylvie, and Hannah had cleared out, then closed the door and turned to face me again.

Here it came.

"What the hell, Angela?" she said. "You just shot your own career in the head."

"I'll be fine," I said.

"And it's all my fault," A.A. went on.

"Wrong again," I said. "Nobody did this but me. And that asshole deserved everything he got. I regret nothing."

She looked hurt.

"You know what I mean," I said. "I'm going to miss the hell out of you, but I'll only be a few minutes away."

A.A. didn't answer. I guess I wasn't the only one who could wield a strategic silence, because I was feeling guiltier by the second.

"Has he texted you?" I asked.

"Only about eighteen times," she said.

"And?"

"I didn't answer," she said.

"Good," I said. "Knowing him, it'll only take another thirty-two tries before he gets it."

"He's really pissed, you know," she said. "He had to replace his whole hard drive."

I could tell A.A. was fighting between tears and laughter at that point, but her face darkened when she met my eyes again. I stared back, waiting for the inquisition, part two.

"What's wrong with you, Angela?" she said. "Real question."

"Where should I start?" I asked, but A.A. didn't even crack a smile. "Nothing's wrong," I said. "I'm fine."

"No. You're not, and don't try to tell me you are," she shot back. "You're crazy like a rooster in a cage, and I don't get it."

A.A. knew me well. Sometimes too well. It's the cost of a real friendship. The whole thing was like a giant paradox, because everything really was fine, and everything really was a complete mess, all at the same time.

"I'll be fine," I insisted. "Just not today. Okay?"

"Angela—" she said before I kissed her. Not on the cheek. On the mouth, just to shut her up. It was either that or we were both going to start crying, and one of the many things A.A. and I shared was a complete distaste for cheap drama. So I kept things moving instead.

"I'll talk to you soon," I said. Then I grabbed my bike off the wall and wheeled it out the door.

"Hey!" she called after me. "You left your crew shirt."

"Keep it," I said just before the door swung shut behind me.

CHAPTER 5

THAT VERY EVENING, I was summoned to Eve Abajian's town house for what I could only assume would be a world-class dressing down. Eve was the person I most dreaded talking to about the MIT "situation," even worse than telling my parents. I didn't know how she'd already heard about it, but Eve always had a lot of ears to the ground.

"What in the blue hell, Angela?" she said over the intercom at her front door.

"I brought food!" I answered. Eve and I shared a certain obsession with the fried chicken and ginger waffles from Myers and Chang, not far from her place in South Boston. It was like bringing a water pistol to a gunfight, but it was all I had.

When I didn't get any answer, or even a buzz-in, I beeped myself through with the keypad and headed inside to face the music. I knew this had to happen, sooner or later. Emphasis on the *sooner*. Eve Abajian was not one to be kept waiting.

Eve was also the one who got me into MIT in the first place. I'd met her when I was sixteen, at the summer robotics program there, where she taught coding and applied theory as a volunteer instructor. Ever since, she'd been a mentor to me, steering me toward Carnegie Mellon and then putting in a strongest-possible word with the graduate admissions committee back at MIT after that.

In other words, everything Eve had spent the last six years helping me accomplish had just gotten rerouted straight down the toilet. I wasn't looking forward to this conversation.

As I came up and into the town house's main living space on the second floor, I saw that Eve was parked behind her four-screen array. I could barely see her for all the equipment, which was just as well. Even the sound of her keyboarding was angry.

I paused there, not really sure how to proceed. When the silence stretched on for an uncomfortably long time and I still wasn't sure what to say, I took the food into the kitchen and started plating it up. Maybe I could still ply Eve with a little sweet and salty deliciousness.

"Do you want to hear my side, or just yell at me first?" I called out from the safety of the galley kitchen.

"You know you could have had your pick of jobs in two years?" Eve said. "With a fat paycheck, too."

"Yeah, doing incident response for some Fortune 500 company," I said. "Making sure the employees at GE stay off the porn during the workday. No, thank you."

"Excuse me, but you don't get to be the smartest one in the room. Not tonight," she said. She still wouldn't even look at me when I glanced out toward her workspace. Another silence settled over us, and I was starting to feel genuinely guilty now.

But then, when Eve deigned to speak again, the conversation took an unexpected turn. In the best possible way.

"Lay off the garlic sauce with dinner," she said.

"Excuse me?" I said. We were both complete devotees of that garlicky concoction. "Why would I ever do that?"

"Because you have an interview tomorrow morning at eight thirty, and nobody wants to smell garlic at that hour," Eve said.

My mind spun, processing this new information, or at least trying to. Eve was one of the few people on the planet who always managed to stay a step or two ahead of me.

"What are you talking about?" I asked, loading two plates with a little of everything, one of them minus the sauce. "Where am I interviewing?"

As I carried the plates out to the living room, she sat back in her black Aeron chair and really met my eyes for the first time.

"At my office," she said.

"Your office?" I asked. "As in the Boston field office of the FBI?"

It was a dumb question, and she didn't bother to answer it.

"You'll be meeting Assistant Special Agent in Charge Billy Keats, and I'm not sure who else. But you need to be ready."

"Are you kidding?" I asked. Dumb question number two. It was just such a surprise. "I mean . . . wow. I mean . . ."

I didn't know what to say. It was a little early for any happy dances, but this was amazing news.

"What's the job?" I asked.

"It's not a job. It's an internship," she said.

"Paid?" I asked.

"Don't push it, but yes," Eve answered. "It's supposed to be reserved for active students, so you're welcome for that, too."

"Will I be working with you?" I asked. This was getting better by the second.

"I'm only there a few more weeks before Guatemala. Then I go out on maternity," she said.

Eve was waiting on the birth of a little girl in Guatemala City, through an international adoption agency out of Phoenix. Within the month, she was going to be a first-time mom. I guess when she didn't meet Mr. Right On Time, she did what people like us always do: she hacked a solution.

It seemed safe enough to approach the rest of the way now. I finally put a plate of chicken and waffles in front of her and sat with my own in one of the guest chairs.

"Why are you doing this for me?" I asked.

"I'm not doing it *for* you," she said. "This is to make sure that ridiculous brain of yours gets put to good use in the world. And I don't mean making lattes at Starbucks."

I smiled around a bite of waffle. Eve's praise was like gold: valuable and rare. She's not the touchy-feely, hug-it-out type, but neither am I. It was embarrassing, how much I wanted to be exactly like her.

"Thank you, Eve," I said. "Really."

"You can thank me by not screwing it up," she said.

"This is your last favor, and probably one more than you deserve."

"So, you're saying I have to *settle* for a spot at the FBI?" I asked, still grinning in spite of myself.

"I'm *saying* I got you in the door," she told me. "But you're starting somewhere back of square one. Disciplinary action at MIT doesn't exactly bolster your application."

"I've got this," I said.

She didn't contradict me, and I looked down at my food just to keep from showing her how freaking excited I was already. I think I still owed her a little back payment of contrition, but that could come later.

"What exactly am I going to be doing, anyway?" I asked.

Eve went back to her keyboarding.

"Probably just basic penetration testing to start," she said. "But mark my words, Angela. You play your cards right at the Bureau, and things could get very interesting for someone like you, very fast."

SEVEN MURDER VICTIMS.
FOUR ACCUSED ARMY RANGERS.
TWO VERSIONS OF THE TRUTH.
ONLY ONE CAN SURVIVE.

TURN THE PAGE FOR A PREVIEW OF

JAMES PATTERSON

THE SUMMER HOUSE

and BRENDAN DuBOIS

CHAPTER 1

INSIDE THIS DUMP of a home in rural Sullivan, Georgia, Lillian Zachary's rescue mission to save her younger sister and niece isn't going well. Only because of her parents' pleadings did she make the three-hour drive this warm evening from the safety of her Atlanta condo to liberate Gina and her daughter, Polly, from this place.

She nervously eyes the guns that are on open display, their promise of violence making her uneasy. A pump-action shotgun is leaning near the sole door leading outside, a hunting rifle is up against the wall on the other side of the old home, and two black semiautomatic pistols are on the cluttered kitchen counter, next to three sets of scales and plastic bags full of marijuana. Antique oak cabinets and porcelain-lined sinks and metal faucets are on the opposite side of the room.

Lillian is in a part of the home laughingly called a "living room," and there's nothing in here worth living for, save her sister and her sister's two-year-old girl. The place is foul, with empty beer cans, two-liter bottles of Mountain Dew, crumpled-up McDonald's bags, and crushed pizza cartons strewn across a wooden floor worn and gouged from a century of wear.

Built in the small plantation-plain style and named The Summer House, the place was once the getaway destination of a rich Savannah family fleeing city smells and sounds generations before the invention of air-conditioning. Now, decades later, the rich family has fallen on hard times, and their grandly named Summer House is a decaying rental property fit only for this group of lowlifes.

Lillian wonders if the ghosts of the old Savannah family are horrified to see how decayed and worn their perfect summer escape home has become.

Lillian is perched on the armrest of a black vinyl couch kept together with scrap lumber and duct tape, and Gina is sitting next to her, shaking a footless rag doll in front of little Polly, who's on the carpeted floor before her mother, giggling.

Lillian says, "Gina, c'mon, can we get going?"

Her sister shakes her head. "No, not yet," she says. "Polly's laughing. I love it when Polly laughs. Don't you?"

Lillian isn't married, doesn't seem to have that maternal urge to bear children, but something about the bright-blue eyes and innocent face of the chubby little girl in a pink corduroy jumper stirs her. Her little niece, trapped here with her single mom, in a crappy house in a crappy part of the state.

At the other end of the room is another couch in front of a large-screen television—no doubt stolen, she thinks—and three other people who live here are playing some stupid shoot-'em-up fantasy video game where fire-breathing dragons and knights do battle armed with machine guns. She's already forgotten the names of the two lanky, long-haired boys and their woman friend. Shirley? Or Sally. Whatever. And Randy. Yeah. That's one of the losers' names.

The two guys gave her serious eye when earlier she knocked on the door, and she feels vulnerable and out of place with them and their guns. Even though they seem to be having fun on their couch, there's a simmering tension between them that's growing along with the insults they've been tossing at each other.

"Missed it, you fag!" Randy yells.

"Bite me!" the other young man shouts back.

Upstairs in the old home is the other occupant, Gina's on-again, off-again boyfriend, Stuart, who's lying in bed, not feeling well, bitching and moaning like the community college dropout and drug dealer he is.

Plus the father of little and innocent Polly.

"Gina," she says, looking away from the video game players. "Please."

"Just a sec, Lilly, just a sec, okay?"

Lillian rubs her hands across her tan slacks, looking again at the shotgun resting between the television and the door leading outside. All she wants to do is carry the two green plastic trash bags holding the entire possessions of Gina and her daughter through that door. In just a very few minutes she'll get Gina and Polly out of this shithole and back up to Atlanta and leave this crap off-ramp to a loser life behind.

If those increasingly angry young men let her, Gina, and Polly leave, that is. Randy said a while ago, "Hey, you plan on staying for a while, right? We're gonna party hard later on."

Her plump younger sister is wearing black yoga tights and an Atlanta Falcons sweatshirt, but even through her bad complexion, her eyes shine bright with joy and love for her baby girl. That light gives Lillian hope. Gina moved down to this little town with Stuart, promising Mom and Dad she would study dental hygiene at nearby Savannah Technical College, and not telling anyone until a week ago that she dropped out last year.

Tonight it's going to change, Lillian thinks. She has a great job as a purchasing agent for Delta, and she's confident she can get her younger sister a job even if the work is physical, like handling baggage. Gina is a stout, strong girl, and Lillian thinks that will be perfect for her, and much better pay than the night shift at the local Walmart.

Her little niece keeps on laughing and laughing.

There's a sound of a helicopter flying overhead, and Lillian vows to leave in just one minute. Yep, in sixty seconds she's going to tell Gina to get her ass in gear.

Lillian thinks she sees a shadow pass by one of the far windows.

As he moves through the typical Georgia pine forest to within twenty meters of the target house, he raises a fist, and the others with him halt. He wants to take one more good scan of the target area before the operation begins. A helicopter drones, heading to nearby Hunter Army Airfield. The woods remind him some of forests he operated in back in Kunar province in the 'stan, right up against the border to Pakistan. He likes the smell of trees at night. It reminds him of home, reminds him of previous missions that have gone well. Some meters off is a small lake with a shoreline overgrown with saplings and brush.

He slowly rotates his head from left to right, the night-vision goggles giving him a clear and green ghostly view of the surroundings. He can see that the two-story place used to be a fine small home with two front pillars and classy-looking, black-shuttered windows. Now the siding is peeling away, the pillars are cracked and stained, and one of the windows is covered with plastic.

Only one entry in and out between the two pillars, which will be challenging but not much of a problem.

Four vehicles in the yard. Two Chevy pickup trucks and a battered Sentra with a cracked windshield and trunk held closed with a frayed piece of rope. Previous surveillances of the area showed these same vehicles here, almost every night.

But tonight there's an additional vehicle. A light-blue Volvo sedan.

It doesn't fit, doesn't belong, hasn't been here before.

Which means there's at least one additional person—and perhaps up to four—in the target house.

He sighs.

Embrace the suck, move on.

Has he ever been on a mission that went exactly, 100 percent right?

Never.

So why start tonight?

He catches the attention of his squad mates, and they move into position, with him leading the way to the open wooden porch before the solitary door.

He flips up his night-vision goggles, blinks a few times. He can hear music and sound effects from some sort of video game being played inside.

No worries.

He pulls out his pistol, gets ready to go to work.

Lillian puts her hand on Gina's shoulder, is about to say, *I want to get on I-16 before the drunks start leaving the roadhouses,* when there's a sharp *bang!* and the door leading outside blows wide open into the small, old house.

The woman on the other couch screams, and the guy to her right—Gordy, is that his name?—stands up and says, "Hey, what the hell—"

A man in military-style clothing ducks in with a pistol in his hand, and Lillian stands, putting her arms up in the air, thinking, *Oh, damn it, it's a police raid. These morons have finally been caught dealing their dope.*

Funny how all cops nowadays feel like they have to dress up like soldiers, like this one, with fatigues, black boots, belts and harness, a black ski mask over his head.

Gordy says, "Hey, guy, I know my rights—"

He stops talking when the man with the pistol points it at him—and with horror Lillian recognizes there's a suppressor on the end of the pistol, just like in the movies—and in two muffled reports, Gordy falls back onto the couch, his skull blown open in a blossom of brain and bone.

A spray of blood hits the face of Sally, who is now screaming louder, and the other guy on the couch scrambles over the side, toppling the couch. Lillian pushes Gina, screaming, "Run, run, run!"

Gina ducks down and picks up her girl, who's still giggling, and Lillian shoves her sister and niece away as she grabs a dirty couch pillow and throws it at the gunman.

"Gina!" she screams at her sister. "Run!"

Polly in her arms, Gina runs up the stairs, Lillian pounding the steps right behind her.

CHAPTER 2

THE MAIN PART of the old house is cleared within seconds by his squad, and as he goes past the bodies, picking up warm shell casings and carefully digging out spent bullets as he does so, one thought comes to him: how often Hollywood gets this part wrong.

They love showing a squad like his breaking into a residence, screaming *Go, go, go!* or *Down, down, down!* Truth is, you move quietly and with deliberation, clearing and securing everything before moving on.

He heads to the wide wooden stairway, the others following him. Stops at the foot of the stairs. Makes the necessary hand signals, and they go up, sticking to the left side to reduce the sounds of creaking steps.

Halfway up the stairs he pauses, hearing frantic movement overhead.

When they got to the top of the stairs, Gina slammed open the door to the left with her free hand, saying, "Stuart, Stuart, oh, God, Stuart…"

Lillian broke right, going to the other bedroom, sobbing, panting, not wanting to think of what just happened, who that man was, not wanting again to see in her mind the spray of blood from Gordy being shot in the head, and above all, not wanting to think of the man coming up the stairs after them.

She nearly stumbles over the piles of clothing, shoes, and more crumpled boxes and beer cans strewn across the floor. Two beds. One bureau. Trash bags with clothing. Open closet door.

Two windows. One with an air-conditioning unit that's not running.

The other leading out to safety.

Lillian gets to the window, yanks at the bottom.

It won't move.

"Please, please, please," she whispers.

She yanks again.

Nothing.

She senses the man with the gun is nearing the top of the stairs.

Lillian is too scared to turn around, dares not turn around.

Another tug.

A squeak.

It moves, just enough for her to shove her fingers in between the window and the sill.

"Please, please, please," she prays, whispering louder.

She gives the window a good hard shove, leveraging her weight, her shoulders and arms straining from the attempt.

The window grinds open.

Fresh air flows in.

Lillian bends over, ducks her way through, as she hears the other bedroom door slam shut.

He's nearly at the top of the stairs when he hears a window slide open, and then he gets to the landing.

Room to the left, room to the right.

The door is open to the right-side room. The other door is closed.

He looks back at his squad, gestures to the nearest two behind him, points to the left door, and they nod in acknowledgment.

He steps into the room on the right.

Empty.

Trashy, of course, but there's no one he can see.

The window is wide open.

He's focused on clearing this room, but he can't help but hear the door to the other room open, a woman scream, and a man call out, "Hey, hey, hey—" followed by the friendly *thump* of a pistol firing through a sound suppressor.

Then a sentence is uttered, and two more *thump*s wrap up the job.

He moves through the room, dodging piles of clothes and trash. An overhead light from the top of the stairs gives him good illumination.

The closet is empty.

Fine.

He goes to the window, leans over, peers out.

Lillian is biting her fist, trying hard not to breathe, not to sneeze, not to do a damn thing to get noticed. She's under one of the two unmade beds in this room, trembling, part of her ashamed that she's wet herself from fear.

There are slow and measured paces of someone walking through the room, and then going over to the open window.

She shuts her eyes, her mother's voice whispering to her from more than twenty-five years ago: *There's no such thing as the bogeyman,* she would say. *Just close your eyes and pray to Jesus, and everything will be all right.*

Oh, Mamma, oh, Jesus, please, please, please help me.

He leans out the window, lowering his night-vision goggles to take in the view. More trees, more scrub, and a collapsed small wooden building that looks like it was once an outhouse.

Possible. This place is so old it would fit right in.

He looks closer to the side of the two-story summer house.

He's up about six or so meters. Hell of a drop.

And what's below here? Two rusty fifty-five-gallon oil drums, a roll of chicken-coop wire, and a pile of wooden shingles and scrap lumber.

All resting undisturbed.

He flips up the night-vision goggles, ducks back into the room, sees his squad mates have joined him. He holds a finger to his lips.

Moves across the room.

Lillian is still praying, still trembling, still biting into her fist when a strong hand slides under the bed and grabs her ankle, dragging her out.

She shrieks and rolls over and puts her hands up and says, "Please, please, please, no, no, no!"

Someone grabs her shoulders, holds her down. Another man—the one who just shot Gordy—comes down on one knee and looks down at her. Lillian takes a deep breath, hoping it will calm her down.

It doesn't.

The man has military-type viewing equipment on his forehead, he's wearing military fatigues with some sort of harness and belts, and over one pocket where there should be a name tag is a strip of Velcro, meaning the name tag has been stripped off so he won't be identified. The ski mask from before is pulled up, revealing a friendly and relaxed face.

"Please," she whispers.

"Shhh," he replies. "Just a few questions. I promise I won't hurt you."

Lillian just nods. *Answer him,* she thinks. *Don't ask questions. Just answer.*

He says, "There was a man in the bedroom on the other side, with a woman and a child. Downstairs there was a woman and two other men. Is there anybody else here?"

"No," she says, her whole body shaking, the hands of the man holding her shoulders down firm and strong.

"Are you the owner of the Volvo?"

"Yes."

"Did you come down here alone?"

"Yes."

"Is anyone expecting you to return in the next few minutes?"

She doesn't process the question until it's too late, for she answers truthfully, automatically, and hopefully and says, "No."

The man stays quiet for a few long seconds and then lifts his head to nod to the man behind her. When he removes a hand from her shoulder and she feels the cold metal of a pistol barrel pressing against the side of her head, Lillian knows her mamma has always been wrong, that the bogeyman does exist.

CHAPTER 3

AFTER MY "WORKOUT" for the day, I'm resting on my bed at my condo rental just outside the Marine Corps base in Quantico, Virginia, reading *Glory Road,* the second book in Bruce Catton's trilogy about the Union's Army of the Potomac. I'm enjoying the book and hating Quantico, because it's still not home, and it's definitely not New York City.

My ringing iPhone quickly pulls me away from the year 1862, and my hand knocks the damn thing from the nightstand to the floor. Bending over to pick it up, I gasp as my permanently damaged left leg screams at me to stop moving.

And I quickly think of those poor Civil War soldiers, both blue and gray, how a shot in the leg with a bone-shattering Minié ball meant near-certain amputation. Some days I'm envious of them, suffering short-term grievous hurt and then living on without a damaged leg constantly throbbing with burning-hot pain. I declined a chance to get my left limb amputated, and some days I wonder if I made the right decision.

I grab the phone off the floor, then slide my fingers across the screen to answer.

"Cook," I say, and a very familiar voice replies, "This is Phillips. What are you doing right now?"

"Besides talking to you, sir, I'm staring at my left leg and telling it to behave."

Which is true. My left leg is propped up on a pillow. I'm wearing dark-blue athletic shorts and a blue-and-white NYPD T-shirt. My right leg is slightly tanned, slightly hairy, and highly muscular. My left leg is a shriveled mess of scars, burn tissue, and puckered craters of flesh where metal tore through it last year when I was deployed in Afghanistan.

But my left foot looks okay. Thank goodness for heavy-duty Army boots, which protected my foot during the long minutes when my leg was trapped and burning.

Colonel Ross Phillips, who's probably a mile away from me in his office this bright Saturday afternoon, quickly gets to it. "We got a red ball case—a real screamer—down in Georgia."

"Hold on, sir," I say, and from my cluttered nightstand I pull free a small notepad and a pen from the Marine Federal Credit Union. I snap the pen into place and say, "Go ahead."

He coughs, clears his throat, and says, "Sullivan, Georgia. About fifty miles from Hunter Army Airfield, near Savannah. We have four Army personnel in civilian custody, arrested by the Sullivan County Sheriff's Department. Their duty station is Hunter."

"Four?" I ask.

"Four," he says.

"Names and unit?"

"I've got someone tracking that down."

"What are the charges?"

"Multiple homicides."

My pen stops writing. I scribble and scribble and no ink appears.

"How many?" I ask.

"Another thing we're tracking down," he says. "We should know in a few more minutes. What we do know is that it was a house holding a number of civilians and that they were all shot. Some historical place called The Summer House. How original, eh? Our four guys were arrested by the county sheriff about forty-eight hours later, in a nearby roadhouse."

"Who's CID head at Hunter?"

"Colonel Brenda Tringali, Third MP Group," he says. "But this case is no stolen Humvee from a motor pool. Mass killing of civilians by four Army personnel is one for you and your group. So far it hasn't hit the news media, but it will soon enough."

He coughs again. And again.

"Colonel . . . are you all right?"

"Shut up," he says. "I expect you and your crew there by tonight. The sheriff for that county is Emma Williams. Get to her, use your folks to find out what happened, where it happened, and why. Do your job. And get it done. This brewing shit storm is going to rile up a lot of people and groups. Lucky for the Army you and your crew are going to be out there, taking the heat and whatever crap gets flung around."

"Yes, sir," I say.

"Good," he says. "I'll contact you once I have more information."

My supervisor hangs up, and I throw the dead pen across the room, open the nightstand drawer—grimace again as my leg shouts at me—and find a new pen to scribble down a few more notes.

Then back to my iPhone. I need to reach out to the four members of my investigative unit, but there's one call I need to make—and now—even though I'm dreading it.

I tap on the contact number—the number that last year was my home number—and wait for the call to be picked up in Staten Island, about 250 away.

It's picked up after one ring, and the woman says, "What's wrong?"

I rub the side of my head. "Sorry to do this, but I can't come up tonight."

"What about tomorrow?" she asks. "You know how much Kelli is looking forward to seeing you."

"Tomorrow's not going to work, and Monday won't, either," I say, hating to say these words.

"Jeremiah."

"Yes."

She says, "Work again?"

"Yes."

"Germany?"

"No, that was last month. I'm leaving for Georgia later today. Is Kelli there?"

My ex-wife, Sandy, says, "No. But don't you worry. I'll tell her myself. How Dad is missing another volley-ball tournament. And I'll even tell Kevin you're missing his Boy Scouts Court of Honor Monday night. Anything else I can do for you?"

Months ago these words were sharp blades that Sandy used so well, but now, after months of hearing them, the words have dulled some, though they still hurt.

"No, just tell them I'm sorry, that I'll do my best to make it up to them."

Sandy says, "Fine. And you got a call here from Gary O'Toole, wanting to know if you're going to Pete Monahan's retirement next month."

"Pete?" I ask. "Pete's pulling the pin?"

"That's what Gary told me," she says harshly, like I'm questioning her intelligence or her ability to listen carefully. "I guess Midtown South is planning a huge send-off. You should go."

"No," I say.

"You should go," she repeats, "and you should kiss and make up with the chief of d's...You know they were going to give you a nice desk job at One Police Plaza. I hear the offer is still out there, even if you've been a prick ever since you got hurt."

I say, "Sandy, thanks for telling the kids I won't make it. I'll try to talk to them later this week."

With that call out of the way, I send a text message to three members of my crew, giving them the raw basics. Rendezvous point and time to follow.

I pull up the contact of my fourth team member, but before I can call and speak to her directly, my iPhone chimes again. It's Colonel Phillips.

He says, "More information, all bad."

I get my new pen and pad and say, "Go ahead, sir."

"The four Army personnel...they're all Rangers. Assigned to the Fourth Ranger Battalion, stationed at Hunter Army Airfield."

"Shit," I say.

"Yeah," Phillips says. "These aren't four kids fresh out of Basic Training. Nope, these four are pros."

"Names?"

"Jefferson, Barnes, Tyler, and Ruiz. Four-man fire team, part of Second Platoon, Alpha Company. Jefferson is a staff sergeant, fire-team leader."

"Motive?"

"Your guess is as good as mine. And I got a count on the civilian deaths. Seven."

Seven, I think. *Seven civilians, gunned down by four Army Rangers. Jesus Christ on a crutch.*

I'm in a race now, to see who's going to get there first: my investigators and myself or CNN, Fox, MSNBC, and every journalist with a notepad, camera, or video equipment within a thousand-mile radius, ready to try to convict these men in thirty-second sound bites.

"Breakdown?"

He coughs once more. "Three men, three women. All shot at close range."

I stop taking notes.

"Wait," I say. "You said there were seven. And you said three men, three women. What's the correct number?"

His breathing quivers for a long, long second.

"Six adults were shot," he says. "And a two-year-old baby girl."

For a complete list of books by
JAMES PATTERSON

VISIT
JamesPatterson.com

 Follow James Patterson on Facebook
@JamesPatterson

 Follow James Patterson on Twitter
@JP_Books

 Follow James Patterson on Instagram
@jamespattersonbooks

www.melodramapublishing.com

Library of Congress Control Number: 2011946166
ISBN-13: 978-1620780251
Mass Market Edition: January 2014
10 9 8 7 6 5 4 3 2 1

Interior Design: Candace K. Cottrell
Cover Design: Marion Designs
Model: Jaz

Also by

Erica Hilton

Wifey: From Mistress to Wifey (Part 1)
Wifey: I Am Wifey (Part 2)
Dirty Little Angel
10 Crack Commandments
The Diamond Syndicate
Dirty Money Honey
Bad Girl Blvd.

Wifey:

I AM WIFEY

Erica Hilton

Buy

for Melodrama

CHAPTER 1

Jasmine sat silent, stone-faced, and confused.

"Did we answer all of your questions?" Agent Dowd asked her.

She closed her eyes. All she could do was wonder if Nico was fucking Mia at that very moment as she sat in a room full of FBI agents trying to convince her to become a snitch.

"Jasmine, if something is on your mind, now is the time to speak," Agent Battle said to her.

"You wanna know what's on my mind? I ain't no snitch!—That's what's on my mind. What's on my mind is, why the fuck am I sitting here? Why the fuck I ain't see a judge yet? Why the—"

"Jasmine, you're right. You're not a snitch," Agent Dowd said. "What did we tell you twenty minutes ago? We told you that we want you to be a *source*. There is a huge difference between a source and a snitch."

The room went quiet. Jasmine looked at the agent and rolled her eyes.

"So, yeah, like I said, I wanna see a fuckin' judge. Y'all trying to isolate me, like I'm some dumb bitch or something. I don't wanna be your *source*. Lock my black ass up. Do whatever the fuck you feel you gotta do. But I tell you one thing—Y'all better come correct, because I'm gonna make sure my lawyers go so fuckin' hard on y'all asses for embarrassing me at the restaurant and having me in custody for more than twenty-four hours without seeing a judge. Hello! This is New York City. I know my rights. I'm suppose to see a judge within twenty-four hours!"

Agent Battle, the only black agent in the room as well as the only female agent, motioned to the other two agents to keep quiet. She pulled up a chair, placed it right in front of Jasmine, and sat so her torso was facing the back of the chair.

"So you a ride-or-die chick? You gonna ride for your man because he loves you, right?"

Jasmine looked at Agent Battle and didn't say anything.

"Your pussy is just so tight and juicy that you know that nigga loves you, right?"

"Whateva."

"Jasmine, I been where you at—Fuck this badge!" Agent Battle unclipped her gold shield from her belt and threw it on the table behind her. "I'm talking to you straight up as a black woman. You sitting there now with an attitude and think you can handle anything that's thrown at you, but I'm telling you that your life ain't worth no nigga that's fuckin' the next bitch as we speak. You would have to be crazy."

"I would have to be crazy? But how do I know them photos are real and it ain't no Photoshop tricks?"

"The photos of Nico with Mia?" Agent Battle asked, just to be clear.

"Yeah. I mean, those pictures could be old."

"You right. They could be old, they could be fake, but ask yourself this—If your pussy is so good, and Nico is so in love with you, how come you ain't lawyered up right now?"

"Y'all muthafuckas got me in here handcuffed and isolated from everybody, just like I just finished saying. Can't nobody help me if they don't even know where I'm at. What the fuck?"

Deep inside Jasmine wondered if Agent Battle was right.

Agent Battle motioned to Agent Dowd to undo the handcuffs on Jasmine's wrists, and she walked out of the room without saying anything.

"Oh, my God! What the fuck? I'm tired! I'm hungry! I wanna either go home, or I want to see a judge. I got civil fuckin' rights that y'all are violating."

Agent Battle came back into the room and handed Jasmine a cell phone. "Call your man."

Mia loved riding Nico's dick in the reverse cowgirl position. As she ground her pussy so that every inch of his dick was inside of her, she couldn't hold back the tears that streamed down her face. She was glad her back was to Nico because she didn't want him to see her crying.

"Don't answer it, baby," she softly pleaded in a moan

mixed with a teary voice.

Nico lightly tapped her twice on her ass cheeks and told her to get up for a second. He grabbed his cell phone and looked at it without answering it.

Mia ran her hand down her face while she sat on the edge of the bed. She was trying to wipe away the tears. "Everything okay?"

"You was crying?"

She stood up and walked over to Nico. She buried her head into his chest, and her tears instantly began flowing again. She held on to him as she sobbed.

"The fuck you crying for?"

"Because I'm so happy right now. You make me feel so good." She looked up at Nico as she held on to him. "Baby, I am so sorry for what I did. It really was nothing, really nothing at all. I was just tore-up drunk, high, and confused, and things just happened." She kissed his chest. "I love you."

Jasmine ended the call without leaving a message for Nico.

"I need *my* phone. He ain't answering because he don't pick up numbers he don't recognize."

None of the agents replied.

Jasmine decided to try Nico a second time, with no luck. She didn't want to show it, but she was annoyed. She didn't know what to make of it, but she didn't want to assume anything.

"Jasmine, he's not answering because he's concerned with one thing, and that's looking out for himself. You really need—"

"I really need *my* phone," Jasmine said, cutting off Agent Battle.

"No. You really need to look out for yourself and seriously consider what we're asking you to do."

One of the agents who had left the room came back with Jasmine's cell phone and her oversized Gucci bag, which he placed in her hands.

"You're free to leave," Agent Battle nonchalantly said, surprising Jasmine. She handed Jasmine her card.

Jasmine took hold of it, looked at it, and placed it inside her bag. She stood up and prepared to leave.

"Think about the evidence we have stacked against you. Think about your future and give me a call. But, either way, we'll be in touch," Agent Battle said.

"Where's the bathroom?" Jasmine asked.

Agent Battle escorted her down the hall. Jasmine's high heels echoed throughout the halls as she walked behind Agent Battle.

"When you're done, you can take that elevator down to the lobby," Agent Battle said, and she returned to her office.

Jasmine went inside the bathroom, washed her hands, and threw water on her face. She shook her head when she looked in the mirror and saw how ragged she looked with bags under her eyes from lack of sleep. She was thankful she had a pair of sunglasses in her bag. She reached for them and put them on before fixing her hair.

After she used the bathroom, she called Nico again. This time, after the third ring he picked up. A relieved half-smile appeared on her face before she sighed into the phone and spoke.

"Oh, my God, baby, where are you?" she asked, tears beginning to form in her eyes.

"Where the fuck you at?" Nico barked into the phone.

"What you mean, where am I at? I'm in the precinct."

Nico hesitated. He pushed Mia's head away from his dick and motioned for her to stop. "Why your phone echoin' like that?"

"Nico, I don't know. I just want to go home. Come get me."

"Come get you? You with the lawyer?"

"Why are you asking me a million and one fuckin' questions? Shit! Just come pick me up, so I can get the hell outta here. We'll talk when I see you."

"A'ight, I'll hit you right back."

Nico called his lawyer, who explained to him that he was still trying to find out where Jasmine was.

He called Jasmine back. "Where they holding you at, baby?"

"Downtown, on Reade Street."

"What happened to the murder charge? What they saying?"

Jasmine sighed. "They didn't charge me with nothing. NYPD held me for eighteen hours, and then they transferred me down to the feds, and I been down here for eighteen more hours. And I'm tired and dirty and hungry, and I want to get the fuck outta here."

"So all they did was question you?"

Jasmine sucked her teeth.

"A'ight, Reade Street, right? Give me forty-five minutes, and I'll be there."

"Thank you."

CHAPTER 2

Nico wanted to leave and head to his lawyer's office, but Mia's body was looking right, and he wanted to reclaim the pussy she had given to some other nigga in a moment of weakness.

"Turn around," he instructed her.

Mia turned around so that her bare ass was facing him, and she braced herself by placing both of her hands on the bed. Her pussy was soaked and throbbing in anticipation of Nico's dick.

"You feel so good," she turned her head and said to Nico as soon as he slid his dick back inside of her.

Before long she was coming all over his dick, and once again, tears of joy began to flow out of her eyes.

Jasmine was standing on Reade Street in the sweltering sun waiting for Nico to arrive. The fact that she still had on yesterday's clothes was beyond irritating to her. She called Nico. The phone rang twice then stopped ringing.

She looked at her phone and realized that her battery had died. "I can't believe this shit!" she screamed.

Jasmine looked inside her bag and realized that she didn't have her wallet with her, nor a single coin of loose change.

She walked back inside the FBI building, and a black-uniformed officer at the building's entrance asked her if everything was okay. She nodded to him, and after going through the metal detector, she stood still for a moment and thought about what she should do.

Out the corner of her eye she could see out of the lobby and onto Reade Street, where she had just been standing, and she was certain that she'd seen Nico's Maybach. A huge smile appeared across her face. She quickly bolted from the building and returned to the blistering sun.

Jasmine removed her shades so she could see better. The red light changed to green, and the car drove off. Not wanting to seem like a crazy chick, she decided to just stand in the sun and wait for her man.

It seemed like a thousand cars passed her by as she stood on the street corner looking like a panhandler. A half hour had gone by, and to her it felt like two hours.

She walked back into the federal building, and the uniformed officer smiled at her and waved her through the metal detector.

"You sure you all right? You need help with anything?"

She asked the uniformed officer if she could use a phone and explained to him that her cell phone was dead. The officer pointed in the direction of the dinosaur-looking pay phones in the rear corner of the lobby, and spared her the embarrassment of asking for change.

"Thank you so much," Jasmine said, way too exasperated to even smile.

She dialed Nico, and his phone rang out to voice mail. "Nico, my cell phone is dead, so if you call me, you aren't going to get me. But I'm on Reade Street right near Duane Street. Where the hell are you?" Jasmine ended the call. She had no choice but to hang up the phone and go back outside and wait.

"Come inside me, baby," Mia pleaded to Nico. She always knew when he was about to come because his strokes became much more rhythmic.

She was laying on her back with her legs wide open while Nico fucked her, and just as he was ready to come, she wrapped her legs around his body and interlocked her feet and pulled him into her and made sure that he didn't pull out.

"You wild. You know that, right?" Nico smiled and said to Mia after he came inside her pussy.

Mia unclasped her feet, and Nico pulled his dick out of her and stepped back and looked at her. Mia propped both of her feet on the bed. She looked as if she was preparing for a gynecologist to examine her pussy. She told Nico to look at her, and she contracted her pussy muscles until his come began to ooze out of her. Then she scooped up some of it with her middle finger and put it in her mouth and sucked her finger clean, like she was finishing off the last bits of a Popsicle.

It had been a full two hours since Nico was supposed

to pick Jasmine up. As much as she hated to, she went and sat down on a nearby park bench. Jasmine was a germaphobe and hated things like public toilet bowls, train cars, and public seating, but her feet were aching, she was feeling dehydrated, and she knew that if she didn't sit down she was going to pass out.

Five minutes passed by, and before she knew what was up, she'd dozed off on the park bench. She wasn't in a deep sleep, so when she felt something tap her hand, she instantly woke up. She looked around and didn't see anyone standing near her, but she couldn't believe what she did see. She looked at the back of her right hand and saw what looked like bird shit.

"No, this is not happening to me! This is not happening to me!" she screamed.

With her left hand, she took off her shades and looked at her hand, and she confirmed that it was warm, purplish bird shit that had just landed on her. She jumped to her feet in a panic, shaking and trembling in disgust. She used her left hand and rummaged through her bag and found some tissue to wipe the pigeon shit off.

Jasmine marched back into the federal building, and after going through the metal detectors, she found a bathroom. She washed her hands for five minutes straight, but was unable to wash away the icky feeling.

After exiting the bathroom she went back to the pay phone and tried calling Nico again. This time his phone went straight to voice mail. She knew he'd turned his phone off, but a part of her wanted to believe that he was driving through the Midtown Tunnel and didn't have any reception. She put the phone on the receiver and stood with a blank look on her face.

The officer who'd given her the change walked over to her. "Miss, what's your name?"

"What?"

"Your name."

"For what? What difference does it make?"

"Let me help you."

"If you wanna help me, call my man and find out where he's at."

"Oh, you waiting on a ride?"

Jasmine wasn't in a talkative mood, so she didn't reply.

"My shift ends in a couple of hours, so if you still need a ride, I could look out for you."

Jasmine didn't even look him in his face. She walked toward the exit of the building. She thought about taking him up on his offer, but she knew it would look way too crazy if Nico caught wind of a cop dropping her off at the crib.

She walked back to the corner of Reade Street and waited loyally for her man to come scoop her.

Another hour passed by, and still there was no Nico. It seemed like ages had passed since the feds had shown her those photos of him with Mia, and she was wondering if, in fact, those photos were real. She did her best to shake the thoughts from her head. As soon as she was able to convince herself that those photos were a result of Photoshop tricks.

Jasmine walked back into the federal building one last time and stood in front of the pay phone. She was down to her last quarter when she saw an advertisement sticker for a cab service plastered on the pay phone. She knew her best bet would be to use that quarter to call herself a cab.

When the cab arrived, she instructed the cab driver to take her to her mother's house in Queens. She was hoping that either her mother or father would be there so that she would be able to pay for her cab, take a shower, and change her clothes.

As the cab made its way from Manhattan into Queens, all kinds of thoughts ran through her head. Something had told her not to go to Nico's sprawling Long Island estate that she shared with him, so she decided to follow her gut.

CHAPTER 3

After a good night of sleep at her parents' house, Jasmine was in no mood to go to school. She ate breakfast and then headed out to Long Island, where she let herself inside Nico's mansion with her spare key. Nico wasn't home, and Jasmine still hadn't spoken to him. She dialed his number from his home phone, but he didn't answer.

"So you good?" Nico asked Mia.

Mia nodded, and Nico reminded her that he would be sitting in the rental parked right across from the only entrance to the Marriott Hotel in Hartford, Connecticut.

"Baby, I'm good." She gave him a kiss on the cheek and exited the Holiday Inn hotel the two of them had checked into an hour earlier.

Mia left the room with 32 ounces of "China white" heroin in her Louis Vuitton shoulder bag, her heart pounding as she made it to the hotel parking lot. She placed the bag in the trunk of the rented Volvo and got behind the steering wheel, pushed the ignition, and headed downtown to the Marriott, while Nico followed her in another rental.

After the ten-minute ride to the Marriott, Mia parked the car and called and reported the rental car stolen. She left three hundred and fifty thousand dollars worth of pure heroin inside the trunk of the car, she got out and headed to Room 605 on the sixth floor with another Louis Vuitton bag that held inside only her makeup, wallet, and other personal items.

A buff African dude opened the door to the hotel room.

"Twist?" Mia asked.

Twist nodded and invited her into the room. There were two other African dudes in the room seated at a table, smoking cigarettes and drinking Jack Daniel's.

"You drink?" one of the dudes asked her.

"I'm not here to drink and socialize," Mia said in a no-nonsense tone, trying her best to not let her nervousness show.

Twist started speaking in his language, and soon the other two dudes started to laugh.

"Have a seat," Twist said to her.

Mia remembered Nico's instructions. She then told Twist she wanted them to meet at the bar downstairs, near the lobby.

Twist smiled and said something else in his language, and the other two dudes again started laughing.

"Have a drink. Just sit and relax," Twist said to her, while his boy poured a drink for her, and his other boy got up and went to another room.

"Listen. No disrespect, but can you do me a favor and

speak English?"

Twist said with a thick Kunta Kinte-sounding accent, "You're funny."

Mia didn't smile because this wasn't a game to her.

"So where's Nico?"

"Why you asking all these questions? I told you I'm not drinking, and I told you we gotta go downstairs."

Twist's man came back in with a black knapsack and tossed it to him. He unzipped it and showed it to Mia.

Without saying anything, Mia immediately turned and walked out of the hotel room. She knew there was always the possibility that the room could be wired with cameras. She only wanted to talk business at the bar.

"Sweetie, I only talk in bars and lobbies."

Twist nodded, and they made their way down to the bar, where Mia ordered a soda for herself and a Jack Daniel's on the rocks for Twist. After about five minutes, one of the dudes from in the room came downstairs and placed the black knapsack near Twist's feet and walked off. Twist sipped on his drink, and then he looked around the bar and asked Mia who she thought was five-0.

"You tell me," she replied.

Twist motioned his head at someone seated not too far from them. "That's one right there, and see homie that just walked in . . . that's a cop; he's wearing a vest."

Mia looked at Twist and shook her head. She sipped on her Sprite and placed it back down on the counter. "That's my shooter with the vest."

Twist looked at her and smiled.

"It's three-fifty inside the bag, right?"

Twist nodded, and then Mia instructed him to take the car key that was sitting on the counter.

"Walk out front, and in the second row you'll see a gray Volvo. Check the trunk."

Twist was expecting to handle everything inside the hotel room, but he knew that if he wanted the deal to go through, he had to play by Mia's rules or he'd run the risk of spooking her and having her think that he was a cop.

"I ain't going nowhere," Mia told him.

Twist took the key and made his way to the Volvo. He checked the trunk and saw what was inside the Louis Vuitton bag. A smile flashed across his face, his white teeth contrasting with his blue-black skin.

"You think your girl will like the bag?" Mia asked after he'd returned to the bar.

Twist smiled. "She'll love it."

"That's what's up."

Mia placed a twenty on the counter, knelt down and scooped up the knapsack, and headed out of the bar. She tried to walk as normal as possible, but she felt like she was going to shit herself. She prayed federal agents didn't swarm her and slam her to the ground and arrest her.

When she made it to Nico's rental car, Nico moved to the passenger's seat, and she got in the driver's seat. She put the car in drive and drove off. She reached over and kissed Nico on the cheek. "I told you I got you, baby," she said.

Nico looked inside the black knapsack and smiled.

CHAPTER 4

Nico had a lot on his mind. He had an uneasy feeling that Bebo was planning to take him out. Not only did he feel that his life was in danger, he could also sense that he was close to being indicted. He just didn't know how close. His lawyer had warned him to be careful over the next couple of weeks and to avoid talking on the phone.

Despite the warning, Nico reached out to Jasmine on his way back from Connecticut.

"Jasmine."

"Nico, how the fuck could you just leave me stranded in Manhattan like that with no money or nothing, after you told me you was on your way to come get me?"

"Where are you right now?"

"I'm in the house!"

Nico was quiet.

"So are you going to tell me what happened or what?"

"I might pass through later on tonight, but I'm not sure. I got some moves I gotta make." Just as Nico said that, the prepaid phone he had recently purchased began vibrating. It was his right-hand man BJ.

"Yo, let me hit you back," he said to Jasmine.

"Nico, don't hang up this phone!" Jasmine's blood was

boiling, and she really couldn't take any more of Nico's bullshit. "Ugggghhhh!" She slammed her phone down on the bed.

"BJ, what's good?" Nico asked.

"Bebo want us to come through for a meeting tonight."

BJ was also speaking on a prepaid cell, since he too knew that the feds had stepped up their surveillance.

"Call that muthafucka and tell him to suck my muthafuckin' dick!" Nico barked into the phone. "Shit is hot as hell right now, and this muthafucka setting up play-date meetings and shit, like we're fuckin' two-year-old kids."

"A'ight," BJ said. After a moment of silence, he asked, "How that thing go?"

"Everything's good. 'Bout to cross back into New York right now."

"So you want me to go through just to see what Bebo is saying, or what?"

"If you go to that meeting, you ain't coming outta there alive. Trust me on that."

Nico's main cell phone began ringing. It was Jasmine. He picked up. "I'll hit you right back." He ended the call without giving her a chance to say anything.

BJ was about to hang up, thinking that Nico was talking to him.

"Nah, nah, not you. I was talking to Jasmine. She just hit me up on my other phone."

"But, BJ, trust me, if you go to that meeting, I'll be going to your funeral next week. Fuck Bebo! This is my muthafuckin' shit! This is my muthafuckin' crew and my muthafuckin' city!"

BJ and Nico ended their call. Nico didn't have to spell things out for BJ, who knew it was just a matter of time before Nico called on him to murder Bebo.

Nico didn't know that Twist was working for Bebo. The two had met while in prison. Bebo was furious that Nico had crossed him and cut him out of a deal that he thought Bebo knew nothing about. More importantly, he had no clue who was supplying Nico with that 95% pure heroin.

Bebo knew that he had to maintain his rep at any cost, even if it cost him the life of his top lieutenant. Most of his anger stemmed from his envy of Nico. He took it as Nico trying to outshine him.

CHAPTER 5

Nico wanted to stay off the radar until he could figure out for sure what was going on after he came back from Hartford with Mia. He had Mia open up a safe deposit box at a Chase Bank branch in White Plains, where he stashed the three hundred and fifty thousand.

Mia was more than willing to do whatever Nico asked of her, and she was right by his side when the two of them checked into the W Hotel in midtown Manhattan, where they decided to stay for a couple of days before heading out to Las Vegas.

Jasmine still hadn't spoken at length with Nico to find out where his head was at, but she decided to just chill and give him space and not press him.

She had started to get real close with a Puerto Rican girl from her school named Narjara. Narjara was a little younger than Jasmine. She was eighteen, was from Washington Heights, and lived with her man. Narjara had swagger that Jasmine liked. Plus, she sort of looked up to Jasmine like she was the big sister that she never had, always complimenting her on how beautiful she was, and asking her for advice. Narjara's man was a mid-level drug dealer from Newark, New Jersey, and he was real abusive to her.

When Narjara called Jasmine, crying and hysterical after getting her ass beat by her man, Jasmine didn't hesitate to tell her to take a cab to Long Island and come chill with her. Jasmine wasn't really in the mood to entertain company, since she had so much on her mind, but she figured it would be a much-needed distraction for her.

When Narjara arrived at Jasmine and Nico's estate, she called Jasmine on her cell phone, and Jasmine ran out to greet her and to pay for her cab.

Narjara's right eye was closed and swollen shut, and her bottom lip was split and swollen.

"Oh, my God!" Jasmine covered her mouth with her right hand, looking at Narjara's face in disbelief as she escorted her into her house. "You gotta go to the emergency room and get that eye checked out."

"I can't, Jasmine."

"What you mean, you can't? You don't have a choice; I'm taking you myself. You could lose your eye. That shit don't look good at all. That muthafucka can't be putting his hands on you like that!"

Narjara, on the verge of tears, shook her head. "It's always the same bullshit. It's like no matter what I do, I can never make him happy. He always finds something to scream on me about. I get so tired of him reminding me how, if it wasn't for him, I would still be working a stripper's pole somewhere."

"For real, for real, you ain't fuckin' with his ass no more, and I mean that shit. You can just chill here until we figure something out."

Narjara went to the mirror and looked at her face. "It wasn't even this bad when I got in the cab." Right after she said that, she fell to the floor.

Jasmine screamed as she ran to her aid, "Narjara! Narjara, you okay?"

Narjara had fainted, but she quickly came to. "Yeah, I'm okay. Just real dizzy," she said from the floor, trying to sit up.

"See, this is what I mean—Your ass is going to the hospital right now. I was going to drive you, but I'm calling an ambulance."

"Jasmine, no. I'm all right!"

"No, you aren't all right. You fuckin' just fainted. You getting checked out by a doctor."

"And what am I gonna tell them happened to me? That my boyfriend beat my ass? Then they'll call the cops. And I just don't feel like dealing with that drama."

Jasmine shook her head. At that very moment, her front doorbell rang. She wasn't expecting anyone to come by at such a late hour. She was hoping it was Nico, that he had forgotten his key or something.

The bell rang again.

Jasmine told Narjara she would be right back. She looked on the security camera and saw Bebo. A smile came to her face. She knew that Nico was more than likely right behind him.

"Hey, Bebo," Jasmine said, after opening the door. She leaned over to give him a kiss on the cheek, but he brushed past her, not even bothering to say hello. Two dudes she hadn't seen before followed him.

"Where your man at?" Bebo asked.

Jasmine opened her hands and shrugged.

"Jasmine, I asked you—Where your man at?"

"And I said I don't know!" she replied, quickly sensing that something was wrong.

"You shrugged your fuckin' shoulders. Open your mouth and address me with words."

Narjara walked into the living room to see what was going on. She had put on a pair of Jasmine's shades, but her swelling was still slightly visible.

"Are you high or something?" Jasmine asked. "Where the fuck is Nico?"

"I don't know. I thought he would be with you."

Bebo tried to detect if she was being straight up with him. "Nah, he ain't with me. Get him on the phone."

"Okay, hold up. First, tell me what the hell is going on."

Bebo reached into his waistband and pulled out a snub-nosed revolver and pointed it at Jasmine. "Get the muthafucka on the phone!"

Jasmine's heart started racing. Narjara tried to turn and walk out of the living room.

"Don't move, *chica*!" Bebo ordered.

Narjara stopped dead in her tracks.

"Bebo, seriously, I don't know what's going on. I don't.

I mean, I was just about to take my girl to the hospital and—"

"Get the muthafucka on the phone!" Bebo yelled, his booming voice startling Jasmine. "What the fuck? I'm not playin' no games!"

Jasmine knew in her gut not to test Bebo at that moment. She reached for her phone and dialed Nico. She didn't know if she wanted him to pick up, or ignore her calls as he had been doing. "It's going to voice mail," she stated, her heart thumping out of her chest.

"Dial that shit again!"

Jasmine complied, and again it went to voice mail.

Bebo, his gun still aimed at Jasmine walked closer to her and pressed the gun to her temple. "Where the fuck is Nico?"

Jasmine had never been so scared. "Bebo, I swear to you, I don't know. I haven't spoken to him in a few days."

Bebo pressed the gun into her temple with more force, and then he cocked it.

"Bebo, I swear I don't know! I swear on everything!"

Bebo could see Jasmine tremble just slightly. His instincts told him that she was telling the truth, but he still kept the gun to her temple. "Call him again!"

Jasmine held her phone out, so Bebo could see she was really calling Nico, and then she decided to put the phone on speaker.

"See, he's not picking up. Bebo, I swear to you he's been ignoring my calls. I don't know where he's at. I don't know why he's not taking my calls."

"Who the fuck is that?" Bebo asked, referring to Narjara. He took the gun away from Jasmine's temple.

"That's just my homegirl from nursing school."

"Where the fuck Nico keep his shit?" Bebo again raised his gun to Jasmine.

"He don't tell me nothing about what he do," she replied, a combination of desperation and exasperation in her voice.

"Jasmine, this ain't a fuckin' game—Where the fuck is the safe at?"

"I don't know. I swear to you."

WHACK!

Bebo slapped Jasmine across the face with the butt of his gun, and she instantly saw stars and felt woozy, but she didn't fall to the ground.

"Where the fuck is the safe?"

Narjara yelled, "Jasmine!" and rushed to her aid.

One of Bebo's goons stepped up and grabbed Narjara by her hair.

"It's cool. I got this," Bebo said as he held his gun on both Jasmine and Narjara, now standing right next to each other. "Go find the stash. I got these bitches."

While Bebo's boys turned the house upside down, Jasmine quietly pressed the record feature on her BlackBerry.

"Get off of me!" Narjara screamed, trying to fight Bebo off.

Bebo had grabbed her by the throat and pulled her toward him before putting her in the headlock. Her back was to his chest, and now he was pressing his gun against her temple.

"Bebo, she ain't got nothing to do with anything. Let her go!" Jasmine pleaded as Narjara scratched and clawed at Bebo's muscular arms, trying to free herself from his grip.

Bebo's boys were back in the living room.

"We can't find the stash, but look at this shit we found, yo." One of Bebo's henchmen handed him FBI Agent Battle's card.

"What the fuck!" Bebo screamed at Jasmine and Narjara. "You snitchin'? This bitch is a fed?"

Bebo began to apply so much pressure to Narjara's neck, he was almost on the verge of snapping the bones in it. Narjara's face was blood red, and her eyes were bulging out of their sockets.

"No. No, she's—"

BLAOW!

Narjara's limp body fell to the living room floor from the gun blast that had entered the right side of her temple and exited the left, her blood and brains splattered all across the walls and floor of the living room.

"AHHHHH! Oh, my God! Oh, my God!" Jasmine screamed. She couldn't believe what she had just witnessed.

"Bitch, I'm asking you one more time—Where the fuck is the stash at?" Bebo asked like a coldblooded hitman. He wanted to get his hands on that pure heroin that Nico had sold to Twist.

Jasmine wanted to tell Bebo where Nico's two safes were, but she was so afraid for her life, the words simply would not form in her mouth.

She started to backpedal. She was seconds from turning and bolting up the stairs, where she was going to attempt to jump out of a window to safety. She knew she was looking at death, but the only thing she could think of was surviving.

As soon as Jasmine took two steps backwards, Bebo raised his gun and pointed it at her and fired twice.

BLAOW! BLAOW!

Jasmine had raised her hands in the hair in a defensive motion, but that didn't stop the first bullet from ripping through her right hand and causing blood to splatter everywhere. The second bullet pierced her neck and spun her around, and her body went crashing to the floor. She lay face down, motionless, and bleeding about fifteen feet away from her friend.

Bebo surveyed the room one last time, making sure that Narjara and Jasmine were both dead. "Let's get the fuck up outta here and find that bitch-ass nigga."

He used his baggy shirt to wipe his fingerprints off the gun he had just used. He then walked over to Narjara and knelt down beside her, still holding the gun with his shirt. He then took hold of Narjara's limp right hand and positioned it so that she was gripping the gun.

He chuckled. "It's fucked up how that bitch shot Jasmine and then killed herself."

Then he and his two hitmen hustled out of the house, got into an all-black Lexus, and sped away.

CHAPTER 6

Mia and Nico landed safely in Las Vegas, and they took a car service to the Wynn Resort hotel. They checked into a deluxe top-floor corner suite with a panoramic view.

As soon as the couple stepped foot in the room, Mia said, "Oh, my God! Baby, I love this!"

The suite had floor-to-ceiling windows and a fantastic view of the Las Vegas strip. They were up so high, Mia felt like she was on top of the world.

"Nothing but the best," Nico said.

Mia kissed him on the lips, and she went to explore the other parts of the suite.

Nico was exhausted. He sat down on the couch and put his feet up on the ottoman. He smiled when he heard an excited scream come from the bathroom.

"Oversized Turkish towels! I loves it!" she said as she looked at all of the bathroom amenities.

Mia came back into the room and started massaging his neck and shoulders. "You tired, baby?"

Nico ran his hands down his face. "I'm good. Get me a drink?" He then explained that he was going to lie down for about an hour before they headed out to shop and gamble.

Mia liked the plan. After she poured Nico his drink, she went back to massaging his shoulders.

Nico's phone finally charged to the point where it was able to turn itself on, and it began vibrating to indicate that he had messages. He gulped down his drink and put the glass down. He asked Mia to pass him the phone. Immediately he dialed his voice mail and heard three messages from BJ.

"Yo, call me as soon as you get this," was the first.

An hour later, BJ had called back and left another message. *"My nigga, I don't know if you touched down yet or what, but get at me ASAP."*

Nico knew something was up because BJ never left messages like that. BJ hated the phone and only used it when necessary.

BJ left a third message a little over an hour after he had left the second. *"Nico, where are you? Hit me back. This shit can't wait."*

Nico unplugged the phone, took the charger, and walked into the bathroom and plugged the phone back in. He called BJ back.

Mia could sense something was up, but she didn't ask any questions. She poured herself a drink, sat down on the ottoman, and turned on the flat-screen TV.

BJ picked up on the second ring.

"What's good?"

"Where you at?"

"In Vegas. Why? What's up?"

"You need to get back to New York. Muthafuckas ran

up in your crib and shot shit up."

"What the fuck you talkin' about?"

"My dude, shit is on the news and everything. Something went down at your crib, and people got killed. I don't know what the fuck is going on. Five-0 got shit roped off, and you know they won't tell a nigga shit."

"What?" Nico's mind started racing. He knew Jasmine was probably the only person in the house. "You spoke to Jasmine?"

"Her shit been ringing out to voice mail."

Nico immediately thought the worst. He had gotten rid of the security firm he had hired, after dudes had run up in his crib looking for him and Mia was home alone. He was kicking himself at that moment for not keeping the security guards on the premises.

"I'm heading back to New York tonight, and we gonna handle this shit. Find out what the streets is saying. Get Lorenzo and everybody else and tell them niggas to strap up and get ready to go to war."

"We ready right now, my nigga! We just waiting on word from you before we make a move."

"A'ight, that's what's up." Nico ended the call.

Nico stood in shock and disbelief. He thought about all of the mistakes he had made recently. Without a doubt, he knew his biggest mistake was not staying in touch with Jasmine. Maybe she had been trying to tell him about some new drama, but he didn't give her the opportunity.

Nico emerged from the bathroom and walked back into the living room. Mia took hold of the remote control and turned down the volume to *106 & Park*. She asked if everything was okay.

Shaking his head, Nico grabbed his jewelry from on the dining table and started to put everything back on. "I gotta get back to New York tonight."

"Why?" Mia stood to her feet. "What happened?"

"That was BJ on the phone. He told me niggas ran up in my crib, shot the shit up, and people got killed. He said the shit was on the news and everything."

Mia placed her hand over her mouth in disbelief. She didn't want to ask the obvious, but she knew Jasmine was still living at Nico's Long Island estate. She couldn't help but think about how lucky she was because she would have been dead at that very moment had Jasmine never stepped into the picture.

"Listen, just chill here. I gotta get to New York and find out what's up. I'll get back out here as soon as I can, and if I can't, I'll fly you back to New York."

"No, baby. I want to go back to New York with you. I can't let you just go back to New York alone by yourself like that." Mia pressed up close to Nico and held his hand.

"Nah, I need you to stay out here. Just hold me down from out here. Trust me on this. I don't want you in New York until I take care of this and sort everything out."

Mia was perfect at playing her position, so she got on her iPad and started looking for flights for Nico. She found a flight heading out in two hours, and she booked it.

Nico kissed Mia and then made his way down to the lobby, so he could head to the airport.

As soon as he left the suite, Mia went on Google to see what she could find out about the shooting, and without reading the entire article from New York's *Eyewitness News* Web site, she stopped and focused on where the article said that the names of the female victims at the location of the suspected drug kingpin's residence were being withheld.

Mia wouldn't have wished that kind of death on her worst enemy, but she couldn't help but plaster a smile across her face. Her biggest competition had managed to eliminate herself.

She poured herself a drink of Bailey's Irish Cream on the rocks. She sat down on the couch and smiled at the thought of her and Nico's unimpeded future together.

Mia decided to celebrate Jasmine's demise by treating herself to a luxurious spa treatment, so as soon as she finished her drink, she dialed the front desk and had them book an appointment for her.

With a smile that just would not leave her face, she walked over to the floor-to-ceiling windows and looked out at the breathtaking view. She said out loud to herself, "She should have just listened to me. I told that bitch that—'I am wifey.'"

CHAPTER 7

Nico's red-eye flight landed at New York's LaGuardia Airport at five thirty in the morning. He had already spoken to BJ, who would be at the airport when the plane arrived, waiting to drive them to Nico's Manhattan apartment.

Nico unbuckled his first-class seat and waited for the plane to taxi its way to the gate. What normally took no more than ten minutes was taking much longer, and he was getting extremely restless.

The pilot spoke through the intercom and apologized to the passengers, telling them they had arrived safely at the gate but, due to a mechanical issue with the plane's door, they would be delayed in getting off the plane for another fifteen minutes or so.

Everyone on the plane voiced their anger and disgust before returning to their seats.

Nico called BJ and told him what was going on with the plane.

"It's all good. I'm here," he said to Nico.

"What's the word?"

"That muthafucka Bebo."

Nico gritted his teeth. "That's what you hearing?"

"From everybody. And everybody can't be wrong."

"We handlin' this shit today!" Nico said emphatically. "No doubt."

Nico could see one of the flight attendants opening up the front door to the plane. "I'll be out in like five minutes," he told BJ. He looked down at his seat and on the floor to make sure he wasn't leaving anything behind. Then he stepped into the aisle to exit the plane.

As soon as he looked up, he saw five white uniformed Port Authority police officers. Before Nico could blink, they had him surrounded.

One of the officers said, "Mr. Carter, can you turn around and place your hands behind your back?"

A smirk came across Nico's face. "Y'all niggas serious, man?"

"Mr. Carter, turn around and put your hands behind your back!" the young, rookie-looking officer commanded much more forcefully, his face bloodshot red.

"Get the fuck outta here!" Nico tried to brush past one of the officers. "Put my hands behind my back for what?"

Two of the cops instantly drew their Taser guns and aimed them at him, while two other cops ordered everyone to go to the back of the plane. The rookie officer tried to grab hold of Nico's wrist to cuff him as he told him he was placing him under arrest.

"You arrestin' me for what? What the fuck is the charge?"

The people on the plane looked on in shock, wondering if Nico was a "shoe-bomber" or something.

The next thing Nico knew, the rookie cop punched him square in the face and spun him around and had him laying facedown across two seats in row two.

Nico had the rookie cop by at least thirty pounds and knew it wouldn't have taken much to beat his ass, but he didn't want to get tased, or worse, catch a hot one in his back from one of the trigger-happy cops.

The cop applied the handcuffs and yanked Nico up to his feet by his right elbow. In the process he almost pulled Nico's shoulder out of its socket.

Pain shot through Nico's body, but he clenched his teeth and made sure not to let on that he was in any kind of pain. "What the fuck y'all arrestin' me for?"

The cops didn't reply. Two of them flanked Nico and walked him off the plane, through the terminal, and outside to a throng of waiting Port Authority police cars.

BJ watched in disbelief as Nico was stuffed into the back of a squad car in handcuffs. He got as close as he could to the police car, trying his best to get Nico's attention, but Nico never looked his way as the squad car pulled off. BJ ran back to his car and immediately dialed the lawyer and told him what had just happened.

Nico's lawyer sounded as if he had just woken up. He told BJ he had to get dressed, and that he would be in touch with the Port Authority police within fifteen minutes. "Just keep your phone on, and I'll get back to you as soon as I know something."

BJ then got in his truck and headed to his cousin Lorenzo's house to fill him in on what just went down. BJ couldn't believe Nico had just gotten arrested, but like a true soldier, he stayed focused. He had to find out where Bebo was. Dominoes were starting to fall left and right, and he was determined to not get caught slipping.

CHAPTER 8

Jasmine lay on the floor motionless, her right hand numb from the gunshot wound, her jaw throbbing from being slapped with the butt of Bebo's gun, and her neck literally on fire. She felt like she was in a scene from a horror movie. The room was eerily quiet, and the silence freaked her out. She didn't know if she was about to see that bright light that people talk about seeing when they are on the verge of death.

She had to tell herself not to panic and to stay calm. It seemed as if the silence in the room was getting louder and louder, and her neck hotter and hotter, and she was starting to get extremely light-headed.

"Narjara," she said in a whisper. She still hadn't moved her body.

When she didn't get any response, her adrenaline kicked in, and she called out the name a second time. She still got no answer.

She finally had the courage to open her eyes. "Narjara, you all right?" she asked. Again she got no response.

Jasmine still couldn't feel her right hand, but she needed both of her hands to help her sit up. So she placed her palms on the floor, sort of like she was preparing to do a push-up, and tried to push herself up. As soon as she did that, the blood coming from her hand caused her to slide forward, and in the process, she lost her balance and fell forward on the floor. The sight of her own blood scared her.

She struggled to sit up, and when she did, she realized that the sight of her own blood was nothing compared to the huge hole in Narjara's head.

"Oh, my God!" Jasmine screamed in fear as she looked at Narjara lying on the floor, one of her eyes wide open, the other swollen shut, and her brains splattered everywhere.

Jasmine saw that the door to the house was wide open. Fear instantly gripped her. She thought Bebo was going to come walking through the open door at any moment and finish her off.

"Where's my phone? Where is my phone?" she said out loud, scrambling around. She brought her left hand up to her burning neck, and all she felt was her own hot blood. That freaked her out even more.

Jasmine finally found her phone. She quickly headed up the stairs to the bathroom, staining the walls and the banister with the blood on her hands. As soon as she made it to the bathroom, she locked the door, and with her bloody, trembling left hand, she dialed 9-1-1. As the phone rang, Jasmine did a little dance like she had to pee, but she was just nervous. She couldn't believe that 9-1-1 hadn't picked up on the first ring.

The operator answered the call, "Nine-one-one. What is your emergency?"

Jasmine looked at her reflection in a mirror in the bathroom, and she was a bloody mess.

"Hello. Nine-one-one. What is your emergency?"

"I've been shot. I need an ambulance right away." Seeing herself in the mirror brought the horrors to life, making her feel like she was going to faint.

"Ma'am, did you say you've been shot?"

"Yes."

"Okay, miss, what is your location?"

Jasmine gave the operator her address.

"Who shot you? Was this an accident?"

"Someone broke into my house and shot me."

"Okay, are they still in the house with you now?

"No, but I'm afraid they might come back. Please hurry and get someone here. I'm bleeding, and I'm feeling like I'm gonna die. Please hurry."

"Okay, try to remain calm. We have units on their way to you right now. I just need to get more information from you that will help you and help the people who are coming to assist you. Is that okay?"

"Okay. I'm just so scared, my body is trembling. And my friend is downstairs. They killed her." Jasmine broke down crying into the phone.

"What is your friend's name? Is it a male or a female friend?"

"Narjara; she's a girl."

"Okay. You said she was killed. Was she also shot?"

"Yes." Jasmine could hear the operator typing away as she spoke. "Miss, please hurry."

"They're on their way right now. They're about three minutes away, okay, sweetie. You're gonna be safe. I'm going to stay on the phone with you until they get there."

"Okay."

"Ma'am, what is your name?"

"Jasmine."

"Jasmine, do you know who shot you?"

Jasmine paused in gripping fear.

"Jasmine?"

"No, I don't, but it was three people . . . three men."

"Okay. And where did you get shot?"

Jasmine was getting tired of all the questions, but the operator was a comforting voice to her, so she just dealt with it. "I can hear sirens now," she said, feeling tremendous relief at that point.

"Okay, but I need you to stay on the line with me until they are in the house, okay?"

"Okay."

A minute later Jasmine heard cops inside the house. "The police are here. Can I go downstairs?" Before the operator could respond, Jasmine disconnected the call and started to scream out to the cops to let them know where she was at in the house.

Two cops ran upstairs to her, while one cop remained in the living room with Narjara, and another checked all of the first floor and the basement.

Jasmine was never so happy to see a police officer in her life.

"Are you alone?" one of the cops asked her.

"Yes, I think so."

One cop escorted Jasmine to the living room and handed her off to two paramedics, who had just entered the house, and he ran back upstairs to assist his partner in checking the second floor.

The paramedics had Jasmine sit down to evaluate her, and they did their best to stop the bleeding to her hand and neck. Within minutes they had an oxygen mask on her face and had her lying on a stretcher, which they wheeled to the waiting ambulance in front of Nico's house.

"Am I gonna die?" Jasmine asked the paramedic who stayed with her in the back of the ambulance, her words somewhat inaudible due to the oxygen mask.

"Are you gonna live?"

Jasmine nodded her head to indicate to the paramedic that he had heard her correctly, and at that moment a tear rolled out of the corner of her eye and stopped near her ear.

The overweight white male paramedic wiped away Jasmine's teardrop. "Just relax." He grabbed hold of her left hand to comfort her.

Jasmine squeezed his hand firmly, and at that moment another tear rolled out of the corner of her eye just before both of her eyes calmly closed.

CHAPTER 9

The Port Authority police ushered Nico into a holding cell, took his handcuffs off, and slammed the steel cell doors shut.

"I need to make a call," Nico said to the cop who pushed him into the cell.

"Shut the fuck up and sit your nigger ass down!"

The cop then walked off upset that he had to do lengthy paperwork and even more pissed off that his shift wouldn't end until the Nassau County Police Department detectives arrived and took custody of Nico, so they could question him about the shooting at his Long Island estate.

Nico smiled at the racist remark, but he didn't respond.

"Jimmy, can you fingerprint that black nigger for me? I don't want to have to whip his nigger ass," the cop said to one of his fellow officers. He was purposely talking loud so that Nico could hear him.

"Jimmy, your boy don't got no swag. Tell him it's *nigga*, not nigger," Nico said with a smirk.

Officer Jimmy came over to the damp cell that smelled like a wet cat and unlocked it, and then held Nico by the arm and walked him over to a computer cart and began to fingerprint him.

"So how much they pay y'all to do this job?" Nico asked.

The cop didn't answer.

"At least six figures, right?" Nico asked. "I mean, with overtime and all that, you making at least a hundred grand, right?"

The cop methodically continued to fingerprint Nico and also took his mug shot. When he was done, he walked Nico back to the holding cell, slammed the door shut, and made sure it was locked.

"We make an honorable living. We work for everything we get, and we don't sell poison to our communities," Officer Jimmy said to Nico.

An hour and a half later, two Nassau County cops came to his cell accompanied by the racist cop.

"There's your black nigger right there," the Port Authority cop said to the Nassau County detectives.

The detectives introduced themselves, and then they placed Nico in handcuffs and escorted him to an empty room.

"Yo, what the fuck is up?" Nico asked as he took a seat at the table. "Port Authority arrests me, but Nassau DTs are questioning me?"

"Do you want anything to eat or drink?" one of the detectives asked.

"I wanna know what the fuck I'm being held for."

At that moment, a Port Authority sergeant knocked on the door and whispered something into one of the detectives' ears. The detective got visibly upset, his face turning bright red. And he told his partner to step out into the hallway with him.

"His lawyer is here," the detective told his partner.

"What the fuck?" He looked at the sergeant for answers. "We told you guys not to let his lawyer up until we had a chance to question him."

"We never let him use the phone," the sergeant replied.

"That's bullshit! How the fuck is his lawyer here if he didn't make any phone calls?" The lead detective shook his head in disgust.

The larger police departments like the NYPD and Nassau County all looked on smaller police departments like they were inept. And that was definitely what the two detectives were thinking about the Port Authority police at that very moment.

The detective said to the Port Authority sergeant, "So gotdamn incompetent."

The sergeant didn't reply because he wasn't exactly sure if one of his officers had slipped up and allowed Nico to make a phone call.

"Don't just stand there. Get the fuckin' attorney," the detective said with defeated disgust.

Nico's attorney, Ron Thompson, was a very well known and very powerful black attorney from Manhattan that most police departments both feared and respected. A former prosecutor, he had started his own private practice, and represented many high-profile clients.

The sergeant walked Ron over to the two detectives.

"Gentlemen." Ron held out his hand for a handshake.

The detectives shook Ron's hand, and then they all went into the room where Nico was sitting. The detectives took a seat, but Ron remained standing.

A relieved Nico was shocked to see Ron, but he made sure to keep a poker face after nodding to his attorney.

The lead detective was about to talk, but Ron interrupted him. "First thing—remove the handcuffs from my client's wrists."

After the detectives complied, Ron asked them for a moment alone with Nico.

"How did you know I was here?" Nico asked.

"BJ called me from the airport after he saw you in handcuffs."

Nico nodded.

Ron sat down across from Nico. "You didn't sign anything or make any statements, did you?"

"I ain't sign nothing, and I didn't say anything."

Nico went on to explain how they'd arrested him when he was about to step off the plane but never charged him with anything or told him why he was being arrested.

"Well, you know why?" Ron replied. "The shooting is dominating the news, and they are going to see if they can link you to it."

"I ain't have nothing to do with that shit. I was out of town."

His lawyer nodded. Then he asked him where he went.

"I was in Vegas."

"By yourself?"

"Nah. With my lady."

Ron nodded. "And you don't know nothing about this, right?"

"All I know is what the streets is saying, but I ain't got nothing to do with that shit. I ain't gonna sanction my own crib to get ran into and shot up."

"All right." Ron stood up and went to the door and motioned for the detectives to come in.

"You're holding my client, and you didn't charge him with anything? What the fuck is this?"

"We didn't arrest him. We just want to question him," the lead white detective replied.

"Don't play games with me. I know who arrested him. They arrested him on your department's request," Ron shot back as he stood in his three-thousand-dollar tailor-made Italian suit, looking like he was about to give closing arguments in a courtroom.

"Ron, look . . . we got a murder that took place within our jurisdiction at your client's residence, and we want to ask him questions pertaining to that."

"No. What you want to do is swoop down on my client while he's getting off the plane and make a dramatic arrest and then question him and get him to confess to a crime he had nothing to do with, just so you can have him do a perp walk out of this precinct with the news cameras flashing. That's what you really want."

The detective was about to say something, but Ron cut him off.

"Look, are you charging my client with murder or what? If not, then what the fuck are we doing here?"

"We just want to question him."

"You lost that right with the dramatic way you guys decided to handle things. My client isn't talking."

This was what the detectives feared, and that's why they didn't want Nico to lawyer up. The lead detective knew he was stuck. He looked at his partner for help.

"Ron, we just want to question your client, but we can play hardball and lock him up on a conspiracy charge."

Ron shook his head and smiled. "My client was nowhere in the vicinity of New York when the crimes in question took place, and he can prove that. Now, unless you gentlemen have direct eyewitness testimony and statements that implicate my client in a conspiracy of any kind, then I think he's free to go."

The detectives looked at each other, stumped.

"Nico, you're free. Let's go," Ron said, and the two of them walked out of the interrogation room.

Nico felt like a billionaire when he exited the room. He wanted to retrieve his cell phones before his lawyer drove him to meet up with BJ. He approached the racist Port Authority cop, who was still sitting at his desk doing paperwork, and let him know that he needed his phone, wallet, and cash.

Now that Nico was accompanied by an attorney, the slick racist talk was no longer coming out of the cop's mouth. He quickly retrieved Nico's belongings and handed them to him.

After Nico gathered his stuff and put away his cash and his wallet, he said to the cop, "Remember, it's *nigga*, not nigger. You gotta add more *ga* into it, you feel me?" He watched the cop turn red, and then he patted him on the side of his shoulder. "I'm just fuckin' wit'chu, man. Be easy."

CHAPTER 10

While all kinds of drama was going on in New York, Mia was living it up twenty-five hundred miles away in Las Vegas. If she wasn't at the Encore spa getting a massage, she was at the Wynn spa getting a manicure and a pedicure. And when she wasn't pampering herself at the various spas, she was splurging on herself inside Alexander McQueen, the Chanel store, Hermès, Dior, Graff Diamonds, and Louis Vuitton.

There was so much to do to keep her busy, she actually thought it was a blessing in disguise that Nico had flown back to New York because she knew all he would have wanted to do was gamble and fuck.

Mia had a slew of fine dining choices to choose from, and she made sure that she ate well for breakfast, lunch, and dinner. She did it all. Except for the nightclubs on the resort. She wasn't in the mood to get hit on by anyone. She also didn't trust herself anymore when she drank in public. The last thing she wanted was to have a repeat of what happened to her when she flew to Miami and ended up getting drunk and fucking a friend of her archnemesis, Jasmine.

The doctor acknowledged the police officer who stood guard outside Jasmine's hospital room. He walked up to her bed, where her mom stood on one side and her father on the other.

Jasmine's parents were grateful she was alive, but they were angry with her for putting herself in that position where she'd almost been killed. And they were even angrier with her for resisting their demands that she leave Nico alone for good.

"Jasmine, you heard what the doctor said," her father reminded her. "You were a fraction of a centimeter away from having that bullet pierce your jugular vein, and then what? We wouldn't be standing here talking to you right now."

The doctor patiently waited for an opening to interject.

"But I'm okay!"

As it turned out, Jasmine was extremely lucky. The bullet that had hit her in the neck had actually been more of a deep graze wound. But the bullet had managed to tear off a large piece of flesh from the right side of her neck.

Jasmine's mom and dad were taking turns tag-teaming her, and bashing Nico.

Thankfully for Jasmine, her doctor stepped in. "Excuse me. If I may just interrupt," he said.

"Sure, sure." Jasmine's father stepped to the side to allow the doctor to get closer to her.

"I know this is an extremely emotional and traumatic thing that you all have experienced as a family. And although Jasmine's condition had been upgraded to stable, it's important that she gets her rest. The more she can relax without dealing with anything emotional, then the quicker she will return back to normal."

"Thank you for saying that. Now, Mom and Dad, please stop stressing me!"

There was an awkward silence in the room.

The doctor tried to put everyone at ease. "So, does anyone have any medical questions for me?"

"Yeah. When can I go home?"

The doctor smiled. "We're doing our best to get you home as soon as possible."

Jasmine's mother shook her head. She asked the doctor if the surgery was still planned for the next day.

"Yes, it is still on for tomorrow morning. What we are going to do is repair Jasmine's deep ulnar branch."

Her mom asked, "And what is that again?"

"Well, there are two main arteries that enter the hand—the radial artery and the ulnar artery. You can think about those two arteries as being the trunk of the tree, so to speak. And then think of two big tree branches that grow out of the trunk of the tree. We have to repair that branch that grows out of that main tree trunk."

Jasmine's father nodded his head.

"And, if I understand correctly, that branch that you are going to operate on, it also has other smaller branches that stem off of it?"

"You got it." The doctor smiled. "You should have gone to medical school," he joked.

"So is that the only purpose of the surgery?'

"Ugggghh! Ma, what's with all these questions? He's Chinese, so you know he's smart. I'll be fine. Goodness!"

"Yes, that is the only reason for the surgery, and after the surgery, of course, we will have to have a splint for about two to four weeks for the bone fracture in her hand to properly heal."

Jasmine shook her head. "Can I ask you something?"

"Sure."

"I been worried about how everything is going to heal, and I was thinking that what I'll do is just get a tattoo on my hand and on my neck to cover the scars and I—"

"Oh, Lord Jesus, help me!" Jasmine's mother screamed out loud, her right hand held to the sky.

"And I just want to know how soon would I be able to get a tattoo?"

Her father said, "Jasmine, if you get a tattoo on your neck, you better never step foot in my house again! And I mean that."

The doctor said, "Well, why don't we take things one step at a time? Let's deal with the surgery first and see how quickly we can get you back home and back to normal."

"I feel fine now. I'm ready to leave."

The doctor smiled. "You know, many times people hear about gunshot wounds to the leg or to the arm or to the hand, and they dismiss it as being not that serious. But just as in your case, Jasmine, very often major arteries are impacted, and that is what makes the wounds life-threatening. Never forget just how fortunate you were to be able to get medical attention as soon as you did, because there is always the possibility of losing too much blood to the point where it becomes fatal."

"Lord knows I pray for this child every day," Jasmine's mother said. "Can't nobody tell me the Lord doesn't answer prayers."

The doctor and Jasmine's parents left, leaving her alone with her thoughts. The only conclusion she could come to was, after she had gotten arrested, Nico must have figured she was talking to the police, that she had told them he was a co-conspirator in Shabazz's murder. *That's why he wants me dead*, she thought.

Jasmine couldn't help but wonder if Mia was somehow starting to work her way back into Nico's life and reclaim her wifey status. *Oh, my God! I gotta get out of here!*

Her mind was playing all kinds of tricks on her. One moment her mind was telling her that Nico loved her, the next moment Nico had sent Bebo to murder her. Another moment her mind was telling her to just relax, that Nico was just dealing with a lot and that he would explain everything to her as soon as he could. But she kept thinking that Nico was back to fucking Mia.

Jasmine took a painkiller, which made her feel euphoric, but that soon wore off. She fell asleep wondering if she would wake up and see Nico the next day.

CHAPTER 11

After a successful surgery on her hand, Jasmine was recovering in the post surgical unit, resting and trying to decide what she would do when she got out of the hospital. She was wondering if it would make sense to go back and live at Nico's estate. She didn't know how safe it would be living there, or if Nico even wanted her there, since she still hadn't spoken to him.

Her options were limited because she hadn't stashed enough money to get her own place, and she definitely wasn't going to move back in with her parents. She thought about asking her friend Simone if she could live with her for a little while, but she quickly decided against that idea. Jasmine knew it would take all of two days for Simone to do something to piss her off, and they would end up in an argument or in some kind of drama she didn't need.

She reached for the remote control with her good hand and started flipping through the limited channels the hospital had available. As she channel-surfed, she heard a knock on her room door.

Jasmine assumed it was one of the doctors or nurses coming to check on her, but instead she saw Agent Battle walking into her room accompanied by a handsome black man wearing a suit and a tie.

She continued to channel-surf and avoided looking directly at Agent Battle or the man with her.

"Hello, Jasmine," Agent Battle said in a soft, neutral tone.

Jasmine really had no choice at that point other than to acknowledge Agent Battle, so she returned the hello.

"So how are you feeling? I hope you're recovering well."

"I'm good."

"Jasmine, do you mind if we talk for a few minutes?" Agent Battle asked.

Jasmine turned up the volume on the TV once she found ESPN.

The black guy asked her, "You a Lakers fan?"

Jasmine looked at him and rolled her eyes. She didn't know who he was, so she ignored him.

"May I?" Agent Battle reached for the remote control.

Jasmine didn't answer her, nor did she object when Agent Battle took it upon herself to turn off the TV.

"Jasmine, this is Agent Gosling. I asked him to come with me, so I could revisit what we spoke about when we last saw each other."

Jasmine looked at her and didn't say anything.

"Jasmine, look, let's be straight up with one another. I don't know if you believe in miracles, but I think you would admit that your being alive and able to talk to me right now is pretty much a miracle. Wouldn't you agree?"

Jasmine had a nightmare the night before in which she relived the moment when Bebo fired the two gunshots at her.

"So tell me—how many more miracles do you want to live through?"

"You a cop too?"

Agent Gosling looked at Agent Battle and nodded his head. "Yes, I'm a federal agent.

"Cop, federal agent, po-po, fed—it's all the same shit."

"Jasmine, we can talk, right?" Agent Battle asked her in a tone that was trying to get her to lower her guard and talk to her like she was her good friend.

"Yeah. That's what we're doing, right?"

"No. I mean, can we talk black woman to black woman, black man to black woman, no holds barred?"

"Yeah . . . I guess."

"Jasmine, the people who came and shot you, you do know that wasn't just some random shooting, don't you?"

Jasmine shrugged.

"You can shrug your shoulders, but let me just tell you, when you got shot the other day, please understand that that was a targeted hit on you. There was nothing random about it. Hits aren't random; hits are planned. You do follow me, right?"

Agent Battle's words confirmed the thoughts Jasmine had been having about if Nico had tried to have her killed for snitching. Still, she made sure not to show her hand to Agent Battle.

Agent Gosling added, "So whoever did this to you will be coming back to finish the job."

"Okay, and? Tell me something I don't know." Jasmine shook her head. "Cops make me laugh. Y'all never around to arrest nobody when shit happens, and y'all never know who did shit after it happens, and then y'all always come around after the fact, talking about the obvious. How about walking in this room and telling me that y'all arrested the muthafucka who shot me?"

"In many ways you're right, Jasmine, and that's why we're here. We can't effectively do our job without sources."

"You mean, *snitches.*"

"No, I mean *sources.* Snitches do crimes, and then to get their own asses out of a sling, they tell on the people involved with the crime. That's not what our sources do." Agent Battle reached into her jacket pocket and handed Jasmine a photo of Narjara lying naked on a silver coroner's table with a huge hole on either side of her head.

"Why are you showing that to me?" Jasmine hollered. Her blood pressure rose, and her chest began to heave up and down. She dropped the photo on the floor.

"Jasmine, who is that in that photo?"

"You know who it is."

"No. Who was she to you?"

"She was my friend."

"No, she was more than your friend. Yeah, she was your friend who didn't have a felony record, she was your friend who was in college trying to better herself, she was your friend who had all kinds of potential to be whoever she wanted to be. She was your friend who would have been a nurse, and a wife and a mother some day. But you know what?"

Jasmine looked at her and didn't respond.

"Narjara is never going to get the chance to live out her life and chase her dreams. Never. It's over. For Narjara—and you can correct me if I'm wrong—but it was just one random night that ended her life. One night where she was in the wrong place at the wrong time, and just like that"—Agent Battle snapped her fingers—"her beautiful life was snatched away from her through no fault of hers."

Agent Battle took hold of Narjara's picture, and tears came to her eyes. "Jasmine, this could have been my daughter in this picture laying there dead on that table. That could have been you laying on that coroner's table waiting for your parents to come and identify you."

"But it wasn't."

"Exactly. It wasn't. But you know what our sources do? Our sources help us put away the scumbag muthafuckas who have the audacity to do shit like this to beautiful young women who haven't even had a chance to live." Agent Battle handed Agent Gosling the photo, so she could wipe a tear from the corner of her eye.

Jasmine could sense that Agent Battle's tears were real. She couldn't believe that a cop could genuinely care about a victim.

"Jasmine, I'll be honest with you like I was honest with you when you were in the federal building in Manhattan. I could lock you up on a murder charge tomorrow, and a grand jury could indict you with no problem. I am absolutely confident of that. Or you could leave this hospital later today and end up on a coroner's table like your friend. I'm confident of that as well. But whether you leave here and end up dead, or I lock you up and send you to the penitentiary, the end result is just going to be another beautiful life that is wasted. And you know what? Jasmine, I don't want that. I don't want you wasting your life, and when I say that, I mean it."

"Why the fuck do you care so much? I mean, just do what you gotta do and let me do what I gotta do. But I ain't no snitch."

"I care because I have a responsibility to care."

Jasmine held up her hands and looked at Agent Battle with a confused look, as if to say, *"What the fuck are you talking about?"*

"I have a responsibility to care, just like you have a responsibility to care. And the only difference is, I take my responsibility seriously. Like, if I were you and I had a friend in my life like Narjara, I would look at it as my responsibility to do whatever I had to do to put the people away who did this to her."

"Yeah, but I don't know who shot us."

Agent Battle just looked at Jasmine and knew she was lying.

"I'm serious, I don't."

Agent Battle took Narjara's picture from Agent Gosling and attempted to hand it back to Jasmine.

"Don't give me that picture!"

"Jasmine, do what's right for your friend. Do what's right for the millions of parents out there who are trying to avoid their child becoming the next Narjara."

"That's what our sources help us do," Agent Gosling added. "They help us do what's right for everybody. Jasmine, all Agent Battle is asking you is to help us help you, and in doing that, you'll be helping so many other people. You'll be making a difference."

Agent Gosling had done his homework on Narjara and had found out from interviews that he'd conducted with some of her friends that Narjara looked up to Jasmine as a big sister and that she often went to Jasmine during her battering crisis with her boyfriend.

"Help y'all help me?"

"Yes. Just like Narjara would reach out to you for help with her abusive boyfriend."

"How did you know that?"

"When you do good like that, word gets around. Good has a much bigger impact on people than evil. Even in death, Narjara is counting on you to continue to look out for her."

"So if I help you lock up the people who murdered Narjara, you're saying you could help me?"

Agent Battle didn't want to seem too excited, but those were the words she was waiting to hear. "Obviously that would be a start. But what we're proposing is that you become a source of ours, a paid source, and the information that you would help us obtain would be information that would hopefully lead to the arrest of the people who murdered Narjara. We would also be looking for you to help us obtain information that we could use to help us connect the dots on criminal targets we have already identified."

Jasmine had heard of snitches working with the feds and the police in order to work out plea deals and avoid jail time, but she never knew that snitches got paid by the feds.

"So you said I would be a paid source?"

"Absolutely," Agent Battle said.

"As a paid source, I wouldn't have to worry about any criminal indictments coming my way?"

Agent Battle nodded. "That's correct, but—and I stress the word *but*—let me be clear. You wouldn't have to worry about any criminal indictments coming your way from any of your involvement in any past criminal activities. But if we agree on things and you become a source, that doesn't give you a license to commit crimes. It's like you help us, and we can wipe your past slate clean, but your future slate is contingent on you doing what's right and abiding by the law."

Agent Battle knew that the feds and most law enforcement agencies often turned a blind eye to the continued criminal activities of their informants, but there was no way she could just outright say that to Jasmine.

Jasmine slowly nodded, deep in thought as she weighed her options. "Okay, so what kind of money are we talking about?"

"Well, it depends. It's not as if you show up every week and you get a paycheck. It's usually not structured that way. It's more on a per-assignment basis. For example, let's say the information that you source to us leads to us confiscating two kilos of cocaine. Something like that might get you a five-thousand-dollar payment. Or let's say your information leads to us confiscating a million dollars in cash. That might get you a thirty-thousand-dollar payment. Or if we are targeting a specific individual, the payment would depend on the individual. If you got us a high-level drug distributor, that could generate you twenty thousand dollars. And obviously a lower-level drug distributor would get you less."

Jasmine was starting to like the sound of the numbers she was hearing.

Agent Battle went on to explain, "And, just so we're clear, the payments wouldn't always be so extravagant. We might give you a hundred dollars to make a hundred-dollar marijuana purchase, and for something like that, you would be paid dollar for dollar and would earn a hundred dollars for that purchase."

Jasmine was ready to leap out of her bed and do back flips. She never knew that being a snitch could be so lucrative. She could make a hundred-dollar weed purchase all day every day.

"Question," Jasmine said.

"You got questions, we got answers," Agent Gosling replied with a smile.

"Okay, now this is just hypothetical."

Both agents nodded.

"So let's say I was going to go work for BMW and they were going to pay me fifty thousand a year, but then I found out, for the same job, I could make seventy thousand a year working for Mercedes-Benz, wouldn't I be kind of stupid to not go and work for the company that's paying me more money?"

Agent Battle was about to speak, but Jasmine cut her off.

"Okay, what I'm saying is, can other agencies beat the FBI's pay rate for sources? Like, if I could make more with the NYPD or with the DEA, then why wouldn't I just fuck with them? No offense or anything, I'm just asking."

"Actually, Jasmine, that's a very good question," Agent Battle responded. "And all I can say is, there are no written rules about it. But all of the agencies do have unwritten rules where we all respect each other's sources, and we don't make it a competition thing, where sources are only going to the highest bidder."

"But would I be wrong or get in trouble if I became a source for other law enforcement agencies? I just want to know up front."

"No, you wouldn't be doing anything wrong," Agent Gosling explained. "There have been times where sources were handled by different agencies at the same time."

"Just wanted to be clear," Jasmine said with a slight smile that was almost undetectable, since she was trying so hard to suppress it. "Oh, one last thing. I mean, I'm not saying that I will definitely commit and do this whole snitch thing—"

Agent Battle said, "You would be a source, not a snitch. I don't know any other way to convince you."

"Source, snitch, confidential informant, *yada*, *yada*, *yada*—we're talking about the same thing. Okay, but let's say that I did commit to it. Is there any way I could get an apartment or a house out of this? I'm not talking about something that I would own or anything like that. I'm just saying something furnished where I could move into and not have to worry about paying rent or anything. Like, could y'all cover the rent for me?"

Agent Battle and Agent Gosling both knew the answer to Jasmine's question was yes, but they didn't want to give her the impression that they were desperate. See, the FBI had a lot of leeway with their confidential informants. They knew that the money that they paid them wasn't coming from taxpayer dollars, so they could be flexible. All of the money paid to confidential informants was funded from money that had been confiscated from past drug busts and asset seizures.

"Well, that's something we could discuss." Agent Battle began to gather her things, preparing to leave.

Jasmine wondered if she had pushed too far.

"So, Jasmine, I'll leave you with another card and give you some more time to consider everything we spoke about. I don't know if I have more than thirty-six hours for you to think about this, and I would hate to have my agents come visit you with an arrest warrant because, if they do, it would be too late, and the offer we just spoke about would forever be off the table."

Jasmine nodded.

Agent Gosling reached out his hand, and Jasmine shook it with her good hand, and then she reached for the remote control and turned the TV back on to ESPN.

Just as the two agents reached the door to exit Jasmine's room, she said, "You'll hear from me before I hear from you."

Agent Battle paused, looked at Jasmine, and smiled.

When the door closed behind her, Jasmine buzzed the nurses' station and asked them to bring her another painkiller. Within minutes, she popped the painkiller into her mouth, wondering when, if ever, she was going to hear from her man. But her romantic thoughts about Nico were quickly replaced by thoughts of just how she was going to play both sides of the fence.

CHAPTER 12

Nico and BJ showed up together at the hospital to visit Jasmine, but when they got there, they were told that she had checked out about two hours earlier.

"You know who she was with when she left?" Nico asked the petite older white nurse with glasses.

"Oh, sonny, I'm sorry, but I'm not at liberty to give you that kind of information," she replied.

"No, it's all good. See, I live with the patient. I could give you my address," Nico said, trying to convince the lady to not be so tight.

The nurse looked at Nico and sighed. "Okay, let me see some ID, and I'll see what I can do for you."

Nico rarely walked with ID and knew he didn't have any on him at the time, but he made like he was checking for his driver's license anyway.

"Without any ID, I'm afraid I won't be able to give you any information. Privacy policies, you know."

BJ went into his pocket. He always carried a wad of hundreds in his right pocket and smaller bills in his left pocket. He took hold of a crisp one hundred-dollar bill, folded it up, and discreetly slid it to her.

The nurse played it off well. "What did you say your address was again?"

Nico smiled and gave her his address, and in an instant the old nurse started spilling everything, telling him that Jasmine's parents had come to pick her up.

The nurse then motioned for Nico to come a little closer. "You two are kind of cute to be cops—Are you married?"

Nico and BJ smiled.

"That's all right, ma, we good, but thanks for the compliment. And good looking out with that info. That's what's up," Nico replied.

And then he and BJ were off to Jasmine's parents' house in Southside Jamaica, Queens. Nico wanted to call Jasmine instead of seeing her, but he'd held back from doing so because he was certain that her phone was tapped.

As soon as BJ pulled up to Jasmine's house, they saw Jasmine and her mother and father out front talking to one of their neighbors. Nico could sense that there was going to be some kind of bullshit, so instead of getting out of the car, he had BJ pull to the curb and roll down the driver's side window, since the driver's side was closer to where Jasmine was standing.

"Who the hell is that?" Jasmine's father walked toward the car.

Jasmine, her hand bandaged and gauze on her neck, instantly recognized who it was, and a smile came to her face. She also walked toward the car.

"Jasmine, go in the house!" her father yelled, trying to restrain her from getting any closer to Nico. "I told you I don't want this nigga coming to my house."

Jasmine broke free of her father's grip and made it to BJ's car, but her father wouldn't let up.

"Listen, I don't want any drug dealers coming to my house. I don't want any drug dealers interacting with my daughter," Jasmine's dad said, bending over and looking into the BMW.

Jasmine said to her mom, "Ma, would you control him please and tell him to stop!"

"We just came to check on you," Nico said to Jasmine after he got out of the car. He chose to ignore Jasmine's father, not wanting to escalate the situation.

Jasmine's mom grabbed her husband by the arm and tried to persuade him to give them a minute by themselves.

"That nigga almost got my daughter killed, and I'm supposed to be okay with him ringing my bell?"

"Sir, with all respect, I didn't ring your bell. And I'm not here to cause no problems. I'm just checking on Jasmine and making sure she's all right, and then I'm leaving. Is that cool?"

"Get me from around this nigga before I lose it," Jasmine's father said, retreating to his front door and going inside the house.

"I'm so sorry about all of that," Jasmine said to Nico.

"It's all good." Nico hugged Jasmine and gave her a kiss on the lips. He told her, "Get in the car for a minute."

Jasmine got in the backseat, and Nico got in the front.

"Hey, BJ."

BJ turned his head to the back seat and acknowledged Jasmine as she leaned forward and gave him a kiss on his cheek.

"You good?" BJ asked.

Jasmine shook her head. "Y'all don't even know.'

Nico asked BJ to pull away from the house. BJ put the car in drive and then headed toward the McDonald's parking lot on the corner of Sutphin and Linden Boulevards, which wasn't far from Jasmine's house.

"Baby, I'm so happy to see you. I didn't know what was going on or what to think," Jasmine said. At that point tears came to her eyes as she relived the night she almost lost her life.

BJ pulled into a parking spot and brought the car to a stop, and Nico got out of the car and asked Jasmine to walk with him.

Nico and Jasmine walked about fifteen yards away from BJ's car, and then Nico stopped and hugged Jasmine.

"Why you tearing up?"

"Baby, I was so scared. I'm still scared. Oh my God, you don't know." More tears came to her eyes and rolled down her cheeks.

Nico pulled her close to him and held her tight. "I gotchu, baby girl. I'm not gonna let anything happen to you."

"I know," she replied, still crying.

"You know that, right?"

She nodded her head up and down.

"So why you still crying?'

Jasmine wiped her tears with the hand that wasn't bandaged.

"You know them alphabet boys is watching me, so I can't move as free as I want to or be on the phone and shit, and that's the only reason I ain't been around."

"I just didn't know what to think."

"I know you didn't, and that's why I'm here now."

Jasmine felt so good at that point. She wondered if she could still go through with being a snitch for the federal government. "Can I ask you something?"

"What's up?"

"Did you want me dead?"

"Jasmine, what the fuck kind of question you asking me?"

"Baby, all kinds of thoughts just been running through my mind. When I didn't hear from you, I didn't know what to think. And I had never got any answers about why you didn't come pick me up, so I just didn't know." More tears started coming to Jasmine's eyes. "I'm sorry, but I just couldn't help but wonder if it was you who had sent Bebo to kill me."

All of Nico's muscles instantly got tense when he heard those words come out of Jasmine's mouth. See, the streets had been talking and saying that Bebo was the culprit behind the shootings at Nico's house, but before Nico made a move on Bebo, he wanted to be one hundred percent certain that the streets were right with what they were saying. Jasmine's words had just confirmed it.

"I thought you might have wanted me killed because you thought I might say something about the Shabazz thing."

Nico pulled her close to him and held her. "Shhhhhh," he said into her ear. "You stressing for no reason, baby," he added, massaging her back as he held her close to him, checking to see if he felt any wires or a microphone underneath her clothing. "Trust me, I'm gonna handle this shit." He kissed her on ear and then released her from his embrace.

"I know you will." Jasmine reached for her BlackBerry. "I want you to hear something. The cops came to visit me, and I been telling them that I didn't know who shot me. I mean, even though I know it was Bebo, at the end of the day, I'm not a snitch."

Jasmine's words made Nico feel like he could put his guard down just a bit.

"Just listen." Jasmine then pressed play.

"Get off of me!"

"Bebo, she ain't got nothing to do with anything. Let her go!"

"We can't find the stash, but look at this shit we found, yo."

"What the fuck! You snitchin'? This bitch is a fed?"

"No. No, she's—"

BLAOW!

"AHHHHH! Oh, my God! Oh, my God!"

"Bitch, I'm asking you one more time—Where the fuck is the stash at?"

BLAOW! BLAOW!

"Let's get the fuck up outta here and find that bitch-ass nigga."

"It's fucked up how that bitch shot Jasmine and then killed herself."

Nico didn't totally understand everything in the recording, but he'd heard enough.

"That was from the night I got shot. Bebo had kept stressing me to call you, and I kept calling you but you wasn't picking up. So after the last time I tried to call you, something just clicked in my head and told me to just hit the record button on my phone."

"Right, right," Nico said, his mind in deep thought. "That's good. I'm glad you was smart like that. And you said you didn't tell five-*o* about this, right?"

"No. I wanted you to hear it. I told them I didn't know who it was that ran up in the house."

Nico knew who Narjara was. "That shit is fucked up. What did Bebo mean by what he said at the end of the recording?"

"Bebo put the murder weapon in Narjara's hand to make it look like she had committed murder-suicide."

"That's a grimy muthafucka to do some shit like that to chicks," Nico said with gritted teeth.

Nico reached his hand out for Jasmine's and pulled her close to him again.

"I hate seeing you like this, all bandaged up."

"I'll be okay. I'm a trooper."

"Yeah, you a trooper, but I should've been there for you."

Jasmine kept quiet.

"Look at me," Nico commanded, and Jasmine looked up at him. "You trust me, right?"

Jasmine nodded, and then Nico kissed her.

"You not scared anymore, right?"

Jasmine only slightly shook her head, even though she was still scared and knew she would have yet another nightmare later that night.

"I promise you on everything, I'm gonna handle this shit."

Jasmine looked into Nico's eyes and softly said, "Okay."

CHAPTER 13

Bebo was a creature of habit. He hung out pretty much every night of the week and usually didn't start his day until one in the afternoon. Unless he had a chick spend the night, by two in the afternoon, after he had showered and gotten dressed, he could always be found at USA Diner in Rosedale, Queens, where he'd order his favorite—fish and grits with a large orange juice.

Bebo owned a barbershop on Merrick Boulevard in the Springfield Gardens section of Queens, not too far from USA Diner. He would leave the diner and head straight to his barbershop and get his head shaved, watch music videos, and just hang out and bullshit with all of the barbers and everybody who came through.

"How you doing, baby?" the attractive Jamaican waitress asked him.

Bebo looked up and smiled and then reached his hand out and grabbed hold of the waitress. Pauline was a bisexual with a short man-style haircut dyed blonde.

He pulled her close to him. "Pauline, where you been hiding at, sexy?"

"I been around. I was just working the night shift for a few weeks. You want the usual?"

Bebo nodded.

Pauline walked to the kitchen to give the order to the cook. Then she came back to talk to Bebo, since her section of the diner wasn't very busy. "Your boy was in here the other day."

"Who's that?"

"Nico."

"Oh, word?"

Bebo had been looking for Nico, but no one had been able to track him. Nico hadn't been hanging at any of the strip clubs, and he hadn't been seen at any of the spots he frequented. Bebo's interest was definitely piqued, because Nico rarely came to the USA Diner. He knew something was up.

"Yeah, matter of fact, it was two days ago, my last night on the night shift. He was here with BJ and two other dudes I didn't know."

"So when you gonna let me get at that again?"

"That's how you talk to me? You think I'm one of these five-dollar, dirty-pussy strippers from the strip club or something?"

Bebo ran his hand down Pauline's thigh and then back up and stopped at her crotch.

"That's not yours anymore." She slapped his hand away. "You don't know how to call nobody, so I gave those privileges away."

Bebo smiled. "Who you gave it away to?"

Bebo's fish and grits were ready, so Pauline went and retrieved his order. She came back, placed his food in front of him along with his glass of orange juice, and then she reached in her apron and put a straw in front of him. Then she took out her cell phone and scrolled through until she found a picture of her girlfriend butt naked on a bed with her face down and her ass up in the air.

"That's who I gave your privileges away to." Pauline smiled as she handed him her phone.

Bebo stared at the picture. "Waaaowww! That's what the fuck I'm talking about."

"Call me, be nice to me, and stay in touch with me, and I might be able to convince her to let y'all share this." Pauline winked at Bebo before she took her phone back and walked away.

While Bebo flirted with Pauline inside the diner and his driver sat parked and waiting for him in the parking lot, Nico and BJ sat a block away in a black Nissan Altima with dark tinted windows, the engine running. From where they were sitting, they could see Bebo's truck. They had been sitting in the Altima for about a half an hour waiting for him to come out of the diner. Both Nico and BJ had on ski masks, but they weren't planning a stickup.

Finally, after a few more minutes, Nico saw Bebo emerge from the diner. He was standing on the steps of the diner with Pauline.

"Who the fuck is that bitch?" BJ asked.

"I don't give a fuck! Ride on that nigga right now!"

BJ started to drive west on Merrick Boulevard at about five miles an hour.

"BJ, drive this shit. I don't want him to get to his truck."

"But that chick is with him."

"Fuck that bitch! Roll up on that nigga right now!"

BJ hit the gas pedal, and within seconds he was making a right turn onto 243rd Street. Before he could bring the car to a stop, Nico jumped out, ran toward Bebo, and started blasting.

BLAOW! BLAOW! BLAOW! BLAOW!

The first shot hit Bebo in the stomach.

"Ahhh shit! Muthafucka!" Bebo hollered after being hit. He'd left his gun in his truck, so he had no option but to turn and run back inside the diner for cover.

"AHHHHHHHHHH!" Pauline was so scared and in shock, she froze and didn't run.

Bebo clutched his stomach as he pushed open the double glass doors.

BLAOW! BLAOW! BLAOW!

Nico fired three more shots. The first shot missed Bebo and shattered the glass door.

The sound of gunshots and breaking glass instantly sent the patrons inside the diner screaming and scrambling for cover under their tables.

The second bullet hit Bebo in his ass, and the third hit him in his spine and dropped him to floor, writhing in pain.

With Bebo on the ground, Nico ran up on him and stood over him.

"Yo, chill, man! Don't do that shit!"

Nico let off five shots, all of which struck Bebo in the chest. He wanted to empty his entire clip into Bebo, but his gun jammed.

Right on cue, BJ ran up the steps of the diner and almost slipped on the shattered glass. As soon as he caught his balance, he pumped four shots into Bebo's chest and two to his head.

BJ tapped Nico, and the two of them ran down the steps of the diner and hopped into the Altima. BJ sped down 243rd Street, made a left turn on 133rd Avenue, and headed north on the Cross Island Parkway.

BJ and Nico were both breathing heavily. Nico told BJ to get off at the Linden Boulevard exit and to pull the car over as soon as he could and just park on any random street.

"You good?" Nico asked BJ as the car came to a stop.

"Yeah, yeah."

BJ then popped the trunk, took out a container of gasoline from in it, and doused the entire car. After Nico and BJ placed their handguns and masks inside the stolen vehicle, BJ lit a match and set the car on fire. In a matter of seconds, the car was engulfed in flames.

Nico and BJ both fled the scene, jogging about five blocks to Linden Boulevard, where they split up. Nico hopped on the first westbound New York City bus he saw, and BJ hopped on the first eastbound Nassau County bus. Prior to parting ways, they agreed to link up later that night via two brand-new prepaid cell phones they had purchased before the hit on Bebo.

CHAPTER 14

Jasmine was sitting at home on the computer bored as hell and going absolutely stir crazy at her mother's house, where she had been for a full seventy-two hours since leaving the hospital. Other than leaving the house to discreetly meet with Agent Gosling and Agent Battle at a local restaurant to finalize her plans to cooperate, she had been confined to her parents' house. Although she had agreed to help the feds get incriminating information on Nico, she was having second thoughts about her decision. She'd never told them that she had met with him briefly on the day she was released from the hospital.

Jasmine was supposed to be gathering information on Nico, but she was just genuinely afraid to venture out of her parents' house, worried that Bebo would learn of her whereabouts and come and finish her off. And she definitely didn't want to go back and stay at Nico's house until she heard from him again and knew that he would be staying at the house with her. So, she decided to just stay her ass put.

As soon as Jasmine logged on to Facebook, her cell phone started ringing, and she got a bunch of text messages. Everybody wanted to know if she had heard what happened to Bebo.

Jasmine immediately turned on the four o'clock newscast and started watching the story about Bebo being shot multiple times at the USA Diner in Rosedale, Queens.

"It was crazy!" one eyewitness said to a news reporter. *"I was just about to get out of my car with my girl and walk into the diner, and the next thing I know, I see a dude running toward the diner firing his gun, so I just took cover. It was multiple shots. I immediately grabbed my girl and pushed her to the ground and laid on top of her. I just couldn't believe it. And then as soon as the shots stopped, they started again. It was almost like the shots wouldn't stop."*

"Did you get a look at the gunman?" the reporter asked.

"Nah, things just happened too fast, and we hit the ground. From what I hear, people are saying it was two gunmen. I believe it, because there were just so many shots. You feel me?"

Jasmine changed the channel and saw another station reporting on the same story. All she could wonder was if Bebo was dead. After watching the story on a different news channel, she was able to confirm that he had in fact died at the scene of the crime.

She saw the police had roped off USA Diner with yellow crime scene tape, and Bebo's body covered with a white sheet on the lobby floor of the diner.

Jasmine felt instant euphoria. She felt like she could have her life back and walk around in peace without having to look over her shoulder in fear of Bebo. She knew her man had made good on his promise. Nothing was a bigger turn-on to her than a man who would kill for her. She couldn't wait to fuck his brains out for doing only what a king would do for his queen. After all, she was wifey.

The FBI had given Jasmine a special BlackBerry phone that was almost impossible to be hacked into, and it had an FBI-approved app installed on it to track all of her movements via GPS technology. The phone was also going to be the FBI's primary way of contacting her, and she could use it to record incriminating conversations so she wouldn't have to wear a wire.

Jasmine saw that Agent Gosling was calling her phone, but she ignored him as she browsed for a new outfit in the mall, since she and Simone were planning on hanging out later that night.

Finally, at ten minutes past one in the afternoon Jasmine, dressed in a pair of black leggings, open-toe sandals, and a pair of Gucci shades, arrived at Dallas BBQ for her noon meeting. She tilted her shades slightly so she could see inside the dimly lit restaurant.

"Table for one?" the hostess asked her.

Jasmine gave the hostess a stank look. She scanned the restaurant until she spotted Gosling sitting at the bar. She sauntered up to him carrying two bags from Macy's.

Jasmine could see the fury in Agent Gosling's eyes. His look reminded her of the way her father used to scold her without words by simply giving her a stern look of death.

Agent Gosling got up from the bar and made his way over to a booth table he had been sitting at, about five feet away from the bar area.

Jasmine followed behind him, and the two of them sat down. Agent Gosling still had that stern look in his eyes and hadn't said anything to her at that point.

After picking up the menu to look at what she was going to order, Jasmine finally heard words come out of Agent Gosling's mouth.

"Put the menu down."

Jasmine immediately complied.

"Did I not tell you noon?"

"I thought we were supposed to meet at one."

Agent Gosling stared at her. "Jasmine, our meeting was for twelve, and you have the audacity to walk in here almost an hour and a half late? Let me be clear on something—I'm not one of your friends in the street that you can just blow off. You pull some shit like this again, and I'll lock you up on the spot. Are we clear?"

"But—"

"Jasmine, are we clear? There is going to be no do-overs."

"Yes, we're clear."

"And when I call you, I expect for you to call me back within a reasonable amount of time."

Jasmine was about to lie and play it off like she hadn't realized he had called her, but she could sense that Agent Gosling meant business and wasn't going to tolerate any of her bullshit.

"Okay, I will," she replied.

Agent Gosling nodded as he looked at her.

"I apologize," she said humbly.

Jasmine hated to be punked, but she knew she had to toe the line if she wanted to get all of the benefits of being a confidential informant. Even though Bebo was now dead and she could return to Nico's estate and feel reasonably safe, she still wanted to get her free living situation, courtesy of the FBI, squared away.

At that point a waitress came to the booth and asked if they were ready to order. Jasmine looked at Agent Gosling, and he slightly nodded, giving his approval. Jasmine just ordered French fries and a coco-loco. Agent Gosling didn't order anything because he had eaten while he waited for Jasmine to arrive.

"You could have ordered more to eat," he said.

Jasmine shook her head and explained that she didn't like eating food that was messy, like barbecue ribs and things like that.

"What's a coco-loco?"

"I'll let you drink some when it gets here," she replied. "Is Agent Battle coming?"

"No, she isn't coming. Remember, Agent Battle is the case agent, and I'm your handler."

Jasmine reached into the basket of warm complimentary cornbread. She took out a piece and began munching on it.

"So how have things gone the past couple of days with Nico since you've been home from the hospital?"

At that point Jasmine's French fries and drink arrived. She immediately sipped on her drink, no longer caring that she had told Gosling that she would let him try some.

"Things went well. Don't worry, I'll get you the info you need. There's a way I have to operate and talk around Nico so he won't get suspicious."

Agent Gosling took hold of Jasmine's drink and sipped some of it. Jasmine felt like a bull that'd seen red. She wanted to reach across that table and slap him for putting his lips on her drink. She was planning on pouring him some in a separate glass. She was definitely going to order another drink and give him the one he had just put his backwash in.

"But you have hung out with him since you've been home?"

Jasmine knew about the GPS feature on the BlackBerry, so she knew she couldn't lie but so much. "We didn't hang out, like go out anywhere, but I did see him. He came by my mother's house to check on me."

Gosling nodded. "When did you last see Nico?"

"Yesterday I saw him. I've seen him pretty much every day since I came home from the hospital."

"So what is he saying about the Bebo murder, which I'm sure you're aware of?"

"See, you have to understand—The streets isn't a game of show and tell, where little Johnny comes to school every day and just starts opening up about what the fuck him and his friends did the day before." Jasmine paused. "I can't just start asking, 'So, Nico, did you kill Bebo?' I have to bring things up in the natural course. But, don't worry, I'll get you your info."

"So you've seen him every day since being discharged from the hospital?"

Jasmine nodded.

Agent Gosling cut his eyes at her the same way he had done when she had first come into the restaurant late for their meeting.

"What?"

Agent Gosling reached into a dark brown folder and took out four glossy photos and handed them to her.

"That one right there, that's Mia meeting Nico at the airport in Las Vegas," he said. "And that one right there, that's Mia and Nico having dinner together, also in Las Vegas. And this one, this is Mia and Nico shopping together in Las Vegas. And if you'll notice, each day they have on different outfits, and you'll also notice the date and the time on each photo."

Jasmine could feel sweat forming on her brow. She was beyond embarrassed for being busted in a lie, and at the same time she was also heated with Nico.

"Those dates, Jasmine, they cover the past few days right after Bebo's murder, and you just told me that you saw Nico every day at your mother's house. Kind of hard to do that if your mom lives in Queens and Nico is thousands of miles away."

Jasmine knew there was nothing she could say.

"Let me explain something, Jasmine. I want to go home alive every night. So therefore I have to be able to trust you, and your lies could get me killed out here. So if I wasn't clear a few minutes earlier, let me be perfectly clear now—If you lie to me one more time—No, as a matter of fact, if I even suspect that you're lying to me, I am locking your ass up, and you'll be doing twenty-five years in a federal pen somewhere. Is that understood?"

"Yes, it's understood." Jasmine nodded, tired of being chastised. She was ready to get the meeting over with, so she could figure out how she was going to deal with Mia.

"Now we need to discuss what's going on, and we need to formulate an action plan."

"Okay."

"Before I speak about Nico, we both know that Bebo was murdered two days ago."

"Mmm-hmm. We mentioned this already," Jasmine replied, not knowing exactly what Gosling wanted to hear.

"So what are your thoughts on it?"

"I don't know."

Gosling gave her that stern look again.

"Look, you seem to forget that my hand is going to take another week or so to fully heal, and as you can see, my neck is not fully healed yet either. So it's not like I'm just out and about running the streets. It's like you don't seem to realize that. All you seem concerned about is just doing your job."

Agent Gosling went back into his folder and pulled out three more photos. "Do you know any of these guys?"

Jasmine examined the photos closely. "I know him," she said, pointing to the photo on the right. "I mean, I don't know him like we're super cool or anything like that, but I do know him, and he knows me. His name is Black Justice. He hustles uptown, either in Harlem or the Bronx or Yonkers. And these two, I don't know them, but I think I've seen them before at some of the spots around the city."

"That's right. That's Black Justice, more commonly known as Black Jus. Now this guy right here is named Homicide. And this guy right here goes by the name of Prince. He's new on the New York drug scene. He's a Crip from California with an army of New York Crips who'll murder on his orders. Well, with Bebo's murder and with Nico's strength weakening, we think that—"

"What do you mean, 'with Nico's strength weakening'?"

"From our intel, and from some of our other sources, we gathered that in Ghetto Mafia, Nico is the businessman and Bebo was the killer. So now, with Bebo's death, we feel that Nico's strength is going to be tested—that other crews throughout the city are going to muscle in on Ghetto Mafia's territory."

Jasmine listened intently.

"So what we're going to need you to do is get us close to these three guys right here. These three dudes are going to try to fill the vacuum. We would want you to act as a cut-out for me."

"What do you mean?"

"We would need you to make recorded drug buys on my behalf. You'll let them know that it's on my behalf, and after a few buys we'll ramp up the weight of the buys. At that point, the trust should be there where you'll be able to introduce me, and then from that point on, I'll handle my own transactions directly with them, which will allow us to make arrests."

"Oh, okay. I can do it. But the thing is, I'll definitely need a place to live, and I need some money."

Agent Gosling went into his folder and handed her a Visa bank card. "There's twenty-five hundred on that card. I'll call you later and give you the pin number."

She quickly took hold of the card and slipped it into her bag.

"Twenty-five hundred will be your monthly stipend. If you need more than that, you'll have to let me know, and I'll need to put in a request to the suits in Washington, D.C."

Gosling was speaking Jasmine's language, and she loved it. Twenty-five hundred a month, and she didn't have to open up her legs and fuck anybody.

Just then, the waitress came to the table and asked if she could get them anything else.

Jasmine was feeling much better after getting the bank card, so she immediately asked for another coco-loco.

"And for you, sir?"

"I'm fine. Thanks," Gosling replied to the waitress just before she walked away.

"Now, like I was saying, I need you to really hear me on this."

"Okay, I'm listening."

"Whether it's Black Just, Homicide, or Prince, or for that matter, anyone else we're targeting, you cannot fuck them under any circumstances."

"Not even Nico?"

"No, with Nico that's different because you were involved with him before you started cooperating, but with any of the other targets, if you sleep with them, it will be tough to get a conviction because any lawyer would scream entrapment."

"That won't be a problem, because it's not like I just go around opening up my legs to any and every nigga in the hood."

Agent Gosling just gave her a look, and she immediately knew that he was more than likely aware of her prostituting herself on Craigslist in the past.

"Trust me, that won't be a problem."

Agent Gosling's phone rang, and he excused himself to take the call.

While Gosling was talking on his cell phone, Jasmine just couldn't help herself. She took out her phone and sent Mia a one-word text message: *Bitch!*

"Sorry about that," Agent Gosling said. "Okay, so now listen. When you get home, what you need to do is use the bank card to book the next flight to Las Vegas."

Jasmine looked confused.

"Jasmine, this isn't a free lunch. You need to get out to Vegas and smooth things over with Nico because, at the end of the day, if he doesn't trust you, and if he moves on to Mia and leaves you behind, what secrets will he ever spill to you? And if he doesn't spill secrets to you, then the government really doesn't need your cooperation, and we would have no choice but to lock you up for murder."

"Ugghhh!" Jasmine was tired of Gosling always throwing the possibility of jail in her face. It was frustrating to her because she knew no one had seen her actually murder her ex-boyfriend Shabazz. "Why do you keep saying that? It's not like it's helping anything when you say you'll lock me up."

Jasmine was also pissed off that she was going to have to dip into her twenty-five hundred dollars to purchase the plane ticket.

"And when will I get the apartment or the house that you promised me?"

"By the time you're back to New York, we'll have an apartment for you."

"All right."

CHAPTER 15

Mia looked at her cell phone and saw Jasmine's text. She and Nico were walking together on the Las Vegas strip, taking everything in.

"You know what? I wish Jasmine hadn't survived that shooting," she said to Nico.

Nico was eating the fried corn on the cob he had just bought.

"Did you hear what I said?"

Nico again ignored Mia.

Mia sucked her teeth, and the two of them continued to walk with no specific destination, just enjoying the warm weather and taking in all of the sights.

"Get off that insecure shit, Mia."

Mia apologized.

"Nah, you don't have to apologize, but I'm just saying, don't wish death on Jasmine like that." Nico threw the corn into a nearby trashcan. "This shit is nasty."

Nico walked over to a huge fountain, where kids were making wishes and throwing coins. He hopped up on the ledge of the fountain and sat down, his legs dangling about two feet off the ground.

He motioned for Mia to come to him, and she walked over and stood between his legs with her back to him. Nico leaned forward so that his chest was touching her back, and he clasped his hands around her waist and held her tight.

Mia felt so good. She was somewhat shocked because Nico had never shown any public displays of affection toward her.

Nico had to make Mia feel secure because, with the feds watching him so closely, he needed her to take on risks that he couldn't take himself. She had already shown she was willing to do anything for her man, and Nico wanted to keep it that way.

"I'll keep it real with you—I can't say I wish Jasmine was dead, but I do wish she was as thorough as you."

"What do you mean?"

"I mean, with you, I would trust you with my life. I know if them alphabet boys ever put the screws to you, you wouldn't sell me out. With you, I know that, and with BJ, I know that. And loyalty is everything to me."

Mia gave him a peck on his lips and buried her head into his chest. "Baby, it's about love, and it's about trust. You know me and BJ love you, and we trust you, and you love us and you trust us too."

Nico had been back in Vegas for a few days, but Mia had made it a point to not ask him any questions up until that point. She was just hoping that they didn't end up fucking.

"So what was Jasmine saying when you flew back to New York?"

"She wasn't really saying much."

"You did see her though, right?"

"Yeah, yeah, I saw her. I mean, I went by the hospital and all that, but I just got a feeling she workin' with the police."

Mia lifted her head off Nico's chest and pulled away from him slightly. "Why do you say that?"

"It's a lot of shit that just don't add up."

"Baby, I know it's probably not my place to be talking about your business, but it's not hard to tell that Bebo is the biggest hater. He's jealous of you."

Nico nodded. He wanted to see if she knew anything about Bebo's death. If she did, then he would have known that she was being too much of a busybody and couldn't be trusted.

"Baby, seriously, I hope I don't offend you or say nothing wrong or disrespectful, but it just seems like with Jasmine, you shouldn't have her around you because of the way she did Shabazz. I mean, if she could murder him, then why wouldn't she murder you or snitch you out to the feds? And then with Bebo, it's like when he was in jail, you had everything poppin' without him, and you built everything without him. That's where all his hate and jealousy comes from. I think he would snitch you out or set you up in a heartbeat."

Nico nodded.

"You need to dead Bebo and Jasmine. And, again, I don't say that with no disrespect or anything like that. I'm just saying that you need to be able to sleep at night and not always be stressed out looking over your shoulder. To do that, you should just go back to the way things were before Bebo came home and before Jasmine came into the picture."

Nico was shocked to hear Mia talk with such violent overtones. He wondered if she was wired and recording him, so he kept quiet.

Mia turned around so that her back was once again leaning against Nico's chest.

"You right," Nico whispered into her ear, knowing a wire wouldn't have picked up his whispered words.

Mia turned around and kissed him. "I love you, baby."

Nico hopped off the ledge, and the two of them continued to walk down Las Vegas Boulevard. For the entire time, he kept his lips sealed about both Bebo and Jasmine.

Nico loved playing blackjack, so Mia accompanied him inside Harrah's Casino. She stood behind him and watched as he played. Within a matter of minutes, Nico was experiencing a hot streak.

"A thousand dollars a bet?" he turned and asked Mia.

"Go for it, baby." She smiled as she held on to her bamboo-tasseled leather Gucci wallet.

In what seemed like five minutes, Nico had won five thousand dollars, on top of what he had already won. He took two thousand dollars in chips off the table and handed them to Mia.

"Thank you." She smiled and then put the chips into her wallet. Then she told Nico she was going to the bathroom.

Mia didn't have to use the bathroom; she just wanted to reply to Jasmine's text. Her response to Jasmine was simple and to the point: *Bitches get riches. Snitches get ditches.*

CHAPTER 16

After her meeting with Agent Gosling at Dallas BBQ, Jasmine didn't even go back to her parents' home. Instead, she drove to Nico's Long Island estate so she could book her trip to Las Vegas. This was the first time she had been at the house since the shooting. Now that Bebo was dead, she felt a bit safer.

When she pulled up to the Long Island home, things felt eerie to her. She noticed yellow-and-black police tape still littered the front yard of the house. The sight made her cringe. She exited her BMW truck and made her way to the front door. As she closed the door behind her, her heart beat rapidly from nervousness.

Jasmine exhaled as she walked past the spot where Narjara's dead body had been. She couldn't believe that Nico hadn't had a company come in to clean the bloodstains off the floor.

Her heart began to beat even faster after she heard a noise. "Who is that?" she yelled out.

Jasmine paused and listened closely, only to later realize that the noise was just the sound of a PVC fence in the backyard slamming shut in the wind.

"I have to hurry up and get out of here," she said to herself.

She then went on to the computer and turned it on. Then she logged on to Expedia and searched for flights to Las Vegas.

"This is some bullshit," she said to herself after realizing that the cheapest roundtrip flight, which was on JetBlue Airways, was going to cost her a thousand dollars, almost half of her twenty-five hundred dollars. She reluctantly booked the flight, putting the charges on the bank card that Gosling had given her.

Jasmine grabbed a small rolling suitcase she could carry on to the airplane. Then she went upstairs to her closets and began filling the suitcase. She grabbed three of her sexiest pairs of high-heel shoes, one of which she was going to wear on the plane. Then she grabbed a pair of tight-fitting jeans and two additional sexy outfits. She felt that would be enough because she didn't plan on staying in Vegas for more than three days. She also went into her panty drawer and grabbed matching lace bras and panties and two rhinestone-studded thongs.

After taking off the splint on her hand and removing the bandage from her neck, she stripped out of her clothes and took a quick three-minute shower.

As soon as she finished applying baby oil to her body, she once again got spooked. She screamed out loud, and her heart rate picked up. Then she realized it was just her cell phone vibrating. She picked up the phone and saw a text from Mia—*Bitches get riches. Snitches get ditches.*

Jasmine's pressure instantly shot through the roof. She didn't have a ready comeback. If Mia was calling her a snitch, then Nico had to be putting that in her head. She had been afraid that Nico was avoiding her out of fear that she was a snitch, and now that she was officially a snitch, she didn't know what to think.

"This is really some bullshit," Jasmine said to a white man preparing to sit down in the row in front of her. "I paid damn near a thousand dollars for this ticket, and you would think I would be sitting up in the first row of the plane, and here I am all the way in the back of the plane near the fuckin' bathroom."

The white man looked like a straight-laced biology or world history professor. He looked shocked when he heard Jasmine curse.

Jasmine caught on to the fact that she had offended him. "Oh, I'm sorry. Please excuse my language. I'm just frustrated. My hand is hurting, and you know how it goes. Hey, would you mind placing this bag overhead for me? I just had surgery on my hand, and I really can't lift much with it."

The white guy helped Jasmine out. After he helped her with her bag, he told her that she really needed to look into getting some kind of adjustment to her fare because he had only paid two hundred and seventy-five dollars for his ticket.

"Two seventy-five?" she screamed. "See, this is some muthafuckin' bullshit right here!" Jasmine called for one of the flight attendants to come her way.

Within seconds, an argument ensued between Jasmine and a black flight attendant.

The dark-skinned stewardess, "Ma'am, I'm going to kindly ask you one more time to please sit down, or otherwise I will have no choice but to have the authorities remove you from this plane."

"You can call whatever fuckin' authorities you want to call, but I can guarantee you one muthafuckin' gotdamn thing—My black ass ain't going nowhere. And I can also guarantee you that JetBlue is going to refund me my money."

Jasmine knew she had the power to press her distress button on the special BlackBerry phone that Gosling had given her, and within minutes she would have cops and federal agents coming to aid her. Although Gosling had stressed to her that she should only use the distress button in literal life-or-death situations, she was ready to press the button just to check the sassy black stewardess, if she had to.

"Miss, please, can you watch your language? There's children on the plane," one of the passengers yelled out.

Another passenger screamed, "Yeah, sit down and shut up, so we can take off!"

"Fuck all of y'all!" Jasmine shouted back before taking her window seat.

The six-hour flight was the most miserable flight Jasmine had ever been on in her life, and when the plane landed at twelve thirty in the morning, she couldn't wait to get off. It seemed like it took forever for the rows of passengers to exit the plane, and to make matters worse, Jasmine was all the way in the back.

Finally she retrieved her bag from overhead, and her hand hurt like all hell as she got it without any assistance. She made her way to the front of the plane. "Tighten up your weave, bitch!" she said to the stewardess who had confronted her.

Jasmine was beyond stressed out. She needed a drink in the worst way, just to calm her nerves. As she made her way through the terminal she saw Las Vegas Sports Lounge and decided to go in. The Sports Lounge was still inside the terminal, so it was perfect because she didn't have to leave the airport to and wait before getting a drink.

She made her way to the bar, trying to figure out where she was going to sit. She looked around and noticed a bunch of cute guys in the bar. Before she could figure out where she was going to sit down, a light-skinned black dude, about six foot three and buff, with a thin beard and diamond-studded chain stood up from his seat at the bar and offered it to her.

"Thank you," Jasmine said with a smile. She sat down at the bar and positioned her small suitcase next to her.

"I couldn't have you standing there like that," the gentleman said to her as he held out his right hand and introduced himself. "I'm Derek McGee," he said.

Jasmine extended her hand to his for a gentle handshake. "Hi, Derek. I'm Jasmine,"

Jasmine figured she would cut right to the chase and try and determine if Derek was fronting with fake jewels on, or if he was really 'bout it. From his swagger she could tell he wasn't a hustler, because he was way too polite—like he had manners from a two-parent household. And only good dudes with an education would introduce themselves with their full government name.

"Your hands are so soft. Either you don't work too hard, or you have a bunch of women pampering you," Jasmine said, blinded by his diamond-studded Audemars watch.

Derek smiled, and Jasmine noticed that all thirty-two of his Chiclet-looking teeth were perfectly aligned and bright white, another sign that he wasn't a street dude.

"So you stereotyping me based on my hands?" Derek chuckled. "That's a first. What would you like to drink?"

Jasmine told him, and Derek ordered her a coco-loco, and for himself he ordered a Bacardi and Red Bull.

"So you don't work hard, but you look very successful, you have a ton of women, and you look like a model, and you're at a bar at one in the morning. That could be a dangerous recipe," Jasmine said as soon as their drinks arrived.

Derek told her he was a professional football player.

"Okay, so now I have to leave, but thank you for the drink." Jasmine smiled and pretended to be leaving.

Derek stopped her. "What?"

"You're a liar, and if you aren't lying, then that means you're trouble, because all athletes are trouble."

Derek held out his right hand and showed Jasmine his Super Bowl championship ring from the Green Bay Packers.

"Okay, so you're not a liar." Jasmine closely examined the ring. Then she reached for his left hand to see if he had on a wedding ring. "You married?"

Derek shook his head and told her that he was having way too much fun and wasn't even close to thinking about settling down.

"Yeah, I bet." Jasmine downed her drink because she wanted to get buzzed.

Derek quickly ordered her another drink. "So let me stereotype you now," he said to her as her second drink arrived. "You don't work hard, but you look very successful, you have a ton of men, you look like a model, and you're at a bar at one in the morning. That could be a dangerous recipe," he said, mocking her.

Jasmine smiled. "Why would that be such a dangerous recipe?"

"Because that would make you my weakness."

Jasmine smiled and told him she was a nursing student and was stressed out because she had to withdraw from school because of surgery on her hand and neck.

"Wow!"

Jasmine was thankful that he didn't ask her what the surgery was for. Then Derek looked at her hand and asked her if she was married.

"Nope," Jasmine replied, and then she asked Derek if he could watch her bag for her while she went to the bathroom.

Jasmine got up and went to the bathroom, where she pulled out her cell phone and quickly logged on to

Google and typed in the words "Derek McGee Green Bay Packers." Jasmine clicked on the second listing, which clearly showed a headshot of the same Derek she was sitting with at the bar. She scrolled down and read about him being a top wide receiver and signing a twenty-million-dollar contract extension with thirteen million dollars guaranteed last summer.

"Everything good?" Derek asked, when she returned to the bar area.

"Yup."

"So back to what I was asking you—you have a man?"

"Something like that."

"What do you mean?"

"I mean, you know how y'all niggas do—Can't keep your dick in your pants. So every time I think I got the man of my dreams and everything is all good, he ends up fuckin' somebody else. Remember what you just said about having way too much fun? Yeah, well, all my men always seem to still be in the having-way-too-much-fun mode."

Derek laughed. He ordered another Red Bull and rum, and Jasmine ordered another coco-loco.

"Derek, you want to open a tab, baby?" the female bartender with over-spilling cleavage asked.

Derek reached in his pocket and pulled out a roll of hundred-dollar bills. He handed a crisp Benjamin Franklin to her and told her to keep the change.

Jasmine's pussy began to throb. Liquor and a cute guy with money made her pussy jump, and it was twitching and ready to jump out of her pants.

"So where'd you say you were from? New York?"

Jasmine nodded. She was buzzing like crazy from the two drinks and couldn't stop smiling at Derek.

Derek knew he could smash Jasmine that night if he wanted to, which was just what he planned on doing. "New York girls are trouble."

"No, we're not."

"So who you came out here to see nobody?"

"I told you, I was just stressed and I had to withdraw from school, so I decided to just fly out here and chill for a few days and clear my head."

"Where are you staying?"

"At the Wynn Resort."

"Okay."

Derek, originally from Las Vegas, had just flown into town to visit his parents. He had a home in Las Vegas, but he didn't want to take Jasmine there without knowing what she was really about.

"So if we leave, I can go back with you to the Wynn?"

Jasmine just looked at Derek and slowly nodded.

"Can I stereotype you some more?" Derek asked.

Jasmine smiled and said yes.

Then Derek whispered in her ear and told her that she looked like she kept her pussy bald and that she probably only wore thongs.

"You funny." Jasmine sipped some more of her drink. The smell of Derek's cologne was making her so hot, she wanted to grab him by the dick and pull him into the bathroom and fuck his brains out in one of the stalls.

"But am I right?"

"Maybe."

Derek took another sip of his drink, and then he placed fifty dollars on the bar and ordered another round for him and Jasmine. He positioned himself so he was right up on her and no one else could see as he unbuttoned and unzipped her jeans and felt around for the crotch of her panties, which he moved to the side, and slowly slipped his middle finger inside her soaking wet pussy.

Jasmine sighed in ecstasy, trying to be discreet, and then she slapped his hand. She zipped her pants and buttoned them back.

Derek smiled. "So I was right about one thing."

After their fourth round of drinks, Jasmine and Derek made their way out of the bar and out of the airport. Derek called a number that was provided to all of the players who played for the Green Bay Packers that they could use to call a chauffeured car service to pick them up from anywhere in the country if they were ever out late drinking. He wasn't going to put his NFL contract at risk by drinking and driving, or getting arrested for public intoxication.

Fifteen minutes later, Derek and Jasmine found themselves inside of an all-black chauffeur-driven Yukon Denali with tinted windows and headed to the Wynn.

Jasmine loved Las Vegas. She had just stepped off the plane, and without even spending a dime on slot machines, she felt like she had hit the jackpot.

CHAPTER 17

When morning came, Jasmine woke up as Derek moved about the hotel room.

"Hey," she said in a groggy tone from underneath a white bed sheet.

"What's up, girl?"

"You were just going to fuck me and slide out real quiet, I see. You see how y'all pro athletes do?" Jasmine joked as she sat up in the bed.

"Nah, actually I had already stepped out real quick and met my man downstairs in the lobby."

Jasmine stretched and let out an exaggerated groan, trying to fully wake herself.

"You left and came back? I must have been knocked out. I ain't hear nothing."

"Yeah, I had to get my weed."

Derek sat down at the table that was diagonally across from the bed and pulled out an ounce of weed and put it on the table. "You smoke?" he asked, emptying the contents of a cigar into the trashcan.

"Do I? Did I tell you that I am loving you right now?"

Derek smiled and continued to roll the weed up. "I figured we would smoke and then go get something to eat for breakfast before I head out."

"Okay, that's cool. What is that? Haze?"

"Nah, this ain't haze," Derek smiled and said as he continued to roll the blunt like a skilled marijuana surgeon. "You from New York, but I know New York ain't up on this shit. This that exotic weed."

"What is it?" Jasmine sat down across from Derek, wearing nothing but her bra and panties.

"It's strawberry ice. This shit will get you fucked up."

Derek put the finishing touches on the blunt, sparked it, and handed it to her.

Jasmine took a real long pull on the blunt and then handed it back to Derek. "Wake and bake! That's what the fuck I'm talking about."

For a good fifteen minutes Derek and Jasmine sat and smoked and got high as kites. Jasmine then went to take a shower, while Derek rolled up another blunt.

After Jasmine showered and got dressed, she and Derek finished off the second blunt and made their way downstairs to Society Café. At that point Jasmine was totally enjoying herself and could have cared less about her mission of finding Nico and getting close to him.

"Table for two?" the hostess asked Derek and Jasmine.

"Yes, please," Derek replied.

As soon as Jasmine and Derek sat down, Jasmine picked up the menu and stared at it. "Oh, my God! I am so high right now, I can't even see the words on this menu," Jasmine laughed and said.

"I told you, that strawberry ice will do it to you every time."

Forgetting about the menu, Jasmine put it down and reached across the table and took hold of Derek's hand. "This is exactly the type of getaway I was hoping for. I'm so glad I met you."

"I feel you. I'm glad we met too. But why you talking like we not going to see each other again?"

Before Jasmine could respond, an Asian waitress approached the table and introduced herself and asked if they were ready to place their order. Derek spoke up and asked Jasmine if she minded if he ordered for her.

"No, not all. You know I can't see that menu anyway."

Since it was getting close to noon, Derek proceeded to order drunken noodles for the both of them, Pad Thai for himself, and a Thai breakfast omelet for Jasmine.

"Okay, anything to drink? Coffee or juice maybe?"

"Yeah, you can get us two mimosas," Derek replied.

The waitress jotted everything down. "Be right back."

"You trying to keep me twisted, I see. As high as I am, and you ordering me a mimosa?" Jasmine smiled.

Right after Jasmine said that, she went quiet as she directed her attention toward the entrance to the restaurant, where she saw Mia and Nico enter. Mia immediately pointed in the direction of Jasmine and Derek, like she had a Jasmine radar.

"Shit," Jasmine said under her breath.

"What's wrong?"

"Nothing. I was just thinking about something."

The hostess seated them on the opposite side of the restaurant, where both couples could see each other.

Jasmine decided to just ignore Mia and Nico and directed her attention straight ahead to Derek.

At that point the waitress arrived with their mimosas and told them that their food would be out shortly.

"Okay, thank you," Jasmine smiled and said.

Derek was about to drink from his glass.

"Wait. We have to make a toast first," she said.

"My bad."

Jasmine looked at him and waited for him to take the lead.

Derek finally caught on. "I know what I want to toast—I want to toast to your tight-ass *chocha*!"

"Well, then I definitely gotta toast you to that quality dick you gave me and to that good-ass weed that still got me fucked up."

They laughed as they tapped their glasses a second time, and then they both drank some of the mimosa.

Jasmine wasn't looking in Nico's direction, so she didn't see him approaching.

"Honestly, Derek, I'm really glad that we met. I feel like I really want to get to know you. I just feel some kind of chemistry between us, and I'm not just saying that," she said, looking into his eyes.

"That's real talk."

"Yo, what the fuck you doin' here? And who the fuck is this nigga?" Nico said.

Jasmine looked up at Nico, a disgusted look on her face. "Really?" she asked him, her voiced raised.

"Jasmine, you know how I get down. I'll smack the

shit outta you. Now, what the fuck are you doing out here?"

Derek immediately stood up.

Nico took notice of his height and his muscles and his tats but quickly sized him up as soft. The only thing was, he wasn't sure if Derek was strapped.

"My man, is there a problem?" Derek asked.

"Don't do it to yourself, *potna*!" Nico gave Derek an ice grill and moved closer to him.

Jasmine stepped in. "Derek, it's okay."

"Oh, you talkin' for this nigga too?" Nico then grabbed Jasmine by her arm and attempted to lead her out of the restaurant.

"Nico, get your hands off of me!" she screamed, trying to break free from his vise grip.

Other people in the restaurant began to take notice of the altercation.

Mia got up from her seat and quickly joined in the melee. "You a stalker bitch now?"

Nico hollered, "Mia, what the fuck did I tell you?"

At that point Derek grabbed hold of Jasmine and tried to shield her from Nico.

"I don't care! I'm so tired of this stalker bitch! I'm about to fuck her up!"

Nico snatched up Mia and bitch-smacked her hard two times across the face. "I told you to just chill. Now go the fuck upstairs!" he screamed and then pushed her hard toward the exit of the restaurant.

Mia was shocked and embarrassed. Yeah, she hadn't listened to Nico, but she didn't understand why he always seemed to side with Jasmine.

"Oh, my God! Derek, I am so sorry about this. I'll be okay. Just leave me for now, and I'll call you later. I am so sorry."

"Jasmine, I'm not leaving you."

Nico gestured like he was reaching for a gun in his waistband.

"Nico, no!" Jasmine screamed and then rushed Nico and grabbed him.

"Come the fuck on then! Fuck around and get both of y'all murdered!" Nico snatched Jasmine up by the arm and marched her out of the restaurant.

"Derek, I'll be okay. I'll call you in a few!" she screamed.

Nico was putting so much pressure on Jasmine's arm, it was really hurting her.

"Nico, get off of me. You're hurting me! Stop acting like a fuckin' fool!"

The two of them made it out of the restaurant and to an area in the lobby where they were all alone.

"I can't believe you," Jasmine shouted as she marched toward the elevator, trying to make it up to her room.

Nico knew he had spazzed out. "A'ight, listen," he said.

Jasmine paid him no mind and kept on walking toward the elevators.

"Jasmine! Jasmine, I'm fuckin' talking to you," Nico hollered as he continued to follow her to the elevator.

Jasmine could see herself in the mirror-lined elevator.

"Look what you did to me. Look at my fuckin' arm! Shit!"

Nico had Jasmine in solitude like he wanted her. He really wanted to find out just exactly why she was out in Las Vegas, and how she knew what hotel he was in.

"I'm asking you one more time—What the fuck are you doing out here?"

As the elevator doors opened on to Jasmine's floor, she ignored Nico and quickly walked out of the elevator and toward her room. She desperately wanted to get to her government-issued BlackBerry so she could have him on tape.

"Leave me the fuck alone!"

Jasmine used her card key and unlocked the door to her room, and Nico pushed his way in right behind her.

"Hello! Leave me alone, please. I believe your bitch Mia is in another room." Jasmine walked across the room and grabbed her BlackBerry. "Seriously, Nico, leave right now, or I'm calling the cops," she said, discreetly activating the record feature.

"Call 'em."

Jasmine sighed and sucked her teeth. "Okay, you know what? Fuck it!" She walked over to the table that had Derek's weed sitting on top of it and sat down and pulled out a second chair for Nico.

"Since you so hard to find, and now you want to talk all of a sudden, sit down and let's talk, Nico."

CHAPTER 18

Nico's phone began to vibrate. He looked at it and saw that it was Mia, so he hit his ignore button and sent her to voice mail.

"Come on, sit down." Jasmine tapped the cushion with her hand.

Nico kicked the arm of the chair and knocked it over in the process.

WHACK!

He bitch-slapped Jasmine so hard, she saw stars. She had to catch her balance after almost falling out of the chair.

Jasmine tried to throw a punch, but Nico caught hold of her wrist, and bent it backwards, taking her down to the ground.

"Ahhhh! That's my sore hand!" she screamed, writhing in pain on the ground.

Nico applied more pressure to her bent wrist.

Jasmine tried to get to her feet, but Nico let her wrist go, grabbed her by the throat, and slammed the back of her head to the carpeted floor. Jasmine couldn't breathe, and she scratched at Nico's strong muscular right arm, trying to free herself from his grip.

He squeezed harder on her neck. "Now we gonna do shit my way! You understand me, bitch?"

Jasmine felt like she was about to pass out, so she stopped resisting, and tried to nod.

Nico finally loosened his grip from her neck, and Jasmine gasped for air, coughing and grabbing her throat.

"Now tell me what the fuck you doing out here, and how the fuck did you know where I was staying at? And don't bullshit me!"

Jasmine was still coughing, trying to get air in her lungs. "Nico, what you think I'm doing out here? I'm out here because I love you and I wanted to be with you." She immediately started to cry, hoping her tears would divert Nico's attention. "Baby, I'm out here because I was scared, and you make me feel safe. Do you know what it's like for me to almost get killed by Bebo and then not want to go home at night because I'm thinking he might come back and make sure he kills me? And all I want is to know you'll protect me, and it's like all you're doing is running from me. I'm scared, baby! That's all! I'm scared."

"I took care of that situation. I told you I would handle it, and I handled it. Now what the fuck you not gonna do is stand there and make me keep asking you the same shit."

"You handled what? See, this is what I can't take. I'm supposedly your girl, but you don't tell me shit. I don't know where you are at times, and it's just like *uggggghhhhh*. So what did you handle?"

"You know what the streets is talking about. I did that shit, it's done, it's over with. You can sleep at night now."

Jasmine shook her head.

"Answer me, Jasmine."

"You're going to think what you want to think, so I don't care. I knew you was out here because I called around to all of the hotels and the resorts asking for Mia's name. And as soon as I found the hotel she was at, I knew you would more than likely be side by side with her. And guess what? Looks like I was right." Jasmine had no idea if Mia had booked the room, so at that point her heart was pounding.

Nico looked at her as she wiped her tears. "You full of shit."

Jasmine exhaled because she knew Nico hadn't caught her in a lie. "Yeah, I'm full of shit. *Ugggghhh!* Baby, what is wrong? Like, did I do something or what? One minute everything is all good—We at Mr. Chow eating good and living it up—and then the next thing I know, the cops is at our table, I get arrested, and after that, it's like everything just short-circuited. What is going on?" she asked, desperation in her voice.

Tears started to fall from Jasmine's face. She picked up the chair that Nico had kicked over and sat back down. "Nico, be straight up with me and tell me the truth. Were you the one who sent Bebo to kill me?"

"The fuck you talking about?"

"I'm serious, Nico."

Nico plastered a smirk on his face. "What you think?"

"I think you did."

He shook his head and chuckled. "You're funny."

"That's why I'm out here. I came out here saying to

myself that if you're out here with Mia, then there's no way you didn't send Bebo to kill me. You sent him to kill me, and you're out here fuckin' that bitch that you know I can't stand."

"I ain't fuckin' Mia."

"Oh my God! This is what I can't stand! Nico, I'm not stupid. I'm home in New York dealing with my injuries after almost dying, and do I see you or hear from you? You out here fuckin' her while I'm in New York scared for my life. That shit is so fucked up." Jasmine stood up and walked over to a mirror and looked at her neck.

Nico could see the bruises he had caused.

"You choke the shit outta me, you left me stranded at the precinct and never explained to me what that was all about, and you really wonder if I think you had Bebo come to kill me?"

"So whatever happened with that shit? Why did the cops let you go?"

Jasmine sucked her teeth. "Because they didn't have shit on me. It was all bullshit, and we both know that."

"But what did they say?"

"About what? They took me in and they questioned me, but I didn't admit to shit because there was nothing to admit to. And since they wasn't charging me with a crime, they had to let me go. Nico, you know how this shit goes."

Nico walked up to Jasmine and tried to kiss her on the back of her neck, but she moved away.

"I apologize."

Jasmine shook her head. "You apologize? You out

here fuckin' that bitch. You choke me out and you got me home in New York looking like a clueless bird-bitch, and all you can say is 'I apologize'?"

Nico slowly approached Jasmine. "Come here."

"No! Go kiss on Mia. You can't just fuck her and then kiss on me and tell me you apologize. That's supposed to make things right?"

"I'm not fuckin' her."

"So then why is she out here with you? She's transporting kilos for you or something?"

Nico looked hard at Jasmine.

"Nico, it's simple. If you using Mia as a mule to transport your drugs, just say that and I'll know what's up. But if you fuckin' her then just say that too, so I'll know what's up, and I'll know where I stand."

"So who was homie wit'chu down in the restaurant? This his weed on the table?"

"He wasn't nobody. I met him last night at the bar. He was telling me he plays pro football, and he asked me if I would go to breakfast with him."

"So are you fuckin' him?"

"Nico, please don't try to spin this around."

"I ain't spinning shit, but if you wanna keep shit one hundred, let's keep it one hundred."

"I always keep it real, Nico, and you know that."

"Yeah, I know that. And I also know you murdered Shabazz. And if you murdered him, you think my mind don't wander?"

"Oh my God!"

"Babe, I saw you murder your ex in cold blood, and I been riding with you and I ain't ever blink about the shit."

"Hold up, hold up. First of all, you ain't ever see me do shit. And how dare you try to put that shit on me?"

"Nah, hold up, baby girl. You the one slinging murderous accusations, and you need to cut that shit out. Let's be mature adults about this shit. You feel me?"

Nico's prepaid phone started to vibrate at that moment. It was BJ. "My nigga, speak to me," he said and then walked into the bathroom so he could speak in private.

"The coroner finally released the body to homie's family. The funeral is on Friday," BJ explained, referring to Bebo's funeral.

"So whatchu saying?" Nico asked, still being careful not to say much of anything on the phone.

"We need to both be there."

Nico had no plans of ever attending Bebo's funeral, but he trusted BJ's judgment. "I feel you."

"You know what I mean, right?" BJ asked.

"Yeah, I been outta pocket, so the streets been talking."

"No muthafuckin' doubt. They on that conspiracy shit, but if we both there, it'll quiet all that."

"Yeah, yeah. So Friday, huh?"

"Yes, sir. At Gilmore's Funeral Home in Queens, over there on Linden."

"A'ight, speak to his moms and make sure they straight with cheddar and all that. Let them know that we gon' make sure his kids is straight."

"Cool." BJ ended their call.

Nico put his phone back in his pocket and exited the bathroom.

"For the record, I wasn't slinging no murderous accusations. I was just saying that I didn't know what to think," Jasmine tried to explain to Nico.

"Stop running your mouth."

"What are you talking about?"

"I'm just saying . . ."

Jasmine was getting frustrated because she wasn't getting where she wanted to get with Nico.

Nico walked over to the wet bar and poured himself a Jack Daniel's on the rocks and asked Jasmine if she wanted anything to drink. Jasmine just shook her head. He put his drink on the table and gestured for Jasmine to come to him. She went to him, and then he kissed her on the lips.

Jasmine sucked her teeth. "I hate you."

"You hate me?"

"Yes." She felt Nico unbutton her pants..

"You ain't give my pussy away, right?"

Jasmine shook her head no. "You can't fuck me, Nico."

"Why not?" Nico asked, unzipping his own pants.

"Because you don't trust me. You don't tell me—"

"Stop talking."

Nico took another swig of his drink, and then he put it back down. He took Jasmine by the hand, led her into the bathroom, and turned on the shower.

"Take a shower with me," he said to her while he got fully undressed and made his way into the glass-enclosed shower.

Jasmine wanted to resist, but the sight of Nico's naked body turned her on so much, her pussy instantly got wet. She got undressed and joined him in the shower. She started to tongue-kiss him as the water rained down on both of them.

Jasmine didn't know what it was about Nico, but something about the way he fucked her always made her have multiple orgasms and left her weak in the knees.

When they had finished fucking and showering, she was uncharacteristically quiet, dealing with all kinds of emotions and feelings. She had no clue what the hell she had gotten herself into.

CHAPTER 19

Nico ended up staying in Jasmine's room for the rest of the day. Her pussy was sore, but she knew one thing—As long as he was with her, he couldn't be with Mia.

Jasmine had hoped for an opportunity to catch Nico saying something revealing, but with all the fucking they were doing, the opportunity never presented itself. By the time ten o'clock rolled around, they were exhausted and decided to order room service.

After they had finished eating their dinner, Jasmine found herself dozing off in the bed with Nico.

"You still up?" she asked him.

"Yeah."

She turned and faced Nico and kissed him on his chest. "I just wanted to tell you that I love you."

"Oh, a'ight."

Before long, Jasmine was knocked out and in a deep sleep. Nico knew that the weed she had been smoking combined with the liquor and the sex was going to have her out cold for a while. He was tired, but he wasn't about to let himself fall asleep; it was way too early for that.

After about an hour of just laying there, Nico slid out of the bed and went into the bathroom to take a piss.

When he came out of the bathroom, he looked around for Jasmine's cell phone. She had her FBI-issued BlackBerry inside of her open Gucci bag, which was not too far from the bed, and her regular BlackBerry on the nightstand right next to her head.

Seeing the BlackBerry on the nightstand, Nico never thought to look inside her Gucci bag. He walked over and picked up the BlackBerry on the nightstand and walked back into the bathroom with it. Then he locked the door and started searching through the phone. He looked at text messages, incoming calls and outgoing calls, and he figured out how to play back recordings. The only recording he saw was the one that Jasmine had made when Bebo had shot her.

He came out of the bathroom and placed her phone back on the nightstand. He quietly got dressed, got his phone, and made sure all of his cash was in his pocket. Then he took a long look at Jasmine, and as she slept, he reconfirmed how fine she was. Though he felt some relief that she hadn't recorded him, he still had a gut feeling that she was working with the feds.

Nico slipped out of the room headed to the roulette table, but he decided to go to his room first. When he got there, Mia was nowhere to be found, and her bags weren't there. He called her three times, but she didn't pick up. He decided to just go play roulette for an hour, telling himself if Mia wasn't in the room by the time he got back, he was just going to go to the strip club or back to Jasmine's room and fuck her one more time.

Nico had no idea that Mia had already checked out of the room and had checked into an inexpensive hotel room right near the airport. She was tired of him just tossing her to the side whenever he felt like it. She had made up her mind to head back to New York the next day, and she was going to go straight to the safe deposit box Nico had her open up for him and take the three hundred and fifty thousand dollars in there and then disappear.

When Jasmine first opened her eyes, she wasn't exactly sure where she was. So much had been going on in her life, she wasn't sure if she was at her mother's house, at Simone's house, or at her and Nico's house. After about a minute she sat up in the bed, and then she remembered that she was in Las Vegas, and that she and Nico had just spent the majority of the previous day fucking their brains out.

Seeing that the light was on in the bathroom and the bathroom door was closed, she assumed that Nico was in there. She walked over to the bathroom door, knocked on it and called Nico's name, and waited for an answer. When she didn't get one, she tapped on the door again and opened it up and went inside.

Jasmine shook her head as she exited the bathroom. When she realized it was five o'clock in the morning and there was no sign of Nico, she knew he had purposely slid out on her.

Jasmine went back into the bathroom and peed and then washed her hands before getting back into the bed.

The room was still somewhat dark because the sun hadn't risen yet. Jasmine lay in the bed feeling like a whore, knowing that only hours ago Nico had been fucking the shit out of her, and he was now probably fucking Mia the same way.

She reached over and grabbed her BlackBerry. She called Nico, but she got no answer.

"I can't do this shit no more," she said out loud.

She then sent Nico a text message: *So it's like that, Nico? You just fuck me for hours and leave without telling me???*

Jasmine waited five minutes, and when she realized Nico wasn't responding, she texted him again: *You back on that bullshit AGAIN! It's all good, though. Don't worry I WON'T CHASE YOU!!!*

Jasmine tried to go back to sleep, but she couldn't. It had now been a full hour, and Nico still hadn't responded to her missed call or to her texts.

She decided to call Derek. When he didn't pick up, she left him a voice mail: "Hey, Derek. This is Jasmine. I know it's early, but I just really need to speak to you. First, I want to really, really, really apologize for yesterday. I am so sorry. But call me back when you get this, so I can explain. It's way too much to explain in a voice mail."

After about five minutes she decided to send Derek a text message: *Hi Derek, it's Jasmine. I just left you a voice mail. Call me as soon as you can.*

Jasmine grabbed the remote, turned on the TV, and started to flip through the channels. Two minutes later, she heard her BlackBerry vibrating on her nightstand. She quickly reached for it. It was a text message from Derek—*Jasmine, the pussy was good, but I don't need the drama. LOSE MY NUMBER! Thanks!!!*

Jasmine felt like she had just been dropkicked in the gut. She immediately called Derek, but it went to voice mail. She was so mad with Nico at that point because not only was he playing games with her, but he had now managed to fuck up the NFL jackpot that had fallen in her lap.

She got up and went to the wet bar and poured herself a drink. She was done with Las Vegas. After her drink she was going to take a shower, get dressed, eat breakfast, and then head to the airport and see if she could change her ticket or fly standby, so she could get her ass back to New York and reassess everything.

CHAPTER 20

Jasmine made it to the airport and asked to see a JetBlue supervisor. She complained to the supervisor about how rude the JetBlue stewardess had been to her on her flight to Las Vegas, and asked if she could be upgraded to the front of the plane so she wouldn't have to be subjected to the same ghetto treatment.

The white male supervisor began typing into his computer. "Would you like a window seat or an aisle seat?"

"It doesn't matter."

"Okay, just give me one more minute, and I should be—Oh, okay there we go. Would the third-row window seat be good?"

Jasmine smiled. "Perfect."

"Sorry I couldn't get you in the first or second row."

"No, that's fine. You helped me out a great deal."

Jasmine smiled, took hold of her boarding pass, and thanked him again before going to sit down and wait for the plane to start boarding.

A little over an hour later, she found herself boarding the plane and sitting happily in her third-row seat. She had already put her carry-on bag in the overhead compartment and was reading the latest issue of *Essence* magazine while the other passengers boarded the plane.

She looked up and couldn't believe her eyes. She saw Mia boarding the same plane and taking her aisle seat in row two just across the aisle from her. Jasmine's heart started to beat rapidly because she was certain that Nico would be soon boarding the plane. Mia was wearing designer sunglasses that hid her face somewhat, but Jasmine was sure it was her. She intently watched for Nico, but he never walked onto the plane.

Mia turned and saw Jasmine looking at her. She slightly slid her shades downward off her face, just to make sure her eyes weren't playing tricks on her.

"Yeah, it's me, bitch!" Jasmine shouted.

Everybody seated in the front of the plane was surprised at Jasmine's language, not to mention confused.

Mia smiled and calmly walked toward Jasmine and stood over the white lady sitting next to her. "You're frustrated. I understand, sweetie. You'll be okay," she said in a soft, nonthreatening tone.

"If you were smart, you would sit your ass down."

"Ladies, is everything okay?" a gay black male flight attendant walked up and asked both Mia and Jasmine.

"Everything is fine," Mia replied right before taking her aisle seat. "She's just going through a little of life's frustrations."

For the remainder of the almost six-hour flight, Jasmine and Mia both ignored each other. When the flight was approaching the airport, Jasmine sent Simone a text and asked her if she could pick her up from LaGuardia Airport in thirty minutes, and Simone agreed.

Simone rolled down the passenger side window. "Hey, girl." She popped the trunk, so Jasmine could put her bag inside.

"Thank you so much. I flew out of Kennedy Airport, and I got my truck parked there. But there was so much drama, I ended up flying back in to LaGuardia."

"Oh, okay. So you need me to shoot you over to Kennedy?"

"Yeah, if you can."

Simone gave Jasmine a look. "If you didn't have your car parked at Kennedy, then I would be driving you home. So what's the difference?"

"No, I'm just saying I don't want to be all rude and assuming, that's all." Jasmine smiled.

"So you went to Vegas and didn't even tell me?"

"Drama, drama, drama—I can't even begin to tell you!"

"In Vegas? What happened?"

"So I go out there with this dude named Derek McGee. He plays football for the Green Bay Packers—twenty-million-dollar contract, fine as hell, muscles, all that. So . . ."

"And when were you going to tell me about him? Hook a sister up with one of his friends!"

"No, just listen. So me and Derek are at the Wynn Resort. We chillin', smoking good weed, good sex, eating good and all that. So we at brunch at this restaurant, and who the fuck walks in? Nico!"

"No way!"

"I swear to God!"

"How did he know you were there?"

"I got no idea. So Nico comes to the table beefing, like, 'who the fuck is this nigga?' So Derek stands up from the table, and he ain't a street dude, and inside I'm saying to myself, 'Derek, I know you got muscles and all, but I hope your ass knows how to use your hands.'"

Simone chuckled. "Nico ended up knocking his ass out, right?"

"No. So I stand up and I step in between them. But Derek starts talking shit, so next thing I know, I see Nico reaching for his gun."

"Jasmine, no." Simone held her hand over her mouth.

"So I screamed, 'Nico, no!' and I rushed him and held him so he wouldn't do nothing crazy. So Nico is going crazy like, 'What the fuck are you doing out here?' and he's snatching me up, like, 'Come on, let's go.'"

"And what was Derek doing?"

"He was just standing there, asking me if I was all right, so I ended up telling him I would be right back and I was sorry and all that. And Nico marches me out of the restaurant, and it was just crazy!"

"So what else happened?"

"It's too much to tell, but basically I wasn't trying to have Nico murder my ass."

"So you just left Derek out there?"

"Well, his punk ass ended up texting me, talking about my pussy was good and all that but for me to lose his number because he don't need the drama. Look." Jasmine handed Simone her phone to look at the text Derek had sent to her.

"Wow! But, Jasmine, that's twenty million you leaving on the table."

"I know, I know. Don't even remind me. I am *so* through right now."

"So where's Nico?"

"He's still out there. He had some business to take care of. And you know what? I'm glad you asked me that, because you need to come chill with me in Long Island until he gets back in a few days."

Simone looked at Jasmine but didn't say anything. She was well aware of what had happened the last time one of her friends went to her and Nico's house, and she wasn't trying to end up dead.

"Okay, well, at least chill with me for the rest of the day, and then let's hang out later tonight or tomorrow, or something."

Simone agreed.

The two of them ended up driving to Simone's house, where Simone parked her car and got into Jasmine's truck, and they headed out to Bell Boulevard, in Bayside, Queens.

On the plane Jasmine had made up her mind to get a tattoo, and she wanted to do it right at that moment so she wouldn't change her mind.

"You have got to be the wildest chick I know. You just barely healed up good and you getting a tattoo?"

Jasmine smiled and nodded, maneuvering her truck on the Cross Island Parkway toward the Bell Boulevard exit, and before long the two of them were at a tattoo shop called Murder Inc. Jasmine felt her government-issued phone vibrate, and she looked down and realized it was a text from Agent Gosling that said, *That was quick.*

It instantly filled Jasmine with anxiety. She knew that the clock was ticking, in terms of how much time she had to come up with the information they needed, or else her ass was going back to jail. And, to make matters worse, she had to figure out how to delete some of the conversation that she and Nico had, when he basically put Shabazz's murder squarely on her.

She responded, *Yeah, we'll talk. Working on something*

She had to quickly make a move and get her ass in the streets, so she could at least give the FBI some of what they wanted.

Jasmine put her phone away, blew out some air from her lungs, and turned off the ignition. "Let's go do this," she said to Simone, even though Simone wasn't getting a tattoo.

"You are crazy. On your neck? Jasmine, you sure you want to do this?"

"Positive!" Jasmine shot back as they walked toward the shop. "On my neck I am going to get a tattoo in cursive letters that says LOVE IS CURSED. And on my hand I'm going to get a cobra tattoo."

"And you thought about this already?"

"Yup."

Jasmine was excited by how her tattoos turned out. Her excitement didn't last too long, though, because Agent Gosling was texting her again and asking when could they meet.

Jasmine texted back *Soon. Just give me a little more time. You'll be happy.*

And before should could look at her tattoos for a full five minutes, she began plotting and scheming about how she could quickly get close to Black Justice.

CHAPTER 21

Bebo's wake was a mad house, with people wall to wall. There were relatives, baby mommas, friends, undercover police and federal agents, and celebrities. Almost all of the members of Ghetto Mafia were present, but Nico, BJ, and Lorenzo, BJ's cousin and right-hand man, were all noticeably absent.

As people milled about and huddled in their circles, rumors about why Nico wasn't there began to surface. Some people had heard that it was Bebo who had shot Nico's girl, Jasmine. Some dismissed that as nothing but bullshit. Others believed that the two masked men who had gunned down Bebo were BJ and Lorenzo because Nico would send his two lieutenants to carry out his orders for him, instead of doing the dirty work himself.

With about a half an hour left in the wake, a Maybach pulled up to the funeral home and parked illegally. The driver got out and opened the rear door. It was dark outside, and the curtains inside the Maybach were drawn, so no one knew who was inside, until Nico, BJ, and Lorenzo emerged. Immediately the three of them began to get a lot of love from the mourners. It seemed as if everybody wanted to give Nico a pound and a hug; it took them about twenty minutes to make it inside the funeral home.

The three of them made their way to the front row of the mourners, and addressed the family one by one, shaking their hands and telling them that they were sorry for their loss.

"Auntie Rose," Nico said to Bebo's aunt while holding on to her hand, "you was like a mother to Bebo, and you like a mother to me. That's not going to change. Whatever you need, just let me know, and I'll always be there for you." Nico called her auntie because she always cooked tons of food for him and all of Bebo's crew, and she was like an aunt to everybody.

Auntie Rose squeezed Nico's hand and pulled him toward her, so she could speak directly into his ear. "Just promise me you'll find the people who killed my nephew."

Nico didn't know what exactly to say. He felt so fucked up at that moment, knowing that Auntie Rose was looking right at her nephew's killer. "Most definitely." Then he patted her on the shoulder and kept it moving.

By this time BJ and Lo were both already at the Bebo's casket looking at his body. All BJ could think about was the day he had murdered Bebo, and now there he was standing at the casket, looking at his victim. Deep down inside he knew that he had carried out the proper justice because Bebo had broken the street code and therefore deserved to die.

Nico touched the side of the casket—a casket he had paid for—and stared at Bebo.

The three of them stayed at Bebo's casket for about two minutes, and then one by one they turned and walked away from the casket and out of the funeral home.

Lo took out a cigarette and offered one to BJ. Nico didn't want one, but he stood on the steps of the funeral home while Lo and BJ smoked.

"That shit is fucked up," Lo said.

BJ had never even told his cousin Lo that it was him and Nico who had murdered Bebo.

"That's the streets," Nico replied.

"Word up," BJ added.

It was starting to drizzle lightly, and although the wake was nearing its end, it seemed as if there were now more people standing outside the funeral home than at any other time during the wake.

The funeral was scheduled for the next day, Friday morning at 9 A.M., at Allen A.M.E Cathedral, which wasn't too far from the funeral home.

"So in the morning we riding together or what?" Lo asked BJ and Nico as they stood on the steps.

Before either Nico or BJ could answer, an all-black Hummer SUV sped up to the front of the funeral home. The Hummer, driving eastbound on Linden Boulevard, was driving so fast, people had to scurry out of the way to avoid getting hit.

As the Hummer came to a skidding halt on the slick roads, the front and rear passenger side windows both rolled down, and masked gunmen in the front and back seat both stretched their bodies out of the windows and started firing toward Nico, BJ, and Lo.

"Oh shit!" BJ hollered, ducking for cover behind one

of the wooden pillars.

The gunman in the front passenger seat had fired off sixteen shots from a 9mm handgun and was quickly out of bullets. He pulled his body back inside the Hummer and began to urge the driver to pull off. "Drive, nigga! Drive!" he yelled.

The driver didn't listen because he didn't want to pull off too quickly and have his other homeboy fall out of the rear passenger window.

TA TA TA TA TA TA TA TA TA TA TA TA TA TA TATATATATATATATATATATATATATATATAT

TA TA TA TA TA TA TA TA TA TA TA TA TA TA TATATATATATATATATATATATATATATATAT

TA TA TA TA TA TA TA TA TA TA TA TA TA TA TATATATATATATATATATATATATATATATAT

That was the sound of gunfire coming from the second gunman's Calico M960 that had the capability of letting off 750 rounds a minute. Luckily for all of the innocent bystanders, he only had a one-hundred-round magazine in the gun.

After emptying the magazine, the gunman slipped his body back inside the truck, and it peeled off down busy Linden Boulevard before making a quick right turn onto 195th Street.

Within seconds, police and ambulance sirens could be heard blaring from every direction.

Lo had been hit multiple times in the back, legs, and ass, and was laying on the steps of the funeral bleeding and writhing in pain.

BJ had also been shot multiple times. He was hit in the stomach and in his right arm. He was doubled over in pain and hiding in bushes he'd jumped behind after stepping from behind the wooden pillar.

Nico had managed to make it inside the funeral home. He was kicking himself for not being strapped. He was trying to figure out which way to go, and then he saw an exit sign, headed toward it, and ran down some steps that led to the basement. In the basement there were about five dead bodies on silver tables and caskets everywhere. Then he saw another exit sign all the way on the other side of the basement, and he bolted toward it, moving as fast as he could.

He knew he shouldn't have come to Bebo's wake. Now he felt like he was going to have to pay for it with his life. He pushed open the other basement door, which that triggered a loud alarm that scared the shit out of him. When he emerged from that door, he realized he was in the back of the funeral home, where he saw people running down the street in a panic.

At that point he didn't hear any more gunshots, but he did hear a ton of police sirens, so he figured he was safe. He leaned against the brick rear wall of the funeral home and tried his best to catch his breath. It was at that moment that he realized that BJ and Lo weren't following behind him.

"Muthafucka!" he yelled out loud. He then started running toward the funeral home, in the opposite direction of all of the people who were trying to get away.

As soon as he made it to the front of the funeral home, he counted twelve people lying on the ground from gunshot wounds, including a four-year-old girl. He saw BJ and Lo, and they both looked as if they weren't moving. "Ahhh fuck!" he hollered.

Cops had quickly roped off the scene with police tape, and where there wasn't police tape, the cops wouldn't let anyone near the funeral home.

Nico's driver had been forced to move the Maybach, so Nico couldn't locate his car. He looked on helplessly at the chaos until he was forced by police to leave the scene, which he reluctantly did. He later learned that fifteen people had been shot—four fatally—and more than twenty people who hadn't been shot were also injured. And he had gotten no word from BJ or Lo, and his calls and texts to their phones went unanswered.

CHAPTER 22

The morning after the shooting at the funeral home, Agent Gosling called Jasmine on her government-issued BlackBerry.

"Can you talk?" Gosling asked.

"Yeah, I can talk."

"Talk to me about the shooting last night at Bebo's wake."

Jasmine paused.

"What is Nico saying? The funeral is this morning. Is he going?"

"Listen, things have been so crazy and happening so fast, I haven't even—"

"Jasmine, I need you to treat this like it's a full-time job. You need to eat, drink, shit, and sleep what you agreed to, and cut out this half-ass bullshit you've been offering up."

"But I'm trying."

"Well, try harder. You're not giving me anything. Before you left for Vegas, you had nothing. You go out to Vegas and come back with nothing. There is a major shooting, and you have nothing. You do understand what we agreed to, right?"

"Yes," Jasmine meekly replied.

"Well, then what's the problem?"

Jasmine sighed. "I just need more time."

"That's all I keep hearing."

Getting close to Nico was going to be tough, but she didn't want to tell Gosling that. She also didn't want to tell him that she had found out where Black Justice hung out and that she had formulated a plan to get close to him. What she wanted to do was first get something concrete and then let Gosling know what she had come up with.

"How much time do you need?" Gosling asked in a disgusted tone.

"Two weeks."

"I tell you what. Make it a full thirty days. But in thirty days I don't want any excuses. None. Are we clear?"

A slight smile appeared across her face. "No excuses."

Jasmine had heard that on Friday nights Black Justice could usually be found at a strip club called Sue's Rendezvous, located in his hometown of Yonkers. She convinced Simone to go with her, explaining to her that they had spent too much time fucking with dudes from Brooklyn and Queens.

It turned out that Jasmine and Simone had picked the right night to go to Sue's. Two of the chicks from *Basketball Wives* were scheduled to appear at the club, and a popular porn star was also dancing there that night.

Jasmine didn't want to spend fifteen minutes circling around looking for a parking spot, so she let the valet park her truck for her, and she and Simone made their way toward the entrance of the club.

As the two of them approached the front of the club, a bouncer spotted them and called out to them. "It's just the two y'all? No dudes?"

"Yeah, just me and her." Jasmine smiled.

"Okay, that's what's up. Y'all don't have to wait on line. Just stand right here, and as soon as he's done with them, he'll frisk y'all, and y'all can go right in."

"Thank you," Simone responded.

"Do me a favor and open up your bags, so he can check those too," the bouncer added.

Before long Jasmine and Simone had been frisked, and they both paid their twenty-dollar cover charge to get in. When they walked into the club, they quickly saw how rammed it was.

"This shit is way too packed up in here!" Simone screamed into Jasmine's ear.

Jasmine ignored her. She started looking around to see who she knew and tried to figure out where to go. Simone wanted to go to the bar area next to the main stage, but Jasmine wanted to get closer to the tables, where all the ballers were poppin' bottles.

Jasmine felt somebody tug on her arm. She turned around and saw Ish, who was part of Ghetto Mafia and real cool with Nico. That was just what Jasmine didn't want. She was hoping she didn't see anybody she knew.

"Hey, baby," Jasmine yelled with a smile. She gave Ish a kiss on his cheek. "What you doing here?"

"What the fuck *you* doing up in here?"

"I just needed to get out. I been cooped up in the house ever since I got shot, and this is my first time out."

"Oh, right, right. The streets is crazy right now. You got shot, Bebo got murked, then Lo. Shit is on fire."

Jasmine had heard about BJ and Lo getting shot, but she didn't know if Ish was trying to say that Lo had died, and she didn't want to ask any questions.

"Exactly. That's why I just wanted to get out and get my mind off everything, and when I heard my girl Tami from *Basketball Wives* was going to be here, I had to come."

"Oh, so that's what the fuck you doing here. That *Basketball Wives* shit. I feel you. Nico coming through too?"

Jasmine shrugged her shoulders. "Ish, you ever met my girl Simone?"

Ish squinted his eyes to look at Simone, who was attracted to him from the moment she saw him. Ish had that thugged-out look that she loved. He had a deep caramel complexion and full lips and hazel eyes. Ish was about six two, and two hundred pounds of lean muscle, and his deep-set eyes gave him a very menacing appearance.

"Nah, I don't think I ever met shorty before." Ish smiled as he extended his hand to Simone.

"Well, buy her a drink and a lap dance and then get to know her."

"No doubt, no doubt."

"The drink would be fine, but no lap dances, thank you very much." Simone was "strictly dickly." In fact, on the way to the club she'd told Jasmine that the strippers had better not come near her, trying to grind and dance on her. She followed Ish, and they made their way to the bar.

Jasmine continued to walk through the club, and before long she spotted Black Justice sitting with about five other dudes who were drinking and tossing money at strippers. She got as close as she could to him and his crew, and then she found a seat and started to move her body to the music.

One of the dudes with Black Justice asked Jasmine, "You want a drink, ma?"

Jasmine nodded, and within seconds the dude poured her a glass of Ace of Spades. Jasmine thanked him and started sipping the champagne.

"So what's your name?" he asked.

"Ask your boy. He knows who I am."

"Who? Black Jus?"

Jasmine sipped more of her champagne and nodded. Then she put the drink down and stood up and started dancing by herself to one of Drake's hit songs.

The dude told Black Jus what Jasmine said, and Black Jus looked in Jasmine's direction and stared at her, trying to remember her name. Black Justice was a half-black, half-Colombian pretty boy who had fucked many bad chicks in his lifetime. He was trying to remember if he had ever fucked Jasmine.

The dude who had given Jasmine the drink walked back up to her and told her that Jus wanted to see her. Jasmine nodded and turned around and looked in Black

Justice's direction. She kept dancing and waved at him, and then she signaled for him to give her a minute. She didn't want to seem too desperate. When the song ended, she made her way over to Black Jus, who stood up as she approached.

He looked at the tattoo on her neck. "Love is cursed—I like that. You just got that tat?"

"Thank you. Yeah, I just got it."

"Yo, I know that I know you, but I'm trying to figure out from where."

Jasmine gave Black Jus a disgusted look. "Jasmine."

"Right, right. You from Queens, right?"

Jasmine nodded and smiled.

"You used to fuck with that nigga Shabazz?"

"Yo, I swear me and Shabazz might as well have been married or some shit. Everybody links me to him, and I wasn't even fuckin' with him for that long before he got killed."

"So what's up wit'chu?"

"I'm just doing me right now, trying to make my own moves."

"Whatchu mean?"

Jasmine looked at Black Jus, and then she drank some more of her champagne. "It's too noisy in here. I can't really talk like I want to, but I gotta get wit'chu and discuss something."

"Fuck the music! Let's talk now."

Jasmine didn't want to talk right then and there because she wanted to record the conversation. Turning on the recorder at that point wouldn't have made any sense because the music was too loud.

Jasmine stood on her tippy toes and yelled into Black Justice's right ear. "Here's what it is. I just need a new connect right now. I got this nigga from North Carolina, and I had him going through Ghetto Mafia niggas, but you know how hot shit is right now with them."

"So what's good, ma? Talk to me. He lookin' for weight?"

Jasmine nodded her head.

"I gotchu. You know how I gets down."

Jasmine smiled.

"So you fuckin' with that nigga? It's your man or what?"

"Something like that."

"Whatchu mean?"

"I mean, I ain't trying to tie my pussy down."

Black Justice laughed, and then his man came with a brand-new bottle of Hennessy and handed it to him.

"You want some?" he asked Jasmine.

Jasmine shook her head. "So let me get your number because I see you about to get twisted."

Black Justice took out his cell phone and gave Jasmine his number. "Call me right now, and I'll lock you into my phone, and you can lock me into yours."

Jasmine didn't know which number to give him, but something told her to just give him the FBI-issued number, and that's what she did. She took out her FBI BlackBerry and dialed his number.

"Two five two?" Black Justice commented, referring to the area code of Jasmine's number.

Jasmine froze because she didn't have a ready-made excuse as to why the number was out of state. In fact, that was the first time it had dawned on her that she should have known the number.

"Yeah." Jasmine nonchalantly locked in Black Justice's number.

"Oh, that's that North Carolina area code, right?"

Jasmine's heart began to race. She didn't know what to say because she had no idea if it was in fact a North Carolina area code. She just smiled and nodded.

Jasmine and Simone both ended up having a great time at the strip club. Simone had managed to hook up with Ish, and Jasmine had made the initial inroads into Black Justice.

Jasmine was able to exhale later that night. She knew the "confidential informant gods" were on her side because, as luck would have it, the 252 area code was, in fact, a North Carolina area code.

CHAPTER 23

The following afternoon, Black Justice found himself waking up next to a stripper named Bella, who had recently relocated from Miami. Although Bella had a small frame, she had a huge ass, which was what had attracted Black Justice to her. In spite of Bella's ass, Black Justice found himself unable to get his mind off Jasmine. He got out of the bed and walked over to the vertical mirror attached to the back of his bedroom door.

"We would have some cute kids," Bella said as she partially sat up in the bed with her elbow on her pillow and the palm of her hand supporting her head.

"Yeah, we would have some fly-ass seeds."

Bella got out of the bed, walked up to him, and began rubbing on his dick.

"I'm good, ma."

"You good?" She smiled as she continued to rub on his dick.

"I said I was good." Black Justice pushed Bella away. It wasn't a hard push, but it got her attention. "I'm going to the barbershop, and then I got some moves to make."

"So can I chill here until you get back?"

"I got another shorty coming in about a hour or two; otherwise, I would let you chill with me until I get back."

Bella felt like shit but tried to play it off. "So you a pretty boy playa? Playa, playa, playa," she chuckled and said.

Black Justice smiled as he looked into his mirror. Then he put on some cologne before quickly getting dressed.

"I just do my thing. You feel me?"

Bella nodded as she put on her stilettos. Then she grabbed her bag, walked up to Black Jus, and kissed him on the lips. "Call me if you ever need me."

"No doubt." Black Justice reached into the pocket of the jeans he'd worn the night before and pulled out a wad of cash. After peeling off three hundred dollars, he threw the jeans to the ground and handed Bella the cash.

"Thank you, sweetie." Bella gave Black Jus another kiss.

"Yo, how these kicks look with these jeans?"

"It's official." Bella made her way out of the house and into her Mitsubishi Galant and headed to her Harlem apartment.

Black Jus ignored the missed calls he had on his phone from about five different chicks and called Jasmine.

"Hey," Jasmine replied after answering on the third ring.

"What's good?"

"Nothing. I just woke up."

"So, yo, I'm heading to the barbershop. What you doing later? Why don't you come through?"

"Come through where?"

"To the crib."

Jasmine knew that if she went to Black Justice's crib that he would try to fuck her. She remembered Gosling's warnings about no sexual involvement with any of the targets. "Jus, I told you I got a man. I can't disrespect him like that. You understand what I'm saying?"

"Yeah, yeah, so just come through anyway, so we can chop it up about what we was talking about last night."

Jasmine knew she had to get something incriminating on Black Jus, and therefore she had to play the game on his terms. So she got his address and made plans to meet up with him at his crib at four o'clock.

At four o'clock Jasmine found herself at Black Justice's huge New Rochelle home just off North Avenue in Westchester County.

Black Jus opened the front door to his house. "You found it okay?"

"GPS." Jasmine smiled, her BlackBerry in her bag recording everything. "You have a nice house."

"Yeah, it's cool. It's quiet up here, you know, when you want to get away from all the noise and drama."

Jasmine nodded. "Does Irv Gotti live around here?"

"Yeah, that punk-ass nigga live about two blocks away."

Jasmine chuckled. "I thought so." She had been to a party before at his house and thought the area looked familiar.

"So them Ghetto Mafia niggas is dropping like flies."

"Yeah, that's so fucked up."

Jasmine hadn't spoken to Nico, but with Lo's death, she knew she would hear from him soon and, at the very least, would find out about funeral arrangements and would run into him at Lo's funeral.

"So shit is fucked up with them?"

"Yeah, I mean, I don't exactly know what's going on. I mean, they can get product, but the shit is just real weak, you know?"

Black Jus smiled. He loved to hear about the failings of his enemies. "Muthafuckas don't know what they doin'. See, a nigga like me, I gets that fish scale straight off the boat! You feel me now?" He reached behind a picture frame on the mantle of his granite-finished fireplace and held up a brick of cocaine. "Ain't nobody in New York fuckin' with the quality of this shit right here."

"Jus, you are crazy! You keep them bricks in your crib like that?"

Black Jus nodded once as he put the kilo back behind the picture frame. "It's different up here. You want anything to drink?" He walked into his kitchen and handed her a Corona before she could even respond and took out a Heineken for himself.

Black Jus opened both bottles, and he then got a lime and cut a piece of it and handed it to Jasmine for her Corona.

"What you mean, it's different up here?"

"New York City, you got the biggest gang in the world that you going up against, the NYPD. Them NYPD cats is forty thousand cops strong. That shit is like a small muthafuckin' army. But out here, New Rochelle, they got their own little police department. And that shit is like fuckin' with Boss Hog and that *Dukes of Hazzard* shit. You understand what I'm saying?" He laughed.

"Nah, you lost me."

Black Jus took a swig of his Heineken and then explained to Jasmine that, with a smaller police force like New Rochelle's, it was real easy to get to the top people in the department and have them on the take.

"Ohhh, okay, I gotchu. So they on the payroll?"

"Exactly." Black Jus guzzled down the rest of the Heineken and cracked open another one.

"I got a two-year-old daughter and a four-year-old son, but word is bond, I done already put about five kids through college already. And all they daddies is cops."

Jasmine smiled and sipped on her Corona. Having that admission on tape alone was enough to start an investigation into a corrupt police force.

"You heard of diplomatic immunity? What I got up here in Westchester County, I call that shit 'thugmatic' immunity. You feel me?" Black Jus laughed.

He walked back into the living room and examined his hair in the mirror. "Yo, I hate the way this muthafucka lined my shit up. Every time my barber ain't around and I fuck with one of them young barbers, they fuck my shit up!"

Jasmine had no idea why he was complaining because his hair looked perfect, like he could immediately go do a photo shoot for a Sean John ad campaign or something.

"A'ight, so let's talk business. Your man is really moving weight down there in North Carolina or what? What would he need? He ain't just sticking his toe in the water on some bullshit, is he?"

"I mean, I don't want to talk for him, but I would say definitely like nine ki's or better."

"Nine ki's?"

Jasmine figured that using some random uneven number like nine was the best way to avoid suspicion. Nico had once told her that undercover cops and feds always made the mistake of trying to buy shit in perfectly even numbers, and to him that was a red flag that would make him proceed with caution.

"Yeah, but if you don't got nine, then I'm sure he would—"

"Nah, nah, nah, I got it. That ain't no problem."

"What part of North Carolina you said he was from again?"

Jasmine began to panic because she couldn't remember if she had said a particular area, and she didn't want to make a mistake and get caught in a lie. She blew out air from her lungs.

"Okay, look. Please, whatever you do, when you meet the nigga, don't relay none of this shit, because he would kick my muthafuckin' ass."

"Yeah, yeah. I don't run my mouth like that. What's up?"

"See, you know them colleges like Duke and the University of North Carolina?"

"Yeah."

"That whole college scene, and all them white boys with the rich parents, he got that whole shit on lock."

Black Jus smiled and nodded.

"So listen. He gave me twenty-five hundred to purchase an ounce from you, you know, just so he could sample it and shit."

"That ain't nothing."

"No, but it is. The thing is, I already spent most of the money, and right now all I got is a grand on me."

"So I'll get you half an ounce."

"Okay, thank you."

"I gotchu." Black Jus moved closer to Jasmine. "I wanted to get wit'chu ever since I used to see you out with that nigga Shabazz."

Jasmine moved back. "Oh, really?" She smiled.

Black Jus came closer, but she held out her arm and held him at bay.

She told him, "Don't even do that."

"Do what?"

"Push up on me like that. With the harem of bitches that I'm sure you got, I ain't trying to be in your stable."

"What women?" Black Jus leaned in and tried to kiss Jasmine.

"Jus, as good as you look, stop it."

"Don't nobody got to know nothing. It's just me and you right now. Your man ain't here, and my girl ain't here."

"I know that." Jasmine managed to escape from his clutches and went into her bag. "Let's just keep it about business, though. Here, let me give you this money." She tried to discreetly stop the recording device, but since she couldn't do it without making it obvious, she gave up on the idea. She pulled out the cash and counted off a thousand dollars.

Jasmine knew that Black Jus was now going to go real hard at her and try to fuck her, but she had made up her mind to be strong and not give in to him and to only promise him that she would let him fuck her later, just not then and there. Jasmine knew how to play the game. The best bait was the prospect of him fucking her. In fact, the prospect of pussy was even more powerful than the pussy itself. And it was the prospect of getting at Jasmine's pussy that had allowed Black Jus to let his guard down and walk down the road she wanted him to walk.

CHAPTER 24

Nico had not left Jamaica Hospital since the night of the shooting at the funeral home when both BJ and Lo were rushed to the trauma unit. He was at the hospital when BJ came out of surgery. The doctors told him that the prognosis was good, and it looked like BJ would pull through.

But then a different set of surgeons informed him that they had tried everything they could but weren't able to save Lo. Nico was devastated. He felt all kinds of guilt because he was certain that Lo would be alive and that BJ wouldn't be clinging to life if he'd followed his gut and skipped Bebo's wake.

It was nearly four in the morning when he decided to call Jasmine from the hospital. When she didn't pick up, he decided against leaving a message. He would just drive home to Long Island when he left the hospital and give her the news about Lo face to face.

"You okay?" the head nurse asked Nico after he hung up the phone.

"Yeah, I'm good."

"Listen, I'm not supposed to do this," she said, "but the staffing is real light at this time of night, and the anesthesia should be wearing off right about now, so if you want, I can take you in to see your friend but only very briefly."

"I would appreciate that."

The head nurse stood up from her leather chair and told Nico to follow her. The two of them made it to BJ's room in the intensive care unit, and she opened the door and let Nico inside.

"No more than five minutes, okay?"

"Okay."

Nico closed the door behind him and walked up to the side of BJ's bed. BJ was almost unrecognizable because of all the bandages and surgical tape, and the wires, IVs, and monitors attached to him, and the breathing tube attached to his mouth. He noticed the Velcro handcuffs on BJ's arms, hooking his wrists to the bed railing to prevent him from trying to remove any of the medical equipment.

"BJ, it's Nico. Can you hear me?"

BJ was silent, his eyes closed.

Nico undid the Velcro handcuff on BJ's right wrist and clutched his hand. "BJ, it's me, Nico." He could feel BJ starting to squeeze his hand. That was the best feeling. It felt like a surge of electricity shot through his body when BJ squeezed his hand. "You gonna be all right, my nigga. I promise you that."

Nico could see that BJ was starting to sweat. He looked around and saw a box of napkins, took a few, and then blotted the sweat from BJ's brow. Nico could see BJ trying to motion something to him. BJ couldn't talk if he wanted to, because of the breathing tube attached to his mouth. Nico wondered if he should call the nurse, but then he realized BJ was motioning for a pen or a pencil so he could write something. He quickly left the room and approached the nurse, who gave him a pen and a small notepad, and reminded him that he only had a few more minutes in the room. Nico assured her that he wouldn't be long and quickly made it back to BJ's room, where he put the pen in BJ's hand and held the pad for him.

BJ mustered up all the strength he could and struggled to write the letters *L* and *O*.

Nico held on to BJ's hand and squeezed. He didn't want to tell him anything about Lo at that point because he knew BJ needed to focus on his own recovery.

"Everything is good. Don't worry about nothing. Just relax, so we can get you healed up and outta here."

BJ motioned for the pad, and Nico again positioned it so he could write. BJ then scribbled the words NO KIDS. BJ didn't want his kids to come to the hospital and see him like that.

Nico reassured him that he would get word back to his girl and make sure that she didn't bring the kids with her to the hospital.

The nurse walked into the room and told Nico that he had to go. Nico then told BJ that he would be back to check on him the next day.

Nico felt drained when he left the hospital and made it down to the parking lot, where his driver was waiting for him. He instructed the driver to take him to his crib out on Long Island.

When Nico realized Jasmine wasn't home, he decided to have his driver drop him by Mia's house. Without calling before showing up, Nico arrived and let himself in with his own key.

"Oh my God!" Mia screamed out when she awoke to feel Nico touching her.

Mia wasn't expecting Nico, or anyone else for that matter, and since she had withdrawn bucket loads of cash from the safety deposit box earlier that day, she was terrified that someone had broken into her house to rob her.

"Baby, it's me."

"Ugggghhh! My God! You scared the shit outta me!" She sat up in the bed and turned on the lamp on her nightstand. She saw that Nico looked kind of ragged. "You okay?"

"Lo got killed."

"What? Baby, oh no."

"BJ is in ICU. Shit is so fuckin' crazy right now, I don't know." Nico sat down on the bed and ran his hand down his face.

"What happened?"

"We was leaving Bebo's funeral over on Linden, and muthafuckas pulled up in a Hummer or some shit and just sprayed everybody. Niggas was running, and bitches was screaming and shit. BJ and Lo got hit."

Mia knew not to push for more information. She just wrapped her arms around him and hugged him real tight and told him that she was so glad he was okay.

"It ain't about me, though."

"I know, baby, but if something had happened to you, I couldn't live." Mia then thought about the money hidden inside her freezer. "Do you know who was shooting?"

Nico slowly shook his head as he stood up from the bed. "I don't know, but I'm going to find out."

Mia knew Nico really well and could always read his vibes. "What you thinking about, baby? You can talk to me."

Nico blew out air from his lungs and fell backwards on the bed, his face to the ceiling. "I need you to go down to Miami to take care of some business for me. I'll be down there with you as soon as I can. I gotta handle this shit in New York first, though."

"I'm here for you, baby." Mia got on top of him and kissed him softly on his lips and neck. She then positioned herself next to Nico and lay with her left arm draped over him. "Everything is going to be okay."

CHAPTER 25

Black Justice took Jasmine along with him everywhere he went around town, which allowed her to get a ton of information to take back to Agent Gosling. Black Justice was a dream for Jasmine, in terms of the way he constantly bragged and ran his mouth. He had even shown her one of his two stash houses located around the corner from New Rochelle High School.

It was getting tougher and tougher for her to keep rejecting Black Justice's sexual advances, and she definitely used that to her advantage when it came time for her to meet up with Gosling.

Agent Gosling had actually been forced to go out of town for five days due to a death in his family, so he had to move back his scheduled meeting with Jasmine until the day after he returned from the funeral.

Gosling couldn't wait to meet with Jasmine, and had actually arrived twenty minutes early for their three o'clock meeting at Chipotle in downtown Brooklyn. Unfortunately for him, Jasmine didn't share his enthusiasm, and she showed up late.

"It's three forty," Gosling said to Jasmine.

"Parking is crazy around here. Why did you pick this congested-ass area? And how was your funeral? Who died anyway?"

Gosling shook his head. "I lost my sixteen-year-old nephew in a car accident."

"Oh, I'm so sorry to hear that," Jasmine said with genuine emotion.

Gosling thanked her, and then the two of them went to the counter and ordered food. They took their food to the seating area upstairs, so they could talk with a little more privacy.

"So I told you to give me some time, and I think you'll be happy."

Gosling knew that Jasmine had been spending a lot of time with Black Justice, because he had two agents follow her everywhere she went when he went out of town for the funeral.

"Talk to me."

Jasmine pulled out her BlackBerry with the recorder ready to play at the point she knew would intrigue Gosling. "Listen to this," she said.

"New York City, you got the biggest gang in the world that you going up against, the NYPD. Them NYPD cats is forty thousand cops strong. That shit is like a small muthafuckin' army. But out here, New Rochelle, they got their own little police department. And that shit is like fuckin' with Boss Hog and that Dukes of Hazzard *shit. You understand what I'm saying?"*

"Nah, you lost me."

"Ohhh, okay, I gotchu. So they on the payroll?"

"Exactly."

"I got a two-year-old daughter and a four-year-old son, but word is bond, I done already put about five kids through college already. And all they daddies is cops."

Jasmine stopped the playback and took a sip of her margarita.

"That's Black Justice." She reached in her bag, put an ounce of cocaine on the table, and pushed it across the table to Gosling. "I made that purchase from him, which by the way, you need to reimburse me for, and I got him on tape basically admitting that he got the New Rochelle cops in his hip pocket."

Gosling smiled a huge smile. "Wow! Excellent work, Jasmine! This is powerful, very powerful. Much more than I was expecting."

"I know what I'm doing out here. But I just have to say this, and I need you to really hear me. You need to talk to Agent Battle or whoever you got to talk to and get me that apartment ASAP. I mean, on one hand you tell me that under no circumstances am I to fuck anybody, and I'm good with that. But, on the other hand, I need the right tools. I mean, I was going everywhere with Black Justice. He was parading me around town like he was my man and shit. He drove me past one of his stash houses, and he even had me all up inside his own house and all that. So it gets to the point where him or any nigga is gonna want the pussy."

"Please tell me you didn't go there, Jasmine."

"No, I didn't, but what I'm saying is, if I had my own spot, I could control the rules of the game better."

"Give me three days, and you'll have the apartment." Gosling was certain that Agent Battle would finally sign off on the apartment paperwork. "So you said you know about a stash house?"

Jasmine nodded as she ate some more of her food.

"Did you actually go inside the stash house?"

"No, but I'm confident that it really was his stash house. He runs his mouth like a chick, I swear to God." She chuckled.

Jasmine then let him have it for not letting her know that the phone he had given her had a North Carolina number, but Gosling insisted that he had informed her of that fact.

"You didn't," she said emphatically.

Gosling didn't fight with her.

"Anyway, I did what you told me to. I made the first purchase and set it up where you are my man from North Carolina and you're looking to buy nine kilos. I also told him you got all the colleges in North Carolina on smash."

"So do you think he would meet with me, or does he want everything to go through you?"

"No, he trusts me. But if we don't meet with him soon that could spook him, and he'll think I'm bullshitting."

"Okay, so nine kilos?"

"Uh-huh."

"You're talking several hundred thousand dollars."

"And?"

"What I'm getting at is, there is a process before I can get that kind of cash allocated to me."

"Oh my God!"

"We can get the money, but we need some time."

Jasmine shook her head. "He's going to keep pushing up on me, trying to fuck me."

"Work something out."

Her phone began vibrating. "It's him right here."

"Answer it."

"Hello."

"What's good with your man?" Black Justice asked with his deep, gravelly voice.

"He just got in town today."

"A'ight. That's what's up. So we still doing this or what? Speak to me."

Jasmine wasn't sure how she should answer. Her heart started pounding, but she thought quickly on her feet. "Yeah, everything is a go. But what price you talking?"

"For nine, right?"

"You know what? I don't like talking on the phone like this. I'll hit you back, and we'll figure out where we can link and talk face to face."

"Jasmine, don't take him to nobody else."

"Jus, we good. Not on the phone, though. I'll hit you back, or you can hit me back in an hour."

"No doubt."

Jasmine looked at her phone to make sure the call had ended.

Gosling smiled, impressed with the way Jasmine was handling herself. He would have been lying to himself if he said he wasn't attracted to her.

"Why you looking at me like that?" Jasmine asked, feeling a bit uncomfortable.

"So love is cursed?"

"Oh, you looking at my tattoo? It's fire, right?"

"No comment."

"No comment? Yeah, okay. You better step up your swagger before we meet with Black Justice. Don't come looking as lame as you be looking," she said with a laugh.

Agent Gosling had conducted many undercover assignments, so he wasn't worried. He knew he would be able to pull off a meeting with Black Justice. He had to end the meeting with Jasmine so he could contact several of the North Carolina field offices to get some names of some of their confidential informants to see if they would be willing to vouch for him, just in case Black Justice started to sniff around and inquire about him.

CHAPTER 26

Agent Gosling and Jasmine met up the next day near the Brooklyn Bridge, where Jasmine parked her car, got in the FBI-issued BMW 760 Agent Gosling was driving, and headed uptown to Manhattan. Jasmine had arranged for the two of them to link up with Black Justice at a Dominican storefront restaurant, of which he was part owner, and which was located off Broadway in the Washington Heights section of Manhattan. Black Justice often used a small back office inside the restaurant to conduct business.

When Jasmine and Agent Gosling arrived, they parked their car on the opposite side of the street from the restaurant, crossed the busy street, and made their way inside.

"Hi," a sexy Spanish waitress said to them. "How can I help you?"

The place was small, and there were only six tables where customers could sit down and eat. Mostly it was a take-out restaurant.

Jasmine smiled. "Hi, we're here to see Black Jus."

The waitress nodded and turned around and screamed out something in Spanish to another sexy Spanish lady at the cash register.

"You can have a seat. He should be right out."

Jasmine and Gosling thanked her, and they took a seat inside the tight restaurant.

After about five minutes, a muscular brown-skinned dude standing six foot five and looking like he could play on the defensive line for the New York Giants emerged from the back of the restaurant. Jasmine was surprised when she heard him speak to the waitress in Spanish. The waitress pointed out Jasmine and Gosling, who looked in the direction of the tall dude, and he motioned for them to follow him.

When they made it to the back of the restaurant, he introduced himself as Poppy and shook Jasmine's hand.

"Hi, I'm Jasmine."

Gosling held out his hand for a pound. "Jimmy," Gosling replied. Gosling was a second generation Jamaican who didn't have the slightest bit of a Jamaican accent, yet he'd decided to go with the street name Jamaican Jimmy.

Poppy led them through the kitchen and down a narrow set of metal stairs that led to a basement. As soon as Poppy opened the door to the basement, the sound of loud hip-hop could be heard bouncing off the walls, and a strong smell of weed smacked them in the face.

Black Justice was sitting at a metal rectangular desk in front of a huge cage made out of chicken wire with two large pit bulls inside. Both of the dogs had the hugest heads that Jamaican Jimmy had ever seen on a pit bull before. He was certain that somebody had been injecting the dogs with steroids.

Black Justice was eating a plate of Spanish rice and chicken. He nodded to Jasmine and Jamaican Jimmy and motioned for them to have a seat at the two chairs positioned in front of his desk.

Jasmine had her recorder on, but with the sound of the music blasting, there was no way it would pick up any conversation. Jimmy didn't tell Jasmine, but he also had a recording device strapped to his ankle inside the brand-new construction-style Timberlands he was wearing.

Black Justice motioned for Poppy to lower the volume on the music, and Poppy turned the music off completely.

"I said turn the shit down, I didn't say turn it off," Black Justice hollered. "That was my shit right there."

Poppy turned the music back up, but not as loud as before.

Agent Gosling was glad that Poppy had turned the music down because he was certain his recorder could pick up everything being said.

Black Justice took a pull on the blunt he was smoking and began nodding his head to the music. He then stood up and took another pull before passing it to Poppy.

"Black Justice," he said to Jimmy and extended his hand for a pound.

"Jimmy." Agent Gosling clasped Black Justice's hand.

"What's good, Jasmine?"

Jasmine smiled. "Nothing. You see we here and we ain't front on you."

Black Justice nodded, and then he sat down and ate some more off his food.

Poppy passed the blunt back to Black Justice, who held it out for Jimmy, but Jimmy held up one of his hands and waved off the weed.

Jasmine wanted to cringe, but she held it together. Then she reached over and took the weed from Black Justice and took some pulls on it.

Black Justice asked Jimmy, "You don't smoke?"

Jimmy shook his head.

"He's Jamaican and he don't smoke weed," Jasmine said, trying to ease some of the tension that had suddenly filled the room. "Can you believe that shit?"

"Jamaican Jimmy . . . I like that." Black Justice asked Jimmy if he knew an Italian dude name Joey from North Carolina. "The Italians call him Joey Six-Pack."

"Yeah, I'm cool with him."

Joey Six-Pack was an FBI informant the Raleigh, North Carolina field office had briefed Jimmy on.

"Why you ask?"

Black Justice asked, "How you know him?"

"From the fuckin' streets! What the fuck is all these questions for, my dude?"

Black Justice cocked a half smile, and then he asked Jasmine and Jimmy if they wanted anything to eat.

Jimmy said, "Nah, let's just talk business."

"Jimmy about that bread! My muthafuckin' man." Black Justice stood up, took the remaining scraps of food on his plate over to the dogs, and spilled it into their food bowls. "So what kind of whip is Joey pushing now?"

Jasmine was feeling very uncomfortable. She finished

the weed and dropped the last of the blunt on the basement floor and stepped on it.

"Joey always switching up cars. The last thing I think he was pushing was a white Range Rover."

Black Justice nodded. "And what about you? I see you got the seven sixty parked outside. What else you got?"

Jimmy and Jasmine both were surprised that Black Justice knew what kind of car they had pulled up in because they hadn't even parked directly in front of the restaurant, and it wasn't like Black Justice, or anyone else for that matter, had ever seen Jimmy driving around New York.

Jimmy was starting to wonder if Joey Six-Pack and Black Justice had spoken. And with Jimmy not fully knowing Joey Six-Pack's credibility, he wasn't sure what to make of Black Justice's questions.

"I got the NSX, but my main toy is my muthafuckin' sixty-foot Viking Sport Cruiser. Y'all New York niggas ain't up on that shit."

Jasmine had no idea what the hell Jimmy was talking about.

Black Justice looked at Poppy, and he got no response from him.

"The fuck is that?"

"That's my yacht. You need to come down to North Carolina, and we can party on that shit. Bring some New York bitches wit'chu, and trust me when I tell you them bitches will be taking off their panties as soon as they step on that muthafucka."

"Ahhhh shit! Okay. Fuckin' yachts and shit—That's what's up. What that cost you?"

"Seven figures, brand-new."

Black Justice sat back down at his desk. He went into the top drawer and pulled out what looked like a pound of weed and sat it down on top of the desk. "A'ight, so Jasmine said you lookin' for nine kilos."

Jimmy nodded his head. "Nine, maybe more, depends on what price we talking."

"Thirty-five."

"Thirty-five? I got niggas that can beat that."

"The fuck outta here! Ain't nobody beating that price for fish scale!"

Jimmy ran his hand across his face. "Do it for thirty."

"You saying you got muthafuckas that'll sell you a kilo for thirty? You full of shit."

Jasmine was getting nervous. She couldn't understand why he was haggling like he was at a fucking flea market or something.

"So you got the cash?"

"I wouldn't waste your time."

Black Justice went inside his top drawer once again, and this time he pulled out a vanilla Dutch Masters cigar in a plastic clear wrapper and tossed it to Jimmy. He then pushed the bag of weed across the desk toward Jimmy.

"Do me a favor—Twist that up for me," Black Justice said to Jimmy. "I need to think on your price. My mind functions better when I smoke."

Jimmy put the cigar on the table and reminded Black

Justice that he didn't smoke.

Jasmine knew that Black Justice was testing Jimmy, who was making one false move after another. Her heart was in her throat.

Black Justice looked over at Poppy, who smiled and motioned his head in Jimmy's direction before gesturing toward his own waistband. Black Justice shook his head to indicate to Poppy that he didn't want him to do anything at that moment.

"I'll roll the shit up." Jasmine reached for the cigar. She knew in her gut that Jimmy had never rolled up any weed and was hesitating because he didn't want to look stupid.

Black Justice went into the bottom side drawer of his desk and pulled out a chrome .44 Magnum and placed it on top of his desk. "Nah, Jasmine, I want this nigga to twist that shit up for me."

Jimmy didn't know what to say or do.

Black Justice reached forward and grabbed hold of the gun and held it sideways and pointed it directly at Jimmy and Jasmine. "Roll that shit up right now if you and Jasmine wanna walk outta here alive."

Jimmy stood up to his feet and pushed the cigar and the weed off the table and onto the basement floor, and Poppy immediately made a move toward him.

"Nah, Poppy, I got this shit," Black Justice said, his gun aimed at Jimmy.

The pit bulls sensed that their master was angry and began barking violently.

"Jus, come on, chill," Jasmine pleaded.

"The fuck this nigga think he is?" Jimmy squinted his eyes, trying to muster up the meanest screw face he could. "You gon' shoot me 'cuz I won't roll your fuckin' weed up? Come on then. Shoot me, nigga!" Jimmy yelled, his open right hand pounding on his chest. "You got big balls! Shoot me, nigga!"

"Jimmy, shut up!" Jasmine pleaded. "Jus, please, come on, this ain't necessary." She stood up.

"Jasmine, who the fuck is this muthafucka?" Black Justice stood up.

"He's my man!"

"Poppy, turn that music all the way up!"

Jasmine was ready to shit and piss on herself.

"What? You think I'm a cop? You think I'm fuckin' five-*o*?" Jimmy lifted up his shirt to show that he had no gun on him and that he wasn't wearing a wire.

Poppy turned the music up so loud, the sound of the dogs barking could no longer be heard.

Jimmy's heart was racing as his life flashed before his eyes. Not knowing what else to do, he pulled his shirt all the way up and over his head until he was standing there shirtless. Then he reached for his pants and unbuckled the belt and quickly unbuttoned and unzipped his pants and pulled them down to his ankles.

"I ain't no muthafuckin' cop!" Jimmy yelled as he walked around in circles with his pants pulled down to his ankles, exposing his black briefs, his hands raised above his head.

Jimmy looked as stupid as anyone could look, but his move was brilliant because, in the process of making himself look like an absolute fool, he still managed to hide the wire strapped to his ankle on the inside of his Timberland boot.

Poppy couldn't help but laugh at Jimmy. Black Justice motioned for Poppy to turn the music down.

Jimmy's heart was coming out of his chest as he stood there with his hands still in the air, the dogs still barking very loud.

"Pull your muthafuckin' pants up!"

Jimmy felt somewhat relieved, but he knew he wasn't out of the woods yet. He quickly scooped his shirt up from off the basement floor and put it on and pulled up his pants.

"The lowest I'm going is three hundred thousand for the nine kilos," Black Justice said. "Have the cash tomorrow. I'll have Poppy hit y'all up to arrange the location."

Jasmine said, "Okay."

Poppy held open the basement door that led upstairs to the kitchen, and Jasmine and Jimmy both headed toward the stairs, with Poppy behind them.

"It's disrespectful not to roll up a man's weed for him when you in his spot," Black Justice said out loud, a sinister grin on his face.

Jasmine, Jimmy, and Poppy made their way up the stairs and out.

"No muthafuckin' games! Word up!" Black Justice

shouted out to Jasmine and Jimmy.

Jasmine and Jimmy made it through the restaurant's kitchen and then out the front door. They had never been so happy to see daylight.

"I'll hit y'all and let y'all know what's up," Poppy said to Jasmine and Jimmy just before they walked out of the restaurant.

As soon as they got in the car, Agent Gosling asked Jasmine with a real stern voice. "Where is his fuckin' stash house?"

"I told you to step up your swagger, and you up in there haggling like you at a fuckin' car auction or some shit. He tell you thirty-five, you suppose to roll with that number."

"Where the fuck is the stash house, Jasmine?" Agent Gosling hollered.

Jasmine screamed back at him that it was in Yonkers and that they would have to drive to it and she would be able to point it out.

"Gosling, it's weed we're talking about. Everybody knows how to roll up weed. Oh my fuckin' God!"

"Look, shut the fuck up!"

Gosling drove off, and they headed toward Yonkers. After he had driven about two miles from the restaurant, he pulled the car over, got out, and left it running. He told Jasmine he would be right back.

Gosling called Agent Battle and told her what had just happened at the restaurant. He then told her that he was heading over to Yonkers to drive by Black Justice's stash house and that he would call her back in an hour. He also told he needed her to get a judge to sign off on three emergency warrants—one for the stash house, one for the restaurant, and one for Black Justice's residence. He then cautioned Agent Battle against telling the New Rochelle Police Department about the raids on the stash house and Black Justice's house until all of the FBI teams were in place and were ready to storm the locations.

Gosling was taking a major chance that Jasmine would be right about the location of the stash house; otherwise, it would not only make the FBI look really bad, but it would also put Jasmine's life in jeopardy on the streets of New York. He no longer wanted to wait until the next day and show up with the money to do the deal and then make the arrests. He wanted to get Black Justice off the streets that same day for punking him.

CHAPTER 27

Jasmine was shocked when Gosling told her that Black Justice, Poppy, and ten other members of Black Justice's drug organization had been arrested. She didn't feel one ounce of guilt or remorse for the role she played in setting up Black Justice, but she did have doubts about whether major charges would stick. The feds weren't able to catch him with major drugs, nor were they able to directly link him to the stash house because the house wasn't in his name, but they did catch him with an illegal gun and four pounds of marijuana when they nabbed him at the Dominican restaurant.

Jasmine had expressed some concern that Black Justice would quickly beat his charges, and, within a year or so, be back on the streets looking for her. But Agent Gosling tried to assure her that there was enough rock-solid evidence on Black Justice to get him indicted and convicted on a federal conspiracy charge and send him away for a very long time.

It didn't take long for Jasmine to forget about Black Justice. In fact, three days after he had been arrested, she was reimbursed by the feds for the money she had spent buying the half-ounce of cocaine, and she received another twenty-five-hundred-dollar installment payment. On top of the money, she also had the keys to a ninth-floor loft apartment in the trendy SoHo section of Manhattan.

Jasmine couldn't believe her eyes when she walked into the pristine, newly furnished apartment in a building with a doorman. It was way more than she ever could have imagined.

"You like it?" Agent Gosling asked.

Jasmine was beaming. "Are you kidding me?" She knew that only high-end doctors and top runway models could afford to live in SoHo.

After Jasmine had finished touring the apartment, Gosling had to bring her back to reality.

"The apartment is nice, but remember, you have a job to do, so don't let the apartment become a distraction."

Jasmine nodded.

Gosling reminded her of her next two targets, Prince and Homicide. He gave her a rundown of the different intelligence reports the FBI had accumulated on them, including the cars they drove, the clubs where they hung out, the restaurants where they ate, and the women they were fucking.

Jasmine took in everything that Gosling was saying, and she told him to give her a few days and she would come up with a plan to get close to the two targets.

"I got faith in you."

"Oh, now you got faith in me? A few weeks ago you couldn't stop reminding me about how I was going get locked up and all that shit."

Gosling chuckled. "That was before you proved

yourself."

Jasmine sucked her teeth.

"Seriously though, you're a talent that is hard to find and hard to cultivate, and we really value you."

"Thank you."

"But listen. Be smart, and be very careful out here. These guys are wolves, and you can't take anything for granted."

"You learn how to roll weed yet?"

"Fuck you!" Gosling shot back.

Jasmine walked up to him and innocently began to massage his shoulders. "I'll be smart. I know how to maneuver."

Gosling felt his dick starting to rise, so he stood up from the love seat he was sitting on. "Okay, so I got some work to do. I'm going to head in to the office. I'll check in with you in, say, seventy-two hours."

"I just told you to give me a few days to formulate a plan, and then you tell me you're going to check in with me in seventy-two hours? You don't have to micromanage me."

"Like I said, I'll check in with you in seventy-two hours. But call me if you need me."

"Good-bye, Gosling."

Gosling made his way toward the door, but he didn't leave before asking about Nico.

Jasmine told him that he had called her the day before just to check up on her and to ask her to visit BJ in the hospital.

"Did you go?"

"No, not yet. I'll get over there probably today."

Gosling was about to say something else.

"Good-bye, Gosling!" And then she playfully pushed him toward the door.

"Okay, I'll talk to you later. And, seriously, you be careful out there."

CHAPTER 28

When Jasmine entered BJ's hospital room, she was surprised to see Simone in the hospital room with Ish.

"Hey, BJ." Jasmine's smile was mixed with genuine compassion as she walked up to the head of BJ's hospital bed carrying ten get-well-soon helium balloons and a box of chocolate candy. She bent over and gave him a kiss on the cheek.

"Jasmine, what's good, baby girl?" BJ replied with a smile.

BJ was slowly getting his strength back with each passing day, but he still wasn't able to eat on his own and had to be fed through IV.

"I know you all hard and stuff," Jasmine said, "but you better take these balloons and candy."

BJ chuckled. He thanked her for the balloons and candy and told her where to put them.

"What's up, Ish? And, Simone, what the hell you doing here?" Jasmine gave both of them a kiss on the cheek.

"I'm with my baby."

Jasmine laughed and shook her head. "BJ, I introduced these two at the strip club and, I swear, they been attached at the hip ever since. Every time I call this heifer, she talking about, she'll call me back, because she's with Ish."

"That's how us Ghetto Mafia muthafuckas do," BJ replied. "He put it on her the same way Nico put it on you."

Ish laughed as he walked over to BJ to give him a pound.

"Here we go. See, you ain't even hurt. Get your ass up and get dressed. We taking you home right now," Jasmine said.

BJ asked Jasmine, "What's that shit on your neck?"

"It's my new tattoo. You like it? And look at the one I got on my hand."

BJ looked at it and responded in the same manner as everyone else whenever they saw it, repeating what the tattoo said. "Love is cursed."

"Yup. That shit is hot, right?"

BJ nodded. Then he asked Simone and Ish to give him a few minutes alone with Jasmine. As soon as Ish and Simone were out of the room, Jasmine looked over at BJ like she wanted to cry.

"Oh my God. BJ, I didn't want to say nothing, but you sure you okay, boo?"

"Yo, cut that shit out. There ain't gonna be no fuckin' tears up in here."

"I know, but I don't like seeing you up in here like this."

"Jasmine, I'm gonna be all right."

Jasmine bit down on her lip to prevent herself from crying. She really cared about BJ and loved him like a brother, so her feelings of sadness and concern were genuine. Flashbacks of when she'd almost died added to her sadness.

"So what the hell happened? I mean, I been hearing all kind of shit from the street, but you know how that goes."

"I don't wanna talk in here. I'll be home next week, though. When I get out of here, we'll talk."

Jasmine was hoping he would start talking because she had her recorder going from before she walked into his hospital room. "Okay, no problem."

"Yeah, but I been fighting with these doctors. They been telling me that it's a fifty-fifty chance that I'm going to need a colostomy bag for the rest of my life."

"BJ, don't say that."

"They had to remove part of my large intestines."

"But they did say it's a fifty-fifty chance, so that means that maybe you won't have to." Jasmine wiped some tears from her cheek, trying to maintain emotionally for BJ.

"That's what I'm hoping. I told them niggas I would pay whatever, just as long as they fix my shit up right. Word is bond, they might as well kill my ass if I have to walk around with a fuckin' bag attached to me."

"They probably was just giving you the worst-case scenario. But, believe me, from what I learned in nursing school, as long as you can pay, they'll fix you up right. But let your ass be poor or up in here with a damn Medicaid card, you would be ass out."

BJ laughed. "Yeah, I know. Money talks."

Jasmine walked over to a chair underneath the TV in

the corner of the room and sat down.

"I'm gonna be all right, though. Niggas is gonna die behind this shit. You better believe that."

Jasmine looked at him and nodded.

"So what's up with you? Nico, told me to make sure you was straight. What's that about?"

"BJ, it's like I don't even know Nico anymore. I don't see him, I don't speak to him. It's like—"

"Jasmine, just hold the nigga down. You know how shit go sometime."

"I mean, I am holding him down. It's just I don't know what we got anymore."

"Whatchu mean by that?"

"I mean, am I still wifey or what?"

BJ chuckled. "Jasmine, that nigga love you. Trust me when I tell you. And you know Nico's like a brother to me, so I know what's up."

Jasmine smiled. "I know he loves me, but he don't trust me like he used to."

"It ain't you, Jasmine."

"What is it then?"

"You see where I'm at right now? Laid up in a fuckin' hospital with half of my intestines missing and shit. And you seen on the news how the feds just nabbed Black Justice. He's trying to stay one step ahead of death and jail. You feel me?"

"I feel you, but I still need to—"

"You still need Nico to make you feel like a woman and all that lovey-dovey shit, right?"

Jasmine smiled. "No, it's not that."

"Yes, it is. You wanna feel like wifey, like you just said a minute ago."

"What I mean is, I don't want to come across all needy and shit like that. I know how to play my position. I know what I signed up for. I just need Nico to trust me and be straight up with me. That's all."

"If Nico caught a charge and had to do time, would you do the time with him?"

"Of course, I would."

"You full of shit."

"No, BJ, really I would, because if he was in jail, then I would know where I stand, and I would know what's up."

"Well, listen. Between me and you, I told Nico to stay outta New York for a while. And if anybody wants that nigga in New York right now, it's me. I want him here going to war for me, but I know the game, and I know the streets. Right now, you got the feds coming at us, you got NYPD coming at us, we got snitches in Ghetto Mafia looking to snake us, we got other crews coming for our throat, and we got informants helping the feds. So for right now, it just makes sense for us to get this bread outta town. And we getting it right now in Miami. And when the time is right, Nico will be around, and you'll be feeling like wifey again and all that."

"I understand."

"You ain't hurting for nothing, right?"

"No, I'm good."

"You keepin' your shit tight for Nico, right?"

Jasmine gave BJ a look that told him not to even go there.

"I gotta ask."

"No, you don't. You already know the answer to that question."

BJ chuckled. "Nico will be around when he's around. But we trying to stay off the radar until the time is right. When all these dumb-ass niggas out here go to prison, we gonna be the only smart ones still getting it. You feel me?"

"You leaving town too?"

"Me and Ish gonna be right here keeping an eye on your slick ass."

"What you mean by that?" Jasmine was already feeling self-conscious about the comment that BJ had made earlier about confidential informants.

BJ chuckled. "I'm just fuckin' wit'chu. I gotta deal with these surgeries that I got coming up, so I'm here."

"I'm sorry about what happened to Lo."

"This is our life. You know how it goes."

Jasmine moved closer to him and kissed him on the forehead before telling him she had to go. She was super worried. She was wondering if BJ and Nico were on to her role as a confidential informant. If they were, there was going to be a murder scene in which she would be playing the victim.

CHAPTER 29

"*Sak passé.*"

"*Sak passé,*" Mia replied, smiling as she sat up in her beach chair to take a quick break from tanning her body on Miami's famous South Beach. She was trying her hardest to remember the Haitian girl's name. She didn't want to be rude and ask, so she just continued to play things off as she sipped on her piña colada.

"Yeah, so like I was saying, if you want me to take you around later on and show you some different areas, I can do that."

The name finally hit Mia—Pascale.

"Well, I think I'm just going to let Nico handle that. I appreciate the offer, though."

"Oh, okay. So you want to go shopping or do something else later?"

"I'll let you know." Mia then put her shades over her eyes and reclined in the beach chair, hoping Pascale would leave her alone.

"When I come up to New York, I want you to take me everywhere. I don't want to rest for one second."

Mia kept quiet.

"And I never been to New York. I can't wait! You okay?"

Mia hated being around Pascale, the girlfriend of Nico's right-hand man in Miami, Haitian Jack. She just wouldn't shut up. While Haitian Jack and Nico were out running the streets or at the gym lifting weights, Pascale felt it was her duty to show Mia a good time, but she never gave her time to breathe.

"It's just that time of the month for me," Mia lied, hoping that would explain her silence.

"Oh, do you get really bad cramps?"

Mia nodded her head.

"When we leave here, you have to come with me and let me take you by this herbalist. She is the best. I'm telling you, I used to have the worst cramps, and when I went to see her, she told me what to take, and I never had a problem since."

"Really?" Mia asked, trying to sound like she was somewhat interested.

"Oh, she's the best. We'll go when we leave the beach."

Mia couldn't wait to speak to Nico later that day to let him know that she had to somehow ditch Pascale, or else she was going to go crazy. But putting up with Pascale and her annoying self was a small price to pay in exchange for the good life she and Nico had been experiencing on a daily basis in Miami. Every night she and Nico were going to the best restaurants, and in the morning, they were having breakfast on South Shore Drive. And they were treated like royalty everywhere they went, since Haitian Jack had the city on smash.

Jasmine was trying to decide if she was going to answer Agent Gosling's phone call. He had been blowing up her phone for the past hour. All the same time she knew that now that she had the SoHo apartment, there was no way she would be able to duck him for long.

"Hello," she answered nonchalantly.

"I been calling you."

"I'm sorry. I was 'sleep and didn't hear my phone."

"Well, wake your ass up and get to Madison Square Garden by eight o'clock. We got you seats two rows from the floor—Knicks and Lakers—and you'll be in the same row as Homicide. Work your magic."

Jasmine sighed. "Just one ticket?"

"No, two tickets. Bring somebody with you. Pick the tickets up from the box office window. Both tickets will be under your name."

"Okay."

Jasmine was reluctant to go, but she had no choice. She had signed up for this role and now she had to live it out or risk being thrown in jail and giving up her monthly stipend, her apartment, and all the perks that came with being a snitch.

She sat down on the couch and thought about how she should play things. She thought about calling Simone, but then she remembered her fourteen–year-old cousin who loved basketball to the point where he ate, drank, and dreamt basketball. She figured she would call him and see if he would want to go.

"Jasmine, you lyin'!"

"No, Corey, I'm serious. Good seats too."

"Don't play with me like this, Jasmine."

Jasmine couldn't help but laugh. She loved her cousin's innocence. "You know where Spike Lee sits at, right on the floor?"

"Yeah."

"Well, we're two rows behind Spike and all the celebrities."

"Are you serious?"

"Dead-ass."

"Yo, I love you! I definitely want to go."

Jasmine laughed. It made her feel good that she could make his day the way she did.

"Just let your mother know that you won't need no money or anything and that I'll drop you off at your house after the game. I would come pick you up now, but by the time I get dressed and head to Brooklyn and then drive to Manhattan, we'll get there too late and miss the start of the game."

Corey told her that he would let his mother know and that he was going to get dressed and be on the A train in fifteen minutes.

"Just keep your phone on in case we can't find each other."

By the time Jasmine finished getting dressed, it was close to seven-thirty. So instead of driving her own car, which would have slowed her down and gotten her to the game later than she wanted, she hopped in a yellow cab and got to Madison Square Garden by seven forty-five, where she linked up with her cousin, and before long the two of them had their tickets and were headed into the world's most famous arena to see the Knicks play the Lakers.

CHAPTER 30

"Jasmine, I can't believe this!" Corey gushed. "There go Kobe right there, and there's Carmelo Anthony."

Jasmine smiled like a supermodel in her black oversized Dior shades, her Gucci signature bag dangling from her wrist as they finally reached their seats. She reached into her bag and pulled out a twenty-dollar bill and handed it to the usher who had helped them.

"Thank you," the usher said to her. "Are you familiar with The Ainsworth Prime?"

"No. What is that?"

"It's a restaurant bar that's located on the third-floor terrace level. It's open to all club-seat holders such as yourself. I think you would like it."

"Oh, okay."

Jasmine and her cousin both took their seats under the bright lights. Corey looked at the NBA stars with amazement as they warmed up and got ready for the game.

Jasmine looked around trying to locate Homicide, but she didn't see him or anyone that looked like him. She took out her phone and sent a text to Agent Gosling and asked him if he could send her a photo of Homicide.

Fifteen minutes later the photo arrived on her phone. She opened it up and studied it for about two minutes and then looked around some more to see if she could locate Homicide, but she still didn't see him. She decided to chill and enjoy the game with her cousin and not stress about it.

"You want anything to eat or drink?" Jasmine asked Corey.

He shook his head and told her that he was all right.

Jasmine went into her bag and pulled out a fifty-dollar bill and gave it to Corey. "Here. You don't have to be shy around me. I want you to have a good time."

Corey thanked her and took the money and made his way to the concession stand and to the bathroom. Just as he walked out of the row, two guys began to make their way into the same row Jasmine was sitting in. Immediately she recognized Homicide from the photo. Homicide had on a black snap-back Yankees cap, so it was kind of hard to get a great look at him, but Jasmine was sure it was him.

Homicide was a lot shorter in person than she had imagined. He also had a full beard, even though none of the pictures she'd seen of him depicted him with a beard.

"Pardon me, miss," Homicide said to Jasmine as he carefully made his way past her.

"No problem."

As Homicide and his homeboy took their seats, Jasmine thought of exactly how she was going to approach them. She wasn't sure about what move to make, but she was definitely happy that Homicide had come to the game with another dude and not a chick.

At the end of the second quarter and during halftime,

mostly everyone got out of their seats and headed either to the bathroom or to get something to eat or drink. Jasmine and Corey stayed in their seats, while Homicide and his homie made their way out of the aisle.

"My man, that's your girl?" Homicide asked Corey, referring to Jasmine.

Corey shook his head no.

Homicide gave Corey a pound, and then he looked at Jasmine, who didn't say anything.

"You a CO on Rikers Island, right?"

"Who, me?" Jasmine asked.

Homicide nodded, staring Jasmine down.

"Far from that."

"I know you're a cop or some shit like that. You look too fuckin' familiar."

Jasmine instantly got nervous, but she kept her cool, just slowly shaking her head.

"No?"

"I told you she wasn't no CO," Homicide's homeboy said.

"You look familiar too," Jasmine said to Homicide. "What's your name?"

"Homicide."

Jasmine smiled. "What did your momma name you?"

"Aziz," Homicide replied, and then his cell phone starting ringing. He answered the call, and then he told Jasmine he would be right back, and he and his homeboy walked off.

"So you good?" Jasmine asked her cousin.

"More than good!"

"Oh my God!" Jasmine said in a slow cadence to herself but loud enough for her cousin to hear.

"What's the matter?"

"Oh, nothing," Jasmine replied, not wanting to tell Corey what she was thinking. She pulled out her BlackBerry and looked at Homicide's picture again. *I can't believe this*, she thought to herself before the name Aziz Zahir came to her mind.

Jasmine was certain that Homicide was the same person she'd had a secret childhood crush on since she was in the fourth grade. Her palms started to get sweaty, and she started to get both excited and nervous at the same time. Immediately she deleted his picture from her phone.

Jasmine and Aziz had been in the same class at Public School 22 on St. Mark's Avenue in Brooklyn before she moved to Queens. She wondered if she should say anything to him when he got back to his seat, or if she should just play things cool and see where they led.

The second half of the game started, and a lot of people including Homicide had not yet made it back to their seats from the halftime intermission.

As Corey watched the NBA action, Jasmine combed her mind and thought back to her years in elementary school. She remembered how all of the kids laughed at Aziz's name when their teacher introduced him to the class. She also remembered how the kids teased him because he was two years older than all of the kids in his class. Aziz was a smart kid. He was two years older than everybody because he had started school late in Egypt, where he was born, and when he'd moved to the United States at the age of eleven, he was considered a fourth grader by United States standards.

Jasmine couldn't believe that the former teacher's pet, who was very religious, and a borderline nerd, had grown up to be the feared drug hustler and murderous stickup kid from Brooklyn known as Homicide. After graduating from Public School 22, she'd moved to Queens, and she had not seen or heard from him since.

By the middle of the third quarter of the game, Homicide and his homeboy came back to their seats, both carrying a box of chicken fingers, French fries, and beer.

"Excuse me, sexy," Homicide said to Jasmine.

Jasmine smiled as she stood up so he could get by her. As weird as it was, she had waited more than a decade to hear him call her sexy—since she was a skinny fourth-grader with pigtails.

Homicide and his friend were six seats from her and Corey. Jasmine didn't know what to say or do, but she figured she had to say something. She thought about taking things back to fourth grade, scribbling something on a piece of paper and then passing the note down to Homicide, but she changed her mind about that and just waited.

Before long the third quarter had ended, and Jasmine took off her shades so her face was fully visible. Some people in her section were milling around, standing and stretching their legs, and others stayed put in their seats.

She looked down her row and saw Homicide on his phone. He looked as if he was texting somebody.

Jasmine's heart started racing. She was about to make a move and was hoping that Aziz would remember her. She was able to get the attention of Homicide's homie, and she signaled for him to tap Homicide for her. When Homicide looked in her direction, she smiled and motioned with her index finger for him to come to her, and he got up and made his way toward her.

"What's good, ma?" Homicide asked with a slight smile.

Jasmine looked at him, a huge smile on her face. "I know you."

Homicide looked at her as the two of them stood in the aisle so people could freely walk in and out of their row. "From where?"

"Is your last name Zahir?"

Homicide squinted his eyes as he looked intently at Jasmine. He slowly nodded his head. "How you know my government name?"

"I been sitting here bugging, trying my hardest to remember where I know you from. And you are not going to believe this."

"What?"

"Remember Mrs. Freeman? P.S. 22?" Jasmine continued to smile.

Homicide thought back for a minute. "Ohhhh shit! Get the fuck outta here!" he yelled. "Little skinny Jasmine with the pigtails. Ohhhh shit! What the fuck!"

Homicide laughed, extending his hand to Jasmine, who took hold of his hand, and he pulled her toward him and gave her a firm hug.

When the fourth quarter of the game started, people were rushing back to their seats. Jasmine thought quickly and formally introduced her cousin to Homicide, explaining that she knew him from back in the days. She asked Corey if he would switch seats with Homicide, and he agreed.

"This is crazy, right?" Jasmine said, leaning in to Homicide. The crowd was cheering real loud, so it was hard for them to hear each other.

"Word up. So what's good wit'chu?"

"It's so much to tell you and catch up on."

Homicide took out his phone and asked Jasmine for her number. "We gotta link up," he told her.

Jasmine couldn't stop smiling. "You know you were the first boy I ever had a crush on?"

Homicide looked at Jasmine and didn't say anything in response. All he could do was look at how sexy she looked and imagine what it would be like to fuck her. He wasn't sure if he could fuck her that night, but he was definitely going to try.

"You still a Muslim?"

"No doubt."

"I can see you aren't a nerd anymore."

"Nah, these streets changed a muthafucka."

Jasmine nodded her head.

"As sexy as you is, I know you got a man or something."

"Long story."

"So what you doing after you leave here?"

Jasmine shrugged. "Nothing. I just have to make sure my cousin gets home okay, and I'm free."

"That's what's up. So let me take you to get a drink or something. We can hang out and just kick it."

Jasmine nodded.

As the game went on, neither Jasmine nor Homicide paid any attention to the score or the outcome, they were both just so much into each other.

CHAPTER 31

Jasmine woke up at three in the morning in her SoHo apartment, and for a moment she forgot where she was. It was the first time that she had actually slept there, so the unfamiliar surroundings had thrown her off. In addition, her head was pounding from all the liquor she'd consumed hanging with Homicide after the Knicks game. She gathered herself and realized that Homicide was no longer in the bed with her. She had ended up bringing him back to her apartment and fucking him, and after they had finished fucking, they both fell asleep.

What she didn't realize was that Homicide had never actually fallen asleep. He had just waited for her to fall asleep, so he could case her apartment.

While she slept, he went through her bag, her clothes, and her closets. Going through her phone, he saw the names of a bunch of drug dealers—Nico, BJ, Lorenzo, Ish, and Bebo—so he immediately knew how she got down. He was familiar with BlackBerry phones but had never seen this particular model. He was trying to figure out how to get to her text messages.

Just then, Jasmine walked into the kitchen "Hey," she said, sounding real groggy, her eyes squinting from the light.

"Yeah, yeah." Caught by surprise, Homicide stood up and placed her phone on the counter.

She saw the phone, and her heart started pounding. "Everything okay?" She noticed he was fully dressed.

Homicide walked up to her and gave her a hug. "Listen, I'm about to bounce. Some shit came up, and I gotta get back to BK."

Wearing a long T-shirt with nothing else underneath, she wondered if he could feel her heart pounding. She quickly pulled away from him and retrieved her phone.

"Your phone was vibrating crazy."

"Please tell me you didn't answer it."

Homicide slowly shook his head.

Jasmine wondered just what he knew and what he had seen on the phone. "So you was just gonna leave and not say anything?"

"I'll hit you up later today. Go back in the bed and get some sleep."

"What's wrong?"

"A'ight, I'll keep it one hundred wit'chu."

"Please do."

"We ain't have enough time to chop it up like I wanted to, but yo, the thing is, I got a lot of enemies in this town, and it don't take much to get caught slippin'."

"I'm lost."

"When you fell asleep, your phone was vibrating, and I saw a text message from BJ. So—"

"Uggh." Jasmine was about to flip, but she held her cool.

"So I know that name, and the first thought was, is

it the same bitch-ass BJ I know who almost got killed? So I looked through your phone book, and I see all these Ghetto Mafia niggas' names in your phone."

"Homicide. Okay, first of all, you looking through my phone—that shit is real whack."

"Hold up, Jasmine. On the real, I'm not one of these chump-ass niggas on the street or one of these clown-ass dudes you be fuckin' with."

"I didn't say you was."

"Shut the fuck up when I'm talking!" Homicide shouted. He had a real short fuse, but Jasmine had not been in his life to know that.

"I'm sorry."

"What I'm saying is, I'm up in here laying up in your shit with no burner or nothing. Anybody could walk up in this muthafuckin' apartment and start blastin'. You know what I'm saying? Especially them Ghetto Mafia niggas. Them niggas don't fuck with me, and I don't fuck with them."

"Homicide, this is my apartment, and if I bring you here, you're good. I mean, yeah, did I fuck with them Ghetto Mafia niggas? Yes, I did. And I thought I told you that before we left Madison Square Garden that I was fuckin' with Nico." She realized how stupid she had been to let him fuck her that easily. "Would I bring you up in here and risk my own ass getting killed? No, I wouldn't be that stupid. You're good here."

Homicide's primary occupation was setting up drug dealers to get robbed, so he always saw things from a different lens. He kissed Jasmine on the lips. "I'm out."

At that point Jasmine was wondering if she had just blown her assignment. "Okay, but I really want to see you again. I don't want to just be a fuckin' booty call."

Homicide smirked. "You got my number. Hit me up."

CHAPTER 32

At eight o'clock that morning, Jasmine's ringing doorbell and the knocking at her door woke her up. She hadn't told anyone about her SoHo apartment, so she thought it could only be Homicide. She got up as quickly as she could, feeling extremely tired, and walked to the door to look through the peephole.

"Jasmine, it's me."

Instantly her blood pressure shot through the roof when she realized it was Agent Gosling. Jasmine was still unfamiliar with the locks on her door, but she did her best and ripped open the door as fast as she could.

"Okay, no disrespect, but what the fuck are you doing here?"

Agent Gosling invited himself in and began looking around.

Jasmine closed the door behind him. "Seriously, what are you doing here? You tryin' to get me killed or what?"

Agent Gosling didn't let her know that two other FBI agents had followed her after she'd left Madison Square Garden. They had staked out her apartment building, so they knew exactly what time Homicide and Jasmine arrived at the apartment, and they also knew when Homicide left, and had reported everything back to him.

"So how'd things go with Homicide? Were you able to make any contact with him?"

Jasmine sucked her teeth.

"Is that a yes or no?" Gosling asked sternly.

"Yes, I made contact with him." Jasmine felt really nauseous at that moment, so she rushed off to her kitchen and drank some water to try and settle her stomach.

Gosling followed right behind her.

"I had too much to drink last night. I feel sick right now. I was trying to sleep it off, and I was going to call you when I woke up."

Gosling smelled sex in the air.

"Listen, can we please just get on the same page? I mean, not for nothing, but Homicide was at this apartment and left not too long ago. I don't know how I would have explained your black ass popping up at my door."

"Homicide was here?" Gosling asked, trying to sound like didn't know.

"Yes."

"Jasmine, you apparently had too much to drink, and you know what we discussed, and now you're—"

Jasmine cut him off. "No, I didn't fuck him. I know what you told me, and I'm not trying to jeopardize shit."

"Are you sure you didn't fuck him, Jasmine?" Gosling asked, sounding more like a jealous boyfriend than a concerned FBI case agent.

Jasmine rolled her eyes. "So I'm a slut now?"

"No, no, that's not what I was implying."

Jasmine heard her phone vibrating in the other room,

so she walked out of the room to retrieve it. When she got to it, she saw that it was a text from Simone, who had sent her a picture of a dick.

She shook her head and replied to the text with one word. *Nice*

Simone immediately replied back: *It's Ish's dick. He damn near fucked me into a gotdamn COMA! LOL.*

Jasmine replied right back. *Kind of busy right now. I'll hit you back in an hour or so.*

Gosling, a recovering alcoholic, had been sober for a little over nine years. But something that night before had caused him to slip up and he'd found himself in a Manhattan bar downing way too many shots of Jack Daniel's.

He made his way into Jasmine's bedroom. He couldn't help but think about what it would be like to bend Jasmine over her bed and fuck the shit out of her right there on the spot.

"You okay?" Jasmine asked him as he stared at her.

He nodded.

"Something isn't right. You popped up over here out the blue with this glossy-eyed look. Everything is good? You sure?"

Gosling sat down on Jasmine's bed and assured her that he was fine.

"Listen, I wanted to tell you—Stay completely out of Prince's way. We're taking him off your target list."

"Why?" That was music to Jasmine's ears.

"We're ninety percent certain he was behind the

funeral home shooting."

"You shitting?"

"I'm serious." Gosling took out a breath mint and popped it into his mouth to help mask the smell of liquor. "We would hate to be walking you into a death trap, so until we get more intel, just do your best to keep your distance from him. He's a dangerous dude. If he shot up a funeral home gunning for Nico and his crew, there's no telling what he would do to you if he found out or knew somehow that you're Nico's woman."

"Ahhh, you were so concerned about me that you came over this early in the morning?" Jasmine walked over to her bed and sat next to Gosling and gave him a hug.

Gosling immediately stood to his feet. Pretty women was his second biggest vice, and his womanizing usually followed his nights of drinking. "I have to get to the office," he told her. "We have an important meeting."

"Okay, I'll call you later in the afternoon and fill you in on Homicide."

"Okay, you do that. And we have to start moving to get Nico back in New York. Agent Battle is starting to grow impatient with me being so lax about him being in Miami."

Jasmine nodded.

As Gosling made his way out, he turned and looked at her before opening the door. "You look cute when you just wake up."

"Is that right?"

Gosling slowly nodded. He was seconds from pulling

her toward him and sticking his tongue down her throat.

Right at that moment, Homicide was calling Jasmine, but she didn't want to answer in front of Gosling.

"Good-bye, silly." She playfully pushed him out the door as he laughed and told her good-bye.

"Hello," Jasmine said, quickly answering her cell phone before it stopped ringing.

"You up?"

"Yes," Jasmine replied, not knowing what to think.

"I'ma come through and check you this afternoon."

"Oh, okay," Jasmine said with a smile. "I'll be here. I'm not going nowhere."

"That's what's up." Homicide ended the call.

Jasmine was thankful that she hadn't blown her assignment with him, but she was more thankful that her childhood crush wanted to come back and see her. She couldn't stop thinking about him. She made her way back to her bedroom, got in the bed, and smiled her way back to sleep.

CHAPTER 33

Jasmine woke up at eleven a.m. She decided to jump in the shower and then quickly head to Long Island to get some more of her clothes, since she still didn't have a lot of her things in the apartment. She was trying to rush and be back in SoHo before one o'clock, so she would be there when Ish arrived.

She was on the Long Island Expressway when her cell phone started to ring. Using her Bluetooth, she answered the call, and BJ's voice was soon heard coming through the speakers in her truck.

"Jasmine."

"Oh shit! BJ, I'm so sorry. I saw your text, and I meant to hit you back. I was so hung over. I'm just recovering now," she said, laughing lightly.

When BJ didn't laugh or respond, she could sense that something was wrong. "Everything okay? You doing good?"

"Yeah, I'm good. I got an operation scheduled in about two hours."

"Oh, okay. I'll make sure I say a quick prayer for you."

"Jasmine, I need you to keep it totally one hundred with me."

Instantly her heart started pounding. "Of course. About what? What's up?"

"What the fuck is up wit'chu and Black Justice?"

Jasmine immediately shot back, "Ain't nothin' up with that nigga!" Her mouth started to get dry, and she was trying her hardest to think as quickly as she could.

"You ain't fuck that nigga, did you?"

"Oh my muthafuckin' God! Hell no, I didn't fuck him! Me and Simone saw him one night up in the strip club, that night Simone met Ish. And he was with his boys and he was drunk and pushing up on me and shit, but I knew he was high, so it was nothing. I wasn't trying to pay his ass no attention."

"Jasmine, you sure?"

"Yes! I'm more than sure."

BJ started to cough. He sounded like he was choking.

"Oh, my God! BJ, I know you checking up on me because Nico is your boy. But honestly you don't even need to be stressing yourself with this bullshit. It's just going to distract from you getting better. Just believe me. I mean, this shit is totally from left field somewhere. I do know that I wasn't fuckin' with that nigga."

Through more coughs, BJ continued to talk. "Well, the nigga got locked up, and he's on Rikers Island talking shit. You know how things come back."

Jasmine was beyond stressed and was on the verge of tears, but she had to hold it together. "What kind of shit could he be talking?"

"He telling niggas that he fucked you and that your new name should be Suicide Pussy because every nigga that fucks with you either ends up getting murdered, like

Shabazz, or end up in jail like him."

"You know what? I'ma fuck that nigga up! When I hang up the phone, I'm calling Ish, and me and Ish will ride over to Rikers Island right now, and I guarantee you the muthafucka won't talk that bullshit. These lame-ass dudes always act just like bitches whenever I don't fuck with them."

"Fuck that nigga. Don't waste your time going over there. But I'ma tell you this—Just watch where you go. Niggas is saying they saw you coupled up with Homicide at the Knicks game last night, and with this Black Justice shit, it don't look right, you kna'mean?"

Jasmine couldn't take it anymore, and she broke down and started crying.

"BJ, I am so fuckin' heated right now. It's like, damn, can I live? I can't wipe my ass in this city without people being all up in my shit. First of all, I swear on everything, I was at the Knicks game with my fourteen-year-old cousin. I'll give you his number right now, and you can three-way him and ask him. He loves basketball, so I figured I would surprise him and take him to see the Knicks and the Lakers. Now when we got there, did I see Homicide? Yes, I saw him, but I had no idea he was going to be there. And when I saw him I was like, *He looks real familiar*, so we spoke. Come to find out, I knew him since fourth fuckin' grade when we was in the same class. But I swear to you, before last night, I hadn't seen him in like ten years, if not more than that."

BJ knew there was no way rumors like that could start

circulating without some kind of truth to them. "A'ight. If that's what you're saying, then that's what it is."

Jasmine sucked her teeth. "You know that's not true because if you're calling me then I know I'm going to have to hear Nico's mouth on this, and I ain't even do shit. Uggghhh! I swear, sometimes I just want to move up out of New York because I can't take this shit. The dudes are worse than these jealous-ass females that be hating on me."

BJ remained quiet.

"And let me guess. Homicide is saying that he fucked me too, right? I'm just opening up my legs and fuckin' everybody."

"Nah, I told you what it is. If I was you, I would just stay in the crib, lay low until things blow over and Nico gets back in town. A'ight?"

"A'ight, BJ." Jasmine blew some air into the phone. "Get through your surgery."

"I will."

With that, they ended the call.

When she got to Nico's house, she rolled some weed and smoked it while sitting on the deck overlooking the sprawling backyard. It didn't help get her mind off what BJ had told her.

Her mind racing, she combed through her closets and picked out a bunch of outfits that she piled into her truck. At that point, her desire to see Homicide wasn't nearly as intense as it was before she'd spoken to BJ. But she knew she had a job to do.

Jasmine headed back toward SoHo. As soon as she pulled out of the circular driveway, her phone began to ring. It was Simone. She contemplated if she should answer it or not. A big part of her wanted to send Simone to voice mail because she just didn't want to deal with any more stress, drama, or gossip, but at the same time she felt like she had to know everything that was being said about her and exactly who was saying it. So although she didn't want to, she answered Simone's call and braced herself for any new drama.

CHAPTER 34

As Jasmine drove back to Manhattan, Simone would not shut up even for a moment.

"Look at me, just talking your head off." Simone chuckled, sounding like a swimmer coming up for air. "So, anyway, what's up with you? And how's Nico? I haven't heard you talking about him. And whenever I'm out with Ish, I don't see him anywhere. Y'all still together, right?"

Jasmine rolled her eyes. If she could have reached through the phone and choked Simone until she passed out, she would have.

"Of course, we're still together, Simone. I already told you he was in Miami doing his thing."

"He's still in Miami? You know he's fuckin' somebody down there."

"Thank you, Simone. I really needed to hear that."

"Oh, I'm sorry."

Jasmine could almost feel Simone's smile coming through the phone.

"Yeah, what I'm saying . . . I knew he was still out of town because Ish told me that."

"Do me a favor, Simone—When you're all boo'd up with Ish and y'all talkin' pillow talk or whatever, can you please leave me and Nico's names out of your mouths?"

"No, we wasn't talking about you and Nico like that. Ish was just telling me how he's basically been running everything in Brooklyn and Queens since Nico's been out of town."

Jasmine sighed. "Running everything like what?"

"I don't think I need to spell it out for you, Jasmine."

"Actually, you don't. Listen, I have to go. I'll hit you up later."

Jasmine had had enough of Simone's boasting. In a way though, she was glad because it prevented her from saying anything to her about her and Homicide, or about her apartment in SoHo.

"Okay, make sure you do. We have to hang out again real soon."

"We will," Jasmine replied right before hanging up.

Jasmine didn't see how Simone could be a real friend if she was always in competition with her and always trying to one-up her. She did the best she could to block Simone out of her mind, not wanting any negative energy flowing through her when Homicide came by to see her.

It was five thirty and Homicide hadn't yet come by to see Jasmine, nor called her to tell her if he was still coming by. She was starting to think he was standing her up. She thought about texting him, but she didn't want to come across as needy.

Right at five-forty, the doorman called Jasmine and told her that she had a visitor named Homicide.

"Okay, you can send him up."

Three minutes later Homicide was ringing her doorbell.

Jasmine opened the door with a smile wearing a pair of dark blue biker shorts and a T-shirt that was cut short and exposed her stomach. "You actually told the doorman your name was Homicide?" She laughed.

"I don't give a fuck about him. That's my name." Homicide handed her a white shopping bag. "I bought us some fish and brown rice."

"Oh, thank you. And I'm starving too."

Jasmine took the food to the kitchen and got two plates and forks.

"I ain't think you was coming no more."

"Yeah, I know. I was dealing with some shit, trying to get this bread."

She looked at Homicide and smiled as she fixed the plates. He didn't realize she was looking at him. "Can I get a hug or something?" she said, walking toward him. She hugged him real tight and noticed he was wearing a nice-scented Muslim oil. But she could also feel the gun in his waistband. "What scent is that? Kush?"

Homicide smiled. "Yeah. How you know that?"

"I got some culture." Jasmine laughed. "You want me to warm up your food?"

He shook his head no, so Jasmine handed him his plate and warmed up hers.

"So what you do today?" Homicide asked, about to put a forkful of food in his mouth.

"Nothing—other than trying not to get stressed the fuck out."

"Stressed about what?"

Jasmine got her food out of the microwave and started to eat it. Then she explained to Homicide that BJ had called her, and she told him what he had said.

"So you still fuckin' with Nico or what? Break that shit down for me. Be straight up."

Jasmine was silent.

"What the fuck you quiet for? Either yes or no."

"I'm quiet because I honestly don't know the answer. It's like when he wants to see me, he sees me, and when he wants to fuck with other bitches, he does. Right now, he down in Miami, getting money down there, and he's been down there for a minute. Has he called me since he's been there? Not one time. It's like he's running from me."

"You got that suicide pussy, right?"

Jasmine gave him a serious look.

"I'm just fucking wit'chu." Homicide put a forkful of food in his mouth. "I know why you stressed."

"I know too. I just told you why."

Homicide shook his head. "Nah, you *think* that's why you stressed, but you really stressed because you fuck with weak-ass muthafuckas. Your man is supposed to be more than just your man. He's supposed to be your king and treat you like a queen, no matter what it takes. You feel me?"

Jasmine nodded.

"Like, on the real, if Nico was treating you like a queen, he would have had Black Justice touched from inside them prison walls. You know what I'm saying?"

Homicide ate some more food.

"Black Justice talking shit from behind bars, and Nico got his boys calling you basically on some he-said, she-said shit. And this nigga down in Florida with his feet in the sand while his people is up here in New York laid up in the hospital and having funerals and shit—That's why you're stressed."

Jasmine had to admit that Homicide was making a whole lot of sense.

"Niggas think the chips they holding is what makes them." Homicide shook his head. "But that's not it. What makes a real nigga is the heart he's born with. That shit comes from Allah. You can't manufacture heart. It don't matter how much bread you holding."

"BJ was asking me if I was at the Knicks game with you."

"You should've told that nigga yes, and that you left with me. Fuck that bitch-ass nigga BJ!"

Jasmine loved Homicide's swagger.

"You know how women just on instinct can take care of babies and shit like that?"

Jasmine nodded her head.

"That's because women are earths, and that shit is in y'all nature. But with niggas, we're gods, and gods protect everything. You feel me?"

Jasmine nodded again.

"So if you ever fuckin' with a nigga and you don't feel safe, you fuckin' with the wrong nigga."

"See, I knew since fourth grade that you were a good catch."

Homicide chuckled. "I'm too wild for your ass."

Jasmine walked up to him and kissed him on the cheek and then whispered, "No, you're not."

"So this nigga Nico is out of town, BJ is in the hospital, Lo and Bebo are dead, how the fuck them Ghetto Mafia niggas still eating?" he asked.

"They still getting their money."

"I know, but how?"

"You know Ish?"

Homicide thought for a moment, and then he nodded.

"He's running everything."

"Where that nigga live at?"

"In Rosedale. Why?"

Homicide stood up from the chair and started to feel on her ass. Jasmine reached up and kissed him. He pulled away from her and took out his gun and laid it on the kitchen table. Then he slid her shorts down to her ankles, and she stepped out of them.

Homicide started playing with her exposed pussy. She gasped as soon as he stuck his middle finger inside of her. With his other hand, he undid his pants and let them drop to just above his knees. He then took his finger out of Jasmine's pussy and lifted her up onto the dishwasher, where she spread her legs as wide as she could for him.

Homicide slid his dick into her and started to fuck her real slow, and as her pussy got wetter and wetter, he fucked her harder and harder. Jasmine loved every inch of him, and every second of him fucking her. Unlike the night before when she wasn't totally herself because of the alcohol, this time she was sober and felt totally free. She didn't hold back one bit, and her screams and moans let him know that she was thoroughly enjoying the way he fucked her.

She wrapped her legs around his back then clasped both of her hands around the back of his neck. Homicide pulled away from the dishwasher and supported her by gripping her ass and holding her up in the air. Jasmine loved that position, and she bounced up and down on his dick until she came back to back.

Homicide could feel himself about to nut. After a few more real deep strokes, he pulled his dick out of her and shot come all over her stomach, legs, on her short T-Shirt, and the dishwasher.

After Homicide caught his breath, Jasmine hopped off the dishwasher and grabbed him and hugged him and wouldn't let him go, her head buried in his chest. At that moment she didn't care about Nico and what he was doing, she didn't care about Agent Gosling, and she didn't care about her role as a confidential informant. Homicide made her feel safe and secure, and she just wished that she could stay in that exact same position forever, hugging him with her head placed on his chest, and never have to worry about a thing.

CHAPTER 35

Two weeks later, Agent Gosling was starting to get very suspicious of Jasmine's relationship with Homicide because she had yet to produce any incriminating evidence on him. while he was pressuring Jasmine to produce results, Homicide was also starting to apply pressure on her to have her set up Ish to get robbed. Initially Jasmine wasn't sure if it was the smartest thing for her to do, but after a long day of seriously thinking about it, she realized it was actually a good idea. For one, she was dead tired of Simone constantly boasting about what Ish was doing for her. She also figured that if the robbery was successful, she would be able to go to Gosling and have him ease up the pressure on her by convincing him that the FBI needed to really focus on locking up Ish because he was taking over for Nico as the new kingpin. Setting up Ish would also make Homicide trust her and not question her loyalty to him.

So after Jasmine was convinced she was down with setting up Ish, she started calling Simone more often and reminding her that they needed to go out because they hadn't been out in so long. Itching to show off the new outfits and other gifts Ish had given to her, Simone jumped at the bait.

"Did you move in with Ish yet?"

"I might as well have. I mean, I'm always at his crib. He loves when I cook for him, so I try to be there as much as possible."

"Mmm-hmm."

"What?"

"You know the only reason you be over there is for some dick! You probably ain't cook that nigga one good meal yet. Remember you are the one who texted me a picture of his dick."

"Oh my God!" Simone laughed, trying to sound embarrassed. "That shit do look good though, right?"

"I don't know. I deleted that right after you sent it to me. Picture me trying to explain to Nico why Ish's dick is in my phone."

Simone burst out laughing, completely thrilled to talk about Ish any chance she could. Then she started to talk low and in a real serious tone. "So tell me something—When's the last time you had some dick?"

"Why you asking me, like you trying to get the scoop on something? You already know Nico is out of town."

"Jasmine, you telling me you ain't fuck nobody since Nico been gone all this time?"

"That's exactly what I'm telling you—Unless you know about some dick that I don't know about."

"I'm just saying I don't know how you go for so long."

Simone was still the dark-skinned, round-faced girl with the pig nose who'd only recently started looking decent when she had the money to make herself look better. But she was trying to make it like, for all her life, dudes were in bidding wars over her pussy, and she always had her pick of dicks.

"It ain't that hard, Simone. You act like Nico is doing time in prison or something. He'll be back."

"I hear you. But just as long as you know, after we finish partying or whatever, my black ass is going home to Ish for some dick. So don't be looking for me to come back to chill with you in Long Island."

"Whatever, Simone."

Jasmine literally couldn't take any more of her, so she ended the call, with all of the info she needed to relay back to Homicide.

Jasmine and Simone made plans to hang out at Sway, a white trendy bar lounge within walking distance of Jasmine's apartment in SoHo.

"Who told you about this place?" Simone asked Jasmine after she entered Sway and found her seated at a table by herself.

"I been here before."

"Here?"

"Girl, sit your ass down and let me order you a drink. It'll be poppin' in about a hour."

Simone had a stink look on her face. "I hope so. All these white people . . . I don't party with white people."

Jasmine shook her head, annoyed with Simone already. She managed to get the waitress's attention and ordered two apple martinis.

"None of these white boys better try to talk to me."

"Simone, trust me, these white people in here be on a completely different vibe. They all about having fun and a good time when they go out. Watch how many celebs stroll up in here within the next two hours or so."

"In here?"

"Yes, in here."

The waitress came back with the drinks, and Simone took her drink off of the tray without even waiting for the waitress. She crossed her legs, put the tiny red straw to her mouth, and started to sip on her drink.

"Thank you." Jasmine handed the waitress forty dollars.

"So what's up with school?"

"It's kicking my ass." Jasmine didn't want to tell her that she had withdrawn for the semester.

"That's cool."

Simone put her drink down to respond to a text message. She smiled and texted something back.

"Ish said to tell you what's up. And he said he's been to Sway before, and it's a cool spot."

Jasmine looked at Simone and just shook her head. Suddenly Simone had loosened up and was ready to let her hair down after Ish validated the spot.

"So what was you saying about school?"

"Nothing. Never mind."

Simone ordered some Buffalo wings for them. Jasmine knew it was going to be a long night, but she was working, and that's how she looked at it.

She sat for about two hours and listened to Simone talk about how she was so certain that Ish was going to be getting her an engagement ring real soon and how she couldn't wait for him to ask her to marry him.

"No offense, Simone, but do you really think Ish is the marrying type?"

"Yup."

Jasmine left it alone and didn't try to argue with her.

Before long, Simone was asking Jasmine what she had planned for Saturday, the following day.

"Nothing at all. You don't understand how boring my life is right now. It's like all I do is go to school and come home and study."

"You need to stop acting like you married to Nico and start doing you—That's your problem."

Jasmine just nodded. "So what about you? What's up for tomorrow?"

"I'm probably going to go with Ish to the new casino that opened up in Queens." Simone then excused herself to go to the bathroom and told Jasmine that after that she was probably going to get ready to leave.

"Let me guess—You're heading to Ish's house for some dick?"

Simone smiled and pointed at Jasmine, and then she walked off to the bathroom.

As soon as Simone was out of eyesight, Jasmine pulled out her phone and called Homicide. "We about to leave now, so figure in about thirty or forty minutes."

"That's what's up. I'm good. I'm here," Homicide replied. "Everything sound a'ight?"

"Yeah, everything is good. She talking about she heading there now to get fucked."

"No doubt. Just keep your phone on."

"Okay." Jasmine ended the call.

Homicide and his homeboy, who went by the name of Cash Out, were parked three houses down from Ish's house, sitting in an all-black Audi with tinted windows. Ish lived on a quiet middle-class block, where all of the neighbors parked their cars on the street, so the Audi didn't look out of place at two in the morning. Ish's house was completely dark, and the white Mercedes-Benz S550 that he drove wasn't on the block or in his driveway.

At two fifteen in the morning Simone pulled into the driveway of Ish's house and turned off the engine. It took her about two minutes to get out of the car, and when she did she was talking on her cell phone. Fully engrossed in her conversation, she didn't see Homicide and Cash Out exit their Audi wearing all-black and black ski masks.

Ish's house didn't have a fence or any bushes. It was just wide-open landscape and layout, so it would have been easy for Homicide and Cash Out to be spotted.

Simone ended her call just before unlocking the front door. As she opened the door she felt somebody grab her forcefully from behind, rush her into the house, and close the door behind her.

Homicide's left hand was inside of a black leather glove that completely covered Simone's mouth, and with his right hand he gripped a black semi-automatic weapon and pressed it to her temple. "Shut the fuck up! Stop fighting me, and I won't kill you!"

Simone stopped resisting, but her chest was visibly rising and falling from breathing so hard.

"Who's in the house with you?" Homicide asked.

Cash Out turned on the lights and closed the vertical blinds, so no one could see inside the house.

Simone shrugged her shoulders to indicate that she didn't know who was home. She didn't know who was gripping her from behind, but she could see Cash Out in his ski mask, and the sight of him terrified her.

Cash Out quickly ran through the house and went from room to room just to make sure it was completely empty.

Homicide knew from Jasmine that Simone talked about Ish giving her cash and sending her to the post office to buy money orders for him to pay his bills, so he was sure there was cash in the house.

Homicide slid his hand from her mouth and held her in a headlock, her back leaning against his chest and his forearm applying choke-hold pressure to her neck. "Where the cash?"

"It's downstairs in the basement. Please don't kill me!"

"Where at downstairs?"

"In the stand-alone freezer, under the meat and the food."

Homicide nodded to Cash Out, who went downstairs. Within two minutes he came back with three large stacks of frozen cash. It looked like about twenty or thirty thousand dollars, but it was hard to determine because it was stuck together.

"I know that ain't it! Where the rest of the money at?" Homicide threw Simone to the ground by her hair and aimed his gun at her.

"I don't know, I swear to you, I don't know," she said, trembling.

"You lying to me!"

"I'm not. I swear to you, I'm not." Simone shook her head, and tears began streaming down her face. She knew Ish was on his way home and was hoping he would hurry up and get there before she got raped or killed.

"Where the drugs at?"

Simone was frozen in fear because now she knew she was dealing with dudes who knew Ish.

Homicide nodded to Cash Out.

Cash Out walked up to her and kicked her as hard as he could in her ribs. "Where the fuck is the drugs at?" he hollered.

The kick instantly knocked the wind out of Simone, who doubled over on the living room floor clutching her ribs, gasping for air, and trying to talk all at the same time.

"There's nothing," she faintly replied from the ground, certain she was about to die.

Homicide walked over and picked up her phone and told her to find Ish's number. Simone was barely able to move because of the razor-sharp pain in her side that felt like she was being stabbed with a hunting knife.

He held out the phone, and she quickly scrolled through it until she got to Ish's number. Homicide then sent Ish a text message from her phone: *Where are you?*

"Tie that bitch up!" Homicide ordered Cash Out after he sent the text to Ish.

Cash Out ripped the lamp from the wall. Then he snapped the electrical cord from the lamp and used it to tie Simone's hands behind her back and to the base of the fireplace mantle.

Simone had just gotten her breath back in her lungs from being kicked, and just as she did, Cash Out's stuffed his gun in her mouth. "Where the drugs at, bitch?" he asked while he cocked the gun.

The phone rang, and Ish's name popped up on the caller ID. Homicide didn't want to answer it because he didn't want Simone to start screaming or do anything to tip off Ish. When Ish called right back, Homicide sent him to voice mail.

"Bitch, you got two seconds to tell me where the fuckin' drugs at or your man is gonna come home and find your brains splattered in that fireplace."

"I swear to God, I don't know, but in the kitchen look inside the heating vent. There might be something there."

Ish called back a third time, and again Homicide sent him to voice mail.

Homicide was now wondering if the text had spooked Ish and if he knew something was up. He was ready to bounce because he didn't want to get caught out there outgunned and outmanned if Ish showed up with some of his soldiers.

Cash Out ripped the vent gate from the wall and reached inside and found two pounds of weed. He ran back into the living room and showed it to Homicide, who was pleased with the take but frustrated that the robbery didn't go the way he wanted it. He wanted Ish to walk in on the robbery, so he could hold him hostage and find out where Ghetto Mafia's stash house was.

Homicide walked up to Simone and smacked her across the face with his gun. Simone saw stars. Her face spun and hit the wall, and blood from her mouth splattered onto the floor and wall. Three of her front teeth had just been knocked out.

"We out!" he said to Cash Out. And they made it to their Audi with twenty thousand in cash and two pounds of weed.

When the home phone went to voice mail, Ish knew something was up. He ran the red light he was at and the next three red lights, trying to get to his crib as quickly as he could.

A New York City cop saw him run the light at 147th Avenue and Brookville Boulevard and immediately turned on his lights and started to follow him.

Ish was only five blocks away from house when he was stopped. He tried his best to keep his cool as the cop asked him for his license and registration. He was hoping like crazy that the cop didn't ask him to step out of the car, because of the handgun tucked in his waistband.

CHAPTER 36

Homicide and Cash Out got about five miles away from the crime scene when they pulled the car to the side of the road and turned the heat on full blast although it was warm outside. They wanted to thaw out the frozen stacks of money. Once the money was thawed out, Homicide counted out five stacks of the twenty grand and gave it to his partner in crime, and he kept the rest for himself. He also gave Cash Out one pound of the weed and kept the other pound for himself before they parted ways, promising to hook up again real soon for another caper.

By the time Homicide made it to Jasmine's SoHo apartment it was a little past five in the morning.

"Everything okay?" Jasmine asked nervously.

Homicide handed Jasmine three stacks and told her that everything went off smoothly. He sat down on her couch and ran his hand over his head and down his face.

Jasmine took the money and kissed him and thanked him for it, but in the pit of her stomach, she felt horrible. It was the first time that she could remember money in her hands not feeling good to her.

"I bought some Coronas and some Guinness, if you want one."

Homicide told her to bring him a Guinness, which she did, and she sat down next to him on her couch.

Jasmine pressed him for details on the robbery, but the stone-cold look he gave to her was all it took to stop her from asking a million questions.

Homicide reached for Jasmine's remote control and turned on the flat-screen TV.

"Babe, just tell me one thing—did anybody get hurt?"

"What the fuck you asking me that for?" Homicide stared at Jasmine.

"I'm just asking, baby, that's all."

"Don't worry about that shit." Homicide stood up from the couch and guzzled down the rest of the Guinness.

"I'm sorry."

"Just be yourself. You don't know nothing, you don't say nothing, and you'll be good." Homicide rubbed on his beard, thinking he had fucked up by not being patient. He should have just waited for Ish to come home on his own instead of sending that text to him.

"Okay."

"I'm about to bounce."

"I need you."

Homicide looked into her eyes. "I gotchu. Don't worry about nothing."

Jasmine nodded her head, and then she walked Homicide to the apartment door to see him off.

Five minutes later, she called Agent Gosling.

"Hello," Gosling said in a groggy voice.

"You up?"

"No. But what's up? Are you all right?"

"Yeah, I'm okay. Listen, I just got word straight from Homicide that Ish might be using his crib as a stash house."

"Okay. How sure was he?"

"Gosling, he robs drug dealers, so whatever he knows, he knows."

"So what are you saying?"

"I'm saying Ish needs to be a priority."

"We need something more concrete before we can get a search warrant. Just keep your ear to the ground."

"All right. I'll start calling you more. I think Homicide is comfortable enough with me now where he'll start opening his mouth, so I should have something soon that we can work with."

Gosling went quiet for a moment.

"You still there?"

"Yes, I'm here. Jasmine, listen. What do you think about possibly setting me up and having Homicide rob me?"

"I think I could pull that off with Homicide, but not right now. My name is hot as hell on the streets, and if I walk him into an arrest, I won't be living for much longer."

Gosling wasn't sure what Jasmine was getting at, until she explained to him how Black Justice had branded her with the nickname Suicide Pussy.

"That's the only reason I been moving real slow on Homicide. That nigga would kill me in a heartbeat if he even remotely sensed I was snitching."

"You have to stay alive. I get it." He yawned into the phone. "Jasmine, I'm going back to sleep. It's Saturday."

"Okay, no problem."

CHAPTER 37

Jasmine never went to sleep after she got off the phone with Gosling. She wanted to know if Simone and Ish or anyone else had gotten hurt during the home invasion, but she obviously couldn't just come out and ask her. Since it was too early to call her, she decided to send her a text message: *Girl you won't believe this. I heard after we left Sway that IDRIS ELBA showed up!* Jasmine knew how much Simone loved Idris Elba, so she was certain that she would hit her right back.

Simone's head was pounding, and her ribs and her jaw were killing her, so Ish had suggested that she get X-rays just to make sure nothing was broken. It was a good thing Simone was dark-skinned; otherwise, she would have had visible black-and-blue marks on her side and on her face.

She stood up in her hospital gown and walked over to the single mirror in the emergency room. She looked at her face, and tears rolled down her eyes. "Baby, look at me," she said, her lips swollen and three teeth missing.

Ish tried to calm her down by telling her that the swelling would soon go down and that she could get her teeth replaced.

Simone was in the same hospital that BJ was in, just a different section. Ish had gone up to his room to visit him. He had tried to explain to BJ what had happened, but BJ was too drugged up from another surgery he had just undergone. Things weren't looking good for BJ. The doctors were now certain that he was going to have to wear a colostomy bag for the rest of his life. They had done all they could do to prevent it, but the bullets had just done too much damage.

Ish knew he couldn't rely on BJ or Nico, or anyone else for that matter, to help him protect his own home or to seek revenge for the way he had been violated.

"Simone, you sure nobody knew what was up?"

"I'm sure, baby. I know not to open my mouth."

Ish looked at her and nodded his head as he slowly paced back and forth in the emergency room, while Simone sat on one of the hospital beds waiting for the doctor to come back.

Ish liked Simone, but not nearly as much as she liked him. He had been mainly using her to sign for FedEx packages that contained drugs. See, Ghetto Mafia had a group of corrupt FedEx employees in Miami and in New York's JFK Airport who were able to get drugs on board FedEx airplanes for them and also get them on to specific FedEx delivery trucks.

Ghetto Mafia had been able to get drugs delivered to almost any location in Queens they wanted. They would always switch the drop-off locations to lower the risk of getting busted. They would also always have the package come in the name of a chick that they trusted, and they would have the girl sign for the packages. Just in case they ever got caught, they could always plead that the package wasn't in their name, and therefore they weren't responsible for it.

With BJ in the hospital, Bebo and Lo dead, and Nico laying low in Miami, Nico had been forced to have the FedEx packages go to Ish. Nico never wanted to tell anyone other than BJ exactly where his stash houses were. And even with BJ laid up, he still didn't take the chance on telling Ish the location of the stash houses. Instead, Nico had the FedEx re-up packages come directly to Ish's house, so if anything went wrong, Ish would be without excuses.

Nico started having the FedEx packages delivered to Ish's house right after Ish and Simone had met at the strip club. Right from the jump, Ish knew that Simone was real needy and that she was on his dick, so he was easily able to convince her to have her name on the packages. He also convinced her to be at his house on a regular basis to accept the packages and sign for them.

Ish was thankful that the robbery hadn't happened forty-eight hours later because the robbers would have made off with a couple of bricks of heroin and coke that would have been in the house. The fact that the masked intruders had only taken the two pounds of weed and a relatively small amount of cash made Ish believe that

Simone sincerely didn't have anything to do with the robbery. It would've been very tempting for her to set up the home invasion for the same day that he expected a re-up shipment.

Ish disregarded the hospital rules against talking on cell phones and spoke to Nico on his brand-new prepaid phone. He knew to never use his regular cell phone when talking with Nico, and he also knew to never give out Nico's number.

"Ish, I don't give a fuck what you gotta do, but you gotta find out who those muthafuckas were and handle that shit!" Nico ordered.

Ish tried to explain, as he had done before, that the two dudes had masks on and that Simone hadn't seen their faces.

"Ish, that's your fuckin' problem! We got ten ki's coming on Monday, and you already know that I can't have the shipment stopped. Yo, word on everything, Ish, don't fuck up this re-up!" Nico hung up on Ish.

"You believe this nigga Nico is upset with me over this shit?" Ish said to Simone.

Right at that point the emergency room doctor walked in.

"Okay, so we have good news. The X-rays were negative, no fractures or broken bones of any kind."

Ish's mind was somewhere else, so he paid the doctor no attention.

Simone had questions about her teeth and getting cosmetic surgery done, but since the doctor wasn't a dentist, he explained to her that he wouldn't be able to give her any real answers. He then told her that she could get dressed and that he would write up a prescription for her for painkillers.

"The nurse will be right out with the prescription and to sign you out."

"Don't let Nico stress you, baby," Simone said to Ish while they pulled into the parking lot of Walgreens so she could get her prescription filled.

"Fuck that nigga! He on the phone talking that gangsta shit while his pussy ass is hiding out in Miami."

After they left Walgreens, Simone was too afraid to go back to Ish's house alone. So she asked him to drop her at her own apartment and told him that she would only stay at his house while he was there.

Ish dropped her off and headed straight to the barbershop. He figured, if the streets were talking, he could count on finding out by just listening to what the people in the barbershop had to say.

As soon as Simone locked the door to her apartment, she went right to her bathroom mirror and stared at her face. She couldn't believe how horrible she looked, but at the same time, she knew she was lucky to be alive. She popped one of her painkillers into her mouth. As soon as she did that, her cell phone started vibrating.

"You don't how to text me back or call me?" Jasmine asked.

Simone sucked her teeth. "So you didn't hear what happened?"

"What happened with what?"

"Last night I got robbed."

"When? After you left Sway? And you just telling me now?"

"No. Well, yeah, it was after I left Sway, but it happened at Ish's house."

"You're lying."

"I wish I was." Simone sighed. "Yeah, two dudes pushed their way in and beat me and tied me up and robbed the crib."

"Oh my God! Simone, are you serious? Where are you right now?"

"I'm dead serious. Ish just dropped me off from the emergency room."

"Emergency room? Where are you at?"

"I'm home now."

"Okay, I'll be there in forty-five minutes."

"No! I can't let anybody see me like this. My face is swollen, and I got three teeth missing. I look crazy."

Jasmine really felt bad when she heard Simone say she was missing three teeth because she was sure it was Homicide who caused those teeth to go missing.

"You know I don't care how you look! I'm coming over regardless."

"Jasmine, no. Really, I'll be okay. I'm probably going to shoot back over to Ish's house anyway. I have to be there tomorrow when FedEx shows up."

"Fuck FedEx! You don't know what's going on right now, so you don't need to be over by Ish's crib until you find out what's what."

"I have to sign for FedEx. You know how that goes."

"What are you talking about?"

"The re-up through FedEx."

Jasmine went silent for a moment. Then she said, "Hey, let me call you right back," and then she hung up the phone quickly.

Jasmine had no idea what Simone was referring to about the re-up through FedEx, and she just sensed that she needed to have her recorder going while she spoke to Simone. She retrieved her FBI-issued phone and started to record. She then called Simone back and put the call on speakerphone.

"Sorry about that," Jasmine said when Simone answered the phone. "I thought I heard my doorbell, but it was nothing. So, yeah, you were saying something about the re-up."

"Yeah, I was saying I just have to be there to sign for it."

"Simone, trust me. Let things cool off first before you go back to Ish's house. Don't be hardheaded."

"I can't do that to Ish. Nico was already beefing with

him over the robbery, so if this re-up don't go right, then I don't think Ish would let me forget it. I'm just so glad that the delivery didn't come yesterday. Everybody would be sick right now."

Jasmine wasn't sure how to respond.

Simone sucked her teeth and sighed. She told Jasmine that she couldn't believe what she was going through. "Let me go. I'm trying to find a dentist I can go to today."

"Call me if you need anything at all.

Jasmine sat down on the couch and thought about what Simone had just told her. "FedEx?" she said to herself in disbelief.

After thinking it through, she called Gosling. "Got something for you," she said.

"Speak to me."

"FedEx is making deliveries to Ish that you might want to look into."

"What kind of deliveries?"

"What do you think drug dealers are getting delivered to their house? It ain't no e-commerce merchandise being delivered, I can tell you that."

"Wow! I'll get right on this right now."

CHAPTER 38

Based on Jasmine's tip, the FBI contacted FedEx and made arrangements to have drug-sniffing dogs check the two packages scheduled to arrive at Ish's house on Monday morning. Like Gosling had suspected, both packages came up positive for drugs, so the FBI, Drug Enforcement Agency, and the New York City Police Department all moved quickly to formulate a plan to raid Ish's home.

FedEx allowed one of the FBI agents to pose as a FedEx worker and provided him with a FedEx box truck, a uniform, and a hand-held computer. In the back of the FedEx box truck were additional FBI and DEA agents ready to storm Ish's house as soon as the package was delivered. Sitting five blocks away and ready to provide immediate backup were marked and unmarked New York City Police Department units.

Just before ten a.m., the FedEx truck arrived at Ish's house. The middle-aged black FBI agent dressed as a FedEx worker got out of the truck carrying two ten-pound boxes and a hand-held computer. He walked up to Ish's front door and rang the doorbell.

Ish answered the door and immediately suspected something was wrong because his regular FedEx guy was a Puerto Rican guy named Juan.

"Good morning," the FedEx driver said. "I have two packages for a Simone Simmons."

Ish's heart was pounding as he looked around. Nothing looked out of place, but he could sense something wasn't right. "Oh, okay. Let me go get her for you." He went back inside his house and closed the door.

Simone was at a dentist in Westbury, Long Island, preparing to get her teeth worked on. She had called around to a bunch of different dentists, and ended up choosing the one who could give her the quickest appointment at the most reasonable fee.

Her cell phone rang, and she picked up on the first ring. "Hey, babe. Everything go okay?"

"Yo, there's a dark-skinned, black FedEx dude. You ever seen him before?"

"Never."

Ish heard his doorbell ring. "Fuck!" He told Simone he had to go and would call her back.

Ish went to his bedroom and got his gun. He tucked it into his waistband and pulled it over his shirt then ran back downstairs to the front door. "Sorry about that," he said after re-opening the front door.

"No problem. I don't mean to rush you, but I have one other stop to make before ten a.m., or else I'm going to hear it from my boss."

"Yeah, well, I thought Simone was in the house, but she's not home right now."

The FBI agent had already gone over the different scenarios, so he was prepared. He looked into his computer and pressed a button, and then he pressed another button.

"Oh, okay. I was just double-checking. Well, this will require a signature. I don't know if you want to sign for it. If not, I can take it back, and someone can pick it up tonight after six o'clock at our JFK facility."

Ish nodded his head. Everything seemed all right to him. The FedEx worker didn't seem antsy or overly eager for him to take the package. Ish had never had any packages go back to the FedEx facility for later pickup, so he wasn't feeling too good about that option. He had no idea what the screening process was like once the packages went back to the facility, and he didn't want to screw nothing up.

"It's a package for my tenant. I had some issues with her, so I'm not really sure if I should take it or not. You know what I'm saying?"

"No problem." The undercover FBI agent reached for a door tag. "Take this door tag, leave it for your tenant, and just have her pick it up later tonight. And if she can't make it, we'll automatically redeliver it tomorrow."

"A'ight, you know what? Fuck it. I'll sign for the shit."

The FBI agent placed the packages on the steps and handed Ish the handheld device and the small pen that went with it and showed him where to sign.

As Ish signed his name, he thought about asking for

the normal FedEx guy, but he said nothing.

"What's the last name?" the FBI agent asked.

"Jameson."

"Okay. Wasn't sure if it said Jackson." The FBI agent then touched something on the computer screen right before picking up the packages and handing them to Ish.

Ish's phone started to vibrate just as he took hold of the packages. He couldn't pick up, and it went to voice mail. He went back inside his house and closed the door, feeling somewhat relieved.

BOOM!

The front door burst open, and federal agents quickly stormed the house.

"Shit!" Ish dropped his phone on the ground and went for his gun.

"Gun!" one of the agents yelled.

BANG!

The agent leading the attack had fired his gun before Ish had a chance to fire his own. The shot hit Ish in the right shoulder and caused his gun to fall out of his hand and on to the living room floor. The force of the gunshot caused him to lose his balance and fall backwards, but he didn't fall to the ground.

Two of the agents grabbed hold of him and slammed him face first to the living room floor before handcuffing him.

"Errrgghh!" Ish grimaced in pain on the floor.

Agents flooded the rest of the house.

Outside Ish's house, the block was now crawling with

New York City police, FBI, and DEA, and the sound of an ambulance could be heard approaching the block.

Ish was bleeding from his shoulder and still face down on the living room floor grimacing in pain. His pain wasn't only coming from the gunshot wound, but also his jaw that broke when the agents slammed him to the living room floor. To make matters worse, one of the FBI agents planted his boot onto Ish's neck to make sure he didn't try to move.

CHAPTER 39

The raid on Ish's house and his arrest made the television news and the local newspapers. It was becoming clear to everybody that Ghetto Mafia was falling apart.

Homicide read some of the newspaper stories about the raid and couldn't believe how fucked up his luck was. But the story had energized him to continue to target Ghetto Mafia. He knew they were vulnerable, and he was just waiting to see who was going to step in with Ish now locked up.

During the two weeks that followed the raid on Ish's house, Homicide spent a lot more time with Jasmine. He was genuinely starting to like her, so he wanted to be around her more. And the feelings were definitely mutual.

Homicide also wanted to stay close to Jasmine because he wanted to know everything about Ghetto Mafia as soon as she knew. His trust in her was growing with each passing day, but part of him still wondered just how much loyalty she had for Nico.

To test Jasmine, one day out the blue, he had her take him to Nico's house in Long Island. Homicide wanted to see if she would put up any resistance to him, and also what vibes he could get from the house. He wanted to know if Nico really had been out of town in Miami.

Homicide figured he would be able to tell if the house looked like it had been lived in recently.

Jasmine was caught off guard, but she didn't resist his request. "You want to go there now, as in right now?" she asked him, as the two of them sat inside the Shark Bar eating food.

"As soon as we leave here."

Jasmine was starting to come to grips with the fact that Nico had probably written her off for Mia, so she didn't care where she was seen with Homicide or who was reporting what back to Nico.

It was about ten o'clock on a Thursday night when she and Homicide left the Shark Bar in Manhattan and headed out to Long Island. Homicide had a gold Yukon Denali with dark-tinted windows that he always drove, but whenever he was going out with Jasmine, he always preferred for her to chauffeur him around in her BMW truck. So Jasmine drove while he reclined in the front passenger seat, his snub-nose revolver in his waistband.

At that time of night, the roads were not congested at all, so it didn't take Jasmine any time at all to get to Nico's Long Island estate. She pulled up into the circular driveway and turned off the car's engine. The house was pitch-dark inside.

Homicide was used to being in the city where there was always some kind of lights on. But at Nico's remote estate there was no streetlights to help illuminate the property. It was so dark, Homicide could barely see his own hands when he held them up in front of his face.

"It's black as shit out here," he said to Jasmine.

Jasmine was used to the darkness and the quiet because she had experienced it so many times. She could have walked to the front door of the house with her eyes closed if she had to. She made it to the front door, let herself in with her key, disengaged the alarm system, and turned on the light.

Homicide was thankful for the light that came from inside the house because it allowed him to see where he was walking. "This shit is like living out in the country or some shit." He walked inside the house and looked around.

"You ain't lying." She scooped up the pile of mail that had accumulated and placed it all on the kitchen counter.

Homicide took notice of how good Nico appeared to be living. Having finished a five-year prison sentence just over a year ago, he knew he couldn't come close to balling on Nico's level. The envy started to build up inside of him.

While Jasmine looked through the mail, Homicide opened up the refrigerator and looked around. He saw that the refrigerator wasn't that full, and that the expiration date on the gallon of milk had long since passed, giving him further confirmation that the house had not been lived in for a while.

"You want a drink or something?"

"I'm good." Homicide walked out of the kitchen and walked into the den and looked around in there.

While Homicide was in the den, Jasmine got a call from Simone. She wondered about Simone's timing, but she dismissed it as just a coincidence.

"No sob stories," she said, tired of Simone calling her and telling her how much she missed Ish, how he wasn't calling her from jail, how he had flipped out on her when she went to visit him in jail three days after he had been arrested.

"No, I promise. No more 'Depressed Debbie talk' from me."

"Thank you. You understand what I was saying, right?"

"Yeah, I get where you're coming from."

Jasmine had been telling Simone that death and jail was part of the game; if she was going to mess with drug dealers, she had to get used to that. She reminded Simone how her ex-boo Shabazz had been killed, and she quickly got over it and moved on to Nico.

"So we hanging out tomorrow?" Simone asked.

"Yeah, if you want to." Jasmine smiled, glad that Simone seemed like she was ready to move on.

"And we ain't going back to Sway. I don't care what celebrities be up in there. I just don't really click with that environment."

"Whatever. I ain't even gonna argue with you. So how are your teeth? They look good?"

"They look amazing! Oh my God! I went back the other day and got the veneers bonded. Wait until you see me. I look like a Hollywood actress."

"Okay, so you pick the spot, and we'll go wherever you want to go. And, no, we're not going back to Sue's Rendezvous, so get it out your mind."

"I ain't even thinking about Sue's."

"Okay, so just call me tomorrow."

Simone was mad at herself for not having the courage to mention to Jasmine what she really wanted to tell her. It was really bothering her that Ish didn't trust her and that he really thought that she'd staged the home invasion as a setup to him getting busted by the feds.

As much as she had pleaded with Ish and sworn to him that she had nothing to do with either the robbery or the raid, Ish wasn't buying it, and he promised her that he was going to handle her. He also reminded her that it was her name on the FedEx package.

Simone was desperate to prove her innocence and would stay up at night trying to figure things out, replaying events in her head, but she kept coming up blank.

Then three nights ago, she had finally come up with something she thought was concrete. She figured that the masked gunman who'd had his hand around her mouth had to have a full, bushy beard because she remembered seeing what looked like black hair sticking out from the base of the ski mask he was wearing. She also remembered Ish telling her that BJ was saying that Jasmine was playing Nico by going to a Knicks game with Homicide.

Simone had never said anything to Jasmine about what Ish had told her. She wanted to see if Jasmine would voluntarily bring it up. Since Jasmine never said anything, Simone kept her mouth shut about it because she didn't want it getting back to Ish that she couldn't hold water.

Simone was convinced that it was Homicide who had robbed her. She had asked around about how Homicide looked, and people who knew of him all said that he rocked a full beard. She couldn't wait to tell Ish exactly what she was thinking.

Simone felt equally confident that Jasmine's hands were dirty. She couldn't exactly put her finger on it, but she knew that Jasmine wasn't a psychic. Yet to her it was like Jasmine had warned her that Ish's crib was going to get raided.

She'd replayed Jasmine's words in her mind. "*Simone, trust me. Let things cool off first before you go back to Ish's house. Don't be hardheaded.*" She knew the only reason Jasmine had said to trust her was because she knew what was about to go down the next day.

CHAPTER 40

The day after Homicide and Jasmine were at Nico's house, Jasmine was kicking herself for forgetting to bring some more clothes to her SoHo loft. She and Simone were going to be hanging out later that night, and there was a brand-new outfit and a pair of brand-new shoes she had over at Nico's house that she wanted to wear. Although Jasmine would have wanted to spend her Friday afternoon sleeping and relaxing, she decided to drive back out to Long Island during the early part of the afternoon to avoid the crazy Friday rush-hour and late-night traffic.

She hopped in her truck and made her way out to Long Island by herself. The ride alone did her a lot of good because it allowed her some time to just think about things and to clear her head. It was rare for Jasmine to get quality time by herself because her life was in constant turmoil.

Jasmine made it there relatively quickly. After she parked her truck and went inside, she instantly had a flashback to the time she almost got killed in the house by Bebo. Even though a good amount of time had passed since then, she was still afraid to be in the house alone, even during the daytime.

After closing the door behind her and making sure it was locked, she quickly went upstairs and grabbed the outfit and the shoes she had come for. She also grabbed a couple more outfits to take back with her to Manhattan and threw them on the bed.

Jasmine entered her walk-in closet and searched for more shoes to take with her. While looking around, she heard the front door close. Her heart dropped, and then it quickly started beating again. She froze dead in her tracks and kept still, not wanting to make a sound.

Jasmine was certain that her snitching had caught up to her and that either Ish, Black Justice, or even Nico had someone following her, and they had followed her to the house to kill her as payback for all of her snitching.

"Fuck! Shit!" she said softly. She cursed herself for being so stupid to come alone and without a weapon. She could hear the person downstairs moving around. She felt that she had no choice but to hide in the closet.

As quietly as possible Jasmine started taking clothes off the racks they were on and created one huge pile about three feet high. She sat down in it and pulled clothes over her so that her face and body were completely covered. The whole time, her heart was racing a thousand beats per second. Now that her head was covered and her heart was beating so fast, it made it very hard for her to breathe, and she started to feel claustrophobic. Even though the claustrophobic feelings were making her panic even more, she knew she had to keep her head under the clothes if she wanted to stay alive.

Jasmine heard someone coming up the stairs, and it was like right at that moment she saw her life flashing before her eyes. She knew she was going to certainly die.

"JASMINE! JASMINE! Yo, you up here?"

With all of the clothes surrounding her, Jasmine could barely make out the voice. Then after a few seconds, she didn't hear anything. Then she heard a cell phone ringing. She wanted to die. She was so stupid; she had left herself phone downstairs in the kitchen when she had first entered the house.

"Yo, this me. I just touched down about an hour ago. I'm at the crib."

Then it all hit her. That was Nico's voice. She quickly popped her head through the mountain of clothes, so she could get some air in her lungs. She then stood up and left the clothes on the floor. "Nico?" she said, pushing open the closet door. "You scared the shit out of me!"

Nico didn't say anything and just stared at her. He hadn't seen her in so long, he was captivated by her.

She looked at Nico and noticed that his skin was real even-toned and that he had gotten two shades darker. He looked as sexy as ever.

She went right toward him and gave him a really big hug. "I missed you so much!" Tears instantly started running down her face.

"I'm home now. Stop crying."

"I thought you were through with me, baby."

"I was handling business. You know that."

Jasmine shook her head, and through her tears she

smiled and looked at Nico, slowly shaking her head. "I want to be so angry with you right now. And I can't. I hate that about you. Uggghhh!"

Nico looked around the room, not saying anything.

"You wasn't calling me, you wasn't getting word through your boys or nothing. It's like ever since I had got arrested that night, you just went funny style on me, and you never explained why."

"I wasn't calling because them boys was listening, and I had to stay off the grid. I was protecting you by not calling you and possibly getting you jammed up in my shot."

"I hate your ass! Uggghhh! God!"

Jasmine punched Nico in the chest. She wanted to go so hard on Nico and let him have it. She felt like all that she was going through, being a confidential informant, was all because of him. Had he not left her to take the weight when she got jammed up and arrested that night, she never would have had to agree to be a confidential informant.

Nico reached out and grabbed hold of Jasmine's arm and pulled her toward him. Then he slid his hand inside her sweat pants and started rubbing on her pussy.

Jasmine pulled his hand away. "You don't speak to me, you disappear on me and just go about doing your thing with absolutely no cares about me at all, and now you want to just play with my pussy?"

"Stop fighting me." Nico slipped his hand back inside her pants. He reached inside her thong and felt her pussy lips. He started gently rubbing on her clit. "I did have cares for you. Trust me on that."

"Can we just talk? Seriously, let's just talk and get all issues on the table, so I can really know that you hear me and whether or not you actually give a damn about me. And I can clear up anything that's going through your mind."

Nico guided her to the bed, laid her down, and took off her flip-flops. Then he pulled off her sweat pants and her thong.

Jasmine couldn't believe it was so hard for her to resist him. While she stared at him, he took off his shirt. She could tell that he had been working out while he was in Florida because he looked more buff than usual.

Jasmine's pussy was soon leaking. She enjoyed other dicks, but no other dude gave it to her like Nico did, and no other dude made her as wet. She spread open her legs for Nico, who let his jeans fall to the floor of their bedroom, and he slipped his dick into her pussy and started to fuck her harder than he had ever fucked her. Nico was also the only guy who hit Jasmine's G-spot in such an intense way that it made her squirt.

Over the next hour and a half Jasmine would squirt a total of three times, and each time she did, she became more and more like Silly Putty in Nico's hands.

While Jasmine was in the shower, she started to get a little paranoid and wondered had Nico really come home to kill her or to make sure someone carried out a hit on her. She started to think he probably just wanted to fuck her real good one last time before deading her.

She quickly dried off and applied lotion to her body, and she got dressed and started to gather the shoes and the outfits she wanted to take back with her to SoHo.

Nico came back into the bedroom with just his boxers on and drinking a small glass of Hennessy with no ice. "Where the fuck you going with all that?"

"I'm going out with Simone."

She started to make her way toward the door so she could leave, but Nico held out his hand and stopped her.

Jasmine moved his arm. "Excuse me, babe. I have to hurry up."

"Nah, chill for a minute." Nico sipped on his Hennessy. "What the hell is that tattoo about? And what's this shit I'm hearing about you and Homicide at a Knicks game?"

Jasmine tried to push past Nico. "The tattoo is what I was feeling, and the Homicide rumors is just that—rumors."

Nico grabbed Jasmine's arm, but she pulled away from his grip and walked down the steps to the living room.

"You want all these answers after fuckin' me like I'm your whore. I don't think so, Nico."

"I wasn't fuckin' you like a whore."

"Well, how about what the fuck was you doing in Las Vegas with Mia?" Jasmine wondered why she didn't feel this way when he was fucking her half an hour ago. She made her way to the front door of the house. "Back to that quiet shit again, huh?"

Nico finished the glass of Hennessy he was drinking. "Jasmine, I ain't fighting you."

"And I ain't fighting you either. I came for some clothes and I got that. You got some pussy from me, so everything is good. I'm going out with Simone, and I'll see you real late tonight or in the morning."

CHAPTER 41

When Jasmine walked into her SoHo loft, she saw Homicide doing push-ups bareback in the living room. "Hey," she said. Never did Jasmine think she would get so close to Homicide so quickly that she would feel like she had cheated on him, but that's exactly how she was feeling.

"Just knocking out some sets." Homicide stood up from the floor. He could sense something was up with her mood, but he didn't say anything.

Jasmine walked over to a coffee table and placed her clothes and shoes on top of it. "Nico's back," she blurted out.

Homicide scratched his forehead, and then he went back down to the floor and continued doing push-ups.

"I'm just glad he wasn't there last night when we were there."

"Why's that?" Homicide asked, while doing push-ups.

"It would have been drama."

Homicide hopped up from the floor. "I live for drama! That bitch-ass nigga wouldn't want to go to war with me. Trust me on that. I don't want you sexing that nigga. You understand?"

Jasmine slowly nodded her head.

Homicide walked over to a bottle of water he had placed on the floor near where he was doing push-ups, and he opened it up and started drinking.

Jasmine sighed, and tears started to form in her eyes. "Look, baby, can I tell you something? And please don't get upset."

Homicide stopped drinking to listen to what she had to say.

"I know things are still new with us, but I really love you, and I want you to know that you can trust me."

"I trust you, and I'm just saying I don't want you fuckin' that nigga."

"That's what I'm trying to get at—I just fucked him." Jasmine cringed.

Homicide gave her a real intense look.

"I know it was stupid, baby. I know it. And I was kicking myself the whole way home. And please believe that I really only went out there to get these outfits. I had no idea he was even going to be there." She looked at Homicide to see what his response was going to be.

Homicide said nothing. Jasmine could tell he was tight.

"I just want you to trust me and know that I'll always be honest with you, and I want you to always be honest with me, no matter what."

Homicide nodded his head and drank some more water. "I respect that." No woman had ever been that honest with him. "I respect that because you didn't have to say shit to me."

"I just want us to be able to be completely honest with each other. I'm so tired of these relationships that I been in where no one is totally free to just be who they really are. I don't want no superficial shit between us."

Homicide then asked Jasmine to sit down. "Ever heard of Preme?"

"Supreme?"

Homicide nodded.

"Of course. I never met him, but I know him. Who doesn't know Supreme?"

"Preme damn near raised me. He was like a father to me. He taught me the mathematics and all that. If it wasn't for him, I would have never had knowledge of self."

"I didn't know you were close to him like that."

"Well, the thing is, I woulda took a bullet for Preme without hesitating, and I put that on everything. I would have did a life bid in jail for him. But when we all caught charges and got indicted, he started snitching. He was ready to cut a deal for himself and send me and a bunch of other cats to prison for a long time. I'm talking a minimum of seventy-five years. You understand what I'm saying?"

"Yeah."

"So I ain't never tell nobody this. You the first person I'm ever mentioning this to. And this is something that has to stay between me and you."

"Okay, it will. Don't worry," Jasmine said, unsure where Homicide was going with what he was saying.

"So when I was sitting in jail, I find out Preme is snitching and I got in touch with my lawyer and asked him to see if he could cut a deal for me with the district attorney if I was willing to testify against Supreme. And my lawyer pulled it off for me. And I ended up ratting that nigga out."

"Yeah, but if he was going to snitch on you, you was smart to do that."

A bare-chested Homicide walked up to Jasmine. Smiling, he gently placed both of his hands on her cheeks, guided her head toward him, and kissed her on the lips.

"You get it! That's the only reason I snitched him out. The thing is, I would have done no time in jail had I agreed to have my name on the affidavit, but I wasn't down for that. The affidavit I signed was a John Doe affidavit. The district attorney told me that if I didn't reveal my identity, I would have to do some time. So that's the real reason why I ended up doing five years."

"Wow! I wasn't expecting to hear that from you."

"*Honesty* you said, right?"

"Yep."

"See, real recognize real, and that righteousness you was hitting me with is something I ain't never seen before. You know what I'm saying?"

Jasmine nodded her head. "I got something else to tell you, baby."

"What?"

"Well, you know how you said Preme was going to snitch you out?"

Homicide nodded.

"Well, without making this long drawn-out

explanation, let's just say that being around street dudes like Shabazz and Nico forced me to do what I had to do."

"Whatchu mean?"

Jasmine sighed and looked at Homicide. "Well, there really ain't no easy way to say this, so I'll just spit it out. I'm a C.I."

"Stop fuckin' bullshitting." Homicide chuckled.

"I'm not lying. And you were one of those that the FBI had me target."

Homicide immediately thought to himself that he was going to have to murder her if she was telling the truth.

"I really love you, baby, and you know I would never have told you that if I didn't truly love you."

Homicide shook his head in disbelief.

"Don't worry." Jasmine walked up to him and kissed him. "All those times you gave me that good-ass dick, that was my way of making sure I could never hurt you. From the first day I fucked you, it gave you an entrapment defense against the government."

Homicide smiled and rubbed on his beard. He nodded his head to show that he approved of her. He pulled her close to him, and then he marched her into the bathroom so she could take a shower with him.

Jasmine always thought it would be impossible for someone to make her come harder than Nico did, but that notion was shattered when Homicide fucked her in the shower and gave the most powerful orgasm she'd ever had in her life.

CHAPTER 42

Homicide and Jasmine spoke at length about things. He told her that he could easily make one of her problems go away. Jasmine knew he was referring to killing Nico for her so she wouldn't have to ever worry again about the feds putting pressure on her to get incriminating evidence on him. It was a very enticing proposition for her because, although the apartment and the money was good, she preferred having her life back and didn't want to be accountable to anybody.

But she convinced Homicide that killing Nico at that point in time didn't make any sense. She told him to give her some time to work on Nico so she could find out where he was stashing his drugs. Once she did, it would then make sense for Homicide to murder him because she was certain that he had enough drugs and money stashed that her and Homicide would be able to retire on.

Homicide loved the plan. He was even willing to allow Jasmine to see Nico on a regular basis if he stayed in New York because he knew that would be the only way for her to get close enough to figure out where his stash was.

After Homicide and Jasmine finished talking, Homicide sent her on her way with his blessings to go hang out with Simone. He left the apartment at the same time with her. He was planning on linking up with his homie Cash Out so the two of them could go to Sin City Strip Club in the Bronx.

Jasmine was bored out of her mind on City Island with Simone. They went to a couple of different spots on City Island, and none of them was poppin'.

She regretted letting Simone ride with her. Now she was going to have to drive all the way back to Queens to drop her off at her apartment.

Simone begged Jasmine to come with her to one other spot on City Island so they could try Henny Coladas. Jasmine had never had that before, so she decided to just try it before putting their night of boredom and misery to an end.

"It's good, right?" Simone screamed into Jasmine's ear over the music.

Jasmine couldn't front. The drink was one of the best she had ever tasted, and before she knew it, she'd ordered a second, third, and fourth Henny Colada. With liquor in her system, she lost track of time. It was close to three in the morning and time for last call.

Simone had purposely only had one drink because she was planning on bringing up Homicide's name once she got Jasmine drunk.

"The last round is on me." Simone ordered another Henny Colada and gave it to Jasmine. She pulled out twenty dollars and paid the bartender.

"I'm so drunk right now." Jasmine laughed. "And did I tell you Nico is back home? I put it on that nigga as soon as he walked in the door." Jasmine couldn't stop laughing, even though nothing was funny.

"You should go home when you leave here and give him some more. Wear his ass out!" Simone gave Jasmine a pound. "Fuck marriage and a ring and all that shit. If you want to lock a nigga down, you have to wear his ass out in the bedroom."

Jasmine burst out laughing again. She wasn't able to finish the last drink, and she and Simone went to the bathroom before they made their way out to her car.

"You want me to drive?" Simone asked.

Jasmine gave Simone a look as if to say hell no. She got behind the wheel and made her way off City Island, and soon they were on I-95 South, heading toward the Throgs Neck Bridge. When they got to the E-ZPass lane of the Throgs Neck Bridge, Jasmine's E-ZPass wasn't being read for some reason, and the yellow-armed gate in her lane would not rise up for her to drive through.

"This fuckin' thing!" Jasmine started blowing her horn to get the workers' attention.

A Bridge and Tunnel officer came walking over to Jasmine's side and asked her for her E-ZPass, so he could examine it and make sure it wasn't faulty. As soon as she rolled down her window, the smell of liquor hit him smack in the face.

"Miss, were you drinking tonight?" the officer asked.

"Yes."

"How many drinks did you have?"

"Oh shit, here we go, Simone. I don't know. I think three drinks."

"Okay, miss, I'm going to need you to turn off the engine, and I need you and your friend to step out of the vehicle."

"Step out of the car for what?"

"Turn off the engine and step out of the car right now!" the cop screamed.

"Right now!" Jasmine screamed back, mocking the officer.

"Jasmine, just do what he says." Simone followed the officer's directions and got out of the truck.

The officer got on his radio and called for assistance. Within two minutes, three other officers arrived.

Jasmine started to get belligerent. "I'm not getting out of shit! I'm working for the federal government. Y'all can call Agent Gosling!"

The officers looked at each other. She hadn't shown them a badge or any kind of credentials, so they dismissed what she said.

The uniformed officers were trying to rip open Jasmine's truck door, but they couldn't.

Jasmine took out her BlackBerry and pressed her panic button for the first time, and within five minutes New York City police cars started coming to the scene with their sirens blaring. The FBI had dispatched them to the scene to assess everything until their agents could arrive.

Once all the police showed up, Jasmine got out of the car. And as soon as she did, she was handcuffed and taken down to the ground.

"Call Agent Gosling!" she kept screaming.

The police lifted her off the ground and took her to the Bridge and Tunnel office, which contained a holding cell a mere fifty yards away from the toll lanes and threw her in.

"She works for the government?" one of the officers asked Simone.

Simone shook her head and then confirmed for the officers that Jasmine was indeed drunk.

After about twenty minutes, Agent Gosling and three other unmarked FBI cars arrived on the scene. The officers filled Agent Gosling in on what had happened and why Jasmine was being detained. But the FBI had jurisdiction over her, so she was released into Gosling's custody.

Gosling had one of the uniformed officers drive Simone home and informed them that he would drive Jasmine home. He placed Jasmine in the front seat of his squad car and made sure her truck was driven out of the toll bridge lane and parked in a spot right next to the holding cell.

Once Jasmine's truck was safe, Gosling whisked her away.

"Jasmine, you can't fuck up like this!" Gosling screamed. "You were doing phenomenal. Please don't blow it now. And, for heaven's sake, lay off the liquor!" He looked over at her, and her cleavage and her thighs were turning him on.

"I'm sorry. You're right. I don't know what happened."

He reached over and placed his right hand on her left thigh. "I'm sorry. I shouldn't have snapped at you," he said, caressing her knee.

Gosling pulled over to the shoulder of the Cross Island Parkway. When the car came to a complete stop, he turned toward her and, without asking, started to tongue-kiss her, sliding his hand all the way up her thigh until he got to her pussy. Gosling's dick was so hard, it was almost coming out of his pants.

"Wait, wait, wait! What are you doing, Gosling?"

"I want you. I always wanted you," he said, sliding his finger into her pussy.

Jasmine didn't want to fuck Gosling, but she felt like if she didn't, he might end up later framing her for something she didn't do, to get back at her.

Gosling got out of the car and got in the backseat and told her to come to the backseat with him. Jasmine felt creepy—like she was getting ready to fuck her father or her uncle or something, but she did as Gosling told her.

As soon as she got in the backseat, he pulled her toward him and pulled her titties out so that both were fully exposed. Then he turned her around so that her ass was facing him, positioned her knees on the seat, and bent her down so her head wasn't hitting the ceiling. He then lifted up her skirt and pulled her thong to the side. He took his gun out of the holster and put it on safety and tossed it on the front seat. Then he feverishly got out of his pants, stuck his dick in her pussy from behind, and fucked her raw.

"Don't come in me," she said sternly to him while he pumped his dick in and out of her.

Gosling wanted to last long inside of Jasmine, but with all the pent-up excitement, in less than three minutes, he pulled his dick out and was shooting his load all over the backseat of his FBI-issued car. "Ahhh shit! Ohhhh yeah! Wooooo!"

CHAPTER 43

Agent Gosling cleaned up his come with some tissue he had in the car. Jasmine was dead tired and stayed in the backseat, where she was able to stretch out and close her eyes, and she ended up falling asleep.

While she slept, Agent Gosling reached into his glove compartment and pulled out the bottle of vodka he had stashed there. He took a swig and then put the cap back on the bottle and stuffed it back inside the glove compartment. The swig of vodka gave him an instant rush. He loved the way the liquor felt as it traveled down his throat and into his stomach.

Gosling had two houses, but he preferred the one in Floral Park, Long Island. He decided to take Jasmine there. He knew it was a dumb idea, but he didn't care. He wanted some more of Jasmine's pussy. He had come too quickly when he'd fucked her in the car. He wanted to fuck her one more time so she would remember his dick.

He woke her up and told her where she was, and then he walked her into his tidy two-story brick colonial house.

"Let me make you some breakfast," he said to her when they entered the front door. "Here. Have a seat on the couch."

Gosling sat Jasmine down on the couch and then

went and made her a nice breakfast that included grits, eggs, sausages, and toast. Her stomach was feeling queasy from the liquor, so she wasn't able to really eat the food, but the nibble made her feel better.

"Gosling, what am I doing here? What are we doing? What did we do?" Jasmine shook her head, hoping she could just snap her fingers and then be on an island somewhere far away from all the stress and drama in her life.

"Just relax. You done with your food?"

"Yeah. I can't eat any more of it, but thank you." She walked over to the couch, where she lay down.

"You want to take a shower? Or you can go upstairs and lay down in my bed."

"No, I'm okay. I just want to lay here for about a half hour, and then I need you to take me back to my car."

Gosling then left her on the couch and went to his kitchen cabinet and pulled out an unopened bottle of vodka. Then he went into the medicine cabinet in his bathroom and got his bottle of Viagra, took out a pill and popped it in his mouth.

With the liquor and Viagra in his system, Gosling was more than ready to fuck, and he wasn't waiting for Jasmine to wake back up. He went to her on the couch and quietly and carefully lifted up her skirt, pulled her panties down, and started to lick on her clit.

Jasmine woke up startled. "What are you doing?" She tried to push him away, smelling the liquor on his breath.

"Let me fuck you one more time?"

Jasmine took off her panties and her skirt and just

lay there, determined not to put any effort into fucking him because she didn't want him getting hooked and then calling her every day for some pussy.

Gosling took off his pants, spread her legs open, and entered her missionary-style.

She was hoping he would hurry up and get his nut because she could see sweat forming on his brow. The last thing she wanted was his sweat to drip down on her. She could feel him about to come. "Remember what I said— Don't come inside me."

Gosling pulled his dick out and came before he really started sweating.

Although she was feeling better physically, emotionally she was feeling like shit for letting Gosling fuck her. Though she had confessed some of her past sins to Homicide, there was no way she was going to tell him about what she did with Gosling.

While walking out of Gosling's house, she suddenly remembered screaming out in front of Simone that she was working with the federal government. She knew she'd fucked up. Now she had to find a way to fix that.

CHAPTER 44

Nico still didn't know about Jasmine's SoHo apartment. He also didn't know exactly how much time she had been spending away from the house they shared together. So it was easy to see how he found it strange that she had supposedly gone out with Simone, and now here it was, close to seven thirty in the morning, and she still hadn't come back.

What's up with the snitch?—That was Mia's text to Nico, which actually woke him up and made him realize that Jasmine still wasn't home.

Nico didn't respond to it. He didn't need another lecture or a bunch of texts from her explaining why she was so sure that Jasmine was snitching. He had a plan to test her, to see if she was snitching. If she failed, he was going to first murder both of her parents before killing her.

He couldn't wait around for her to come home because he had moves to make. He was going to see BJ in the hospital, and after that, if he hadn't heard from or seen her, then he would call her and find out where she had been all night long.

While Nico was on his way to Jamaica Hospital to see BJ, Jasmine was on the elevator heading to her apartment. She unlocked her door and walked in. She didn't think Homicide was there, but when she walked into her bedroom, she found him sleeping in her bed. She was surprised to see him there, because he always fell asleep in the living room watching sports.

"Babe, wake up," she said, shaking him. "Baby, I have to tell you something."

Homicide opened his eyes and saw Jasmine looking at him, but it took him about forty-five seconds to figure out where he was, to get his bearings.

"Wake up, baby. I need you. I fucked up big time," she said, real urgent.

"What's up? What happened?"

"I got stopped by the Bridge and Tunnel police when I was coming back from City Island with Simone. Something was wrong with my E-ZPass, so the officer comes to my window and he smelled liquor on my breath. So he's like, 'Get out the car,' and was asking me, had I been drinking and all that shit. Simone gets out of the car, and I stay in the car with the doors locked and the windows up, and I'm like, 'Nah, fuck that! I ain't getting out.' And I was talking mad shit because I was drunk, so it was the liquor talking for me. So, anyway, the next thing you know is, he calls other officers, and other cops come and they force me out. I was trying to tell them that I'm a C.I. and was asking them to call and check me out, so they can let me go. And I was just talking real loud and—"

"And where was Simone when all this was going on?"

"She was standing right there."

Homicide thought for a moment, and then he sat up in the bed. "Where she live at?"

"Queens."

"We have to go see her right now before she starts talking." He scooted out of the bed and put on the same jeans and shirt he was wearing the day before.

"I just hope she went straight home and went to sleep and didn't start calling and texting nobody." Jasmine knew it was a matter of life and death.

When they reached Simone's block, Homicide told Jasmine to walk to the apartment and call Simone to come open the door, and when she opened the door, he would and take it from there.

Jasmine exited Homicide's truck and walked four houses down to Simone's house and called her while standing on her steps. Simone picked up on the second ring.

"Oh my God! Simone, you are not going to believe what they put me through," she said into the phone.

"You okay?" Simone asked.

"Yeah, I'm good. I'm gonna kill you for getting me that drunk off them Henny Coladas."

Simone laughed. "You was talking so much shit, and I was trying to get your attention so I could tell you to shut the hell up."

"Simone, I'm outside your door. They just released me. I have to shit, and my stomach is killing me, so you was closer and I figured I would just stop by you real quick, instead of driving all the way to Long Island."

"I didn't hear the bell."

"I didn't ring it."

"Okay, I'm coming right now."

Within thirty seconds Simone was at the door in her short silk pajamas. "So you gonna come and blow up my bathroom?" She laughed.

"Who you dressed all sexy for?" Jasmine asked, trying to stall her like Homicide had told her to do.

"This ain't sexy. What are you talking about?"

"Let me find out."

"You ain't gonna find out nothing. But hurry up. Come in, so I can close this door."

Jasmine couldn't stall anymore, so she walked in, not wanting to create suspicion.

As soon as Simone tried to close the door, Homicide sprang to the door like an alley cat and stuck his foot in the base to prevent it from closing.

"Who is this?" Simone said with an attitude. She wasn't sure what was going on. Initially she thought it was her landlord who had stuck his foot in the door.

Homicide then grabbed the doorknob and pushed open the door.

As soon as Simone saw Homicide's beard she started to scream.

Homicide grabbed her and repeatedly slapped her in

the face until she fell to the ground. "Shut the fuck up!" he said through clenched teeth. "Don't open your fuckin' mouth!"

He pulled out his gun and pointed it at Simone, who remembered it from Ish's house. She was sure it was the same gun. Simone immediately remembered the voice as being the same voice from the home invasion at Ish's house. She also peeped how calm Jasmine was. She knew Jasmine was in on whatever was going down.

"Please just don't hurt me. Please. Jasmine, you don't have to do this. I swear, you don't. You know how long we go back, Jasmine, and you know I wouldn't say nothing to nobody. Jasmine, I won't hurt you. You know that, Jasmine."

Jasmine kept quiet.

"I told you to shut the fuck up!" Homicide punched Simone squarely in the face, and she dropped to the ground like a rag doll. He then dragged her by her hair into the living room.

Jasmine knew what was about to happen and couldn't watch.

Simone tried to put up a fight, but Homicide kicked her in the ribs the same way he did at Ish's house. She immediately clutched her stomach and doubled over on the ground in pain.

Homicide grabbed one of the cushions from the couch and placed it over her head and mashed her head to the floor, suffocating her. Simone was trying to free herself, and she put up the best struggle she could, but her screams were muffled by the cushion.

Homicide knew the cushion would also muffle the gun blast.

BLAOW!

One gun blast from Homicide's gun sent a bullet right through Simone's head and blood splattering on the floor. Simone's body went limp. When Homicide removed the pillow from her face, it was clear that she was dead. Her eyes were wide open, but there was no life in her body.

"Go find some bleach, and see if you can find some gloves," Homicide instructed.

Jasmine knew Simone was a clean freak, so she went right to her kitchen and found plastic gloves that Simone used to wash dishes, and then she looked in the cabinets and found Clorox, and she brought it for Homicide.

"Get me some water too," he told her.

Jasmine ran and got a large glass of water, and then she ran into the bathroom and grabbed the first two towels she saw. She knew what Homicide wanted to do.

With the bleach, water, and towels, Jasmine and Homicide took about fifteen minutes and wiped all of the doorknobs and surface areas clean of any fingerprints. Once the apartment was wiped clean, Homicide poured bleach all over the couch cushion. Then he looked around to make sure there were no security cameras anywhere.

Jasmine saw Simone's phone on the floor and picked it up. She started to go through her text messages and noticed no recent BBM messages or text messages. Then she looked at her call log and saw that Simone had called her on-again, off-again lover Carlos at five o'clock in the morning and spoke to him for half an hour, and also spoke to him again at seven in the morning.

Homicide asked, "We good?"

"We have to make one more stop." Jasmine showed him the phone.

Homicide nodded and then he and Jasmine left the apartment. They made sure all of the lights were off, all of the shades and blinds were drawn closed, and the door was locked. As they walked back to Homicide's truck, he looked at all the houses in close proximity to Simone's, checking for security cameras. He didn't see any cameras that could have captured him and Jasmine going to or exiting Simone's apartment.

Jasmine and Homicide then headed to Carlos' apartment, where a similar murder scene played itself out, with Carlos also losing his life.

"Dead witnesses are the best witnesses," Homicide joked.

When it was all said and done, it took weeks before Simone's and Carlos' bodies were found inside their apartments. Jasmine cried her eyes out daily over the loss of her best female friend.

Police investigators theorized that there must have been some kind of love triangle gone bad. Although they couldn't link Ish to their deaths, since he had the best alibi in the world by being in jail, his name still emerged as the main person of interest.

CHAPTER 45

Jasmine explained to Homicide that she needed to go to Long Island for a few days to get the info on Nico. The truth was, she really needed to get a few days to herself and not feel like she was going to go crazy and have a nervous breakdown. Homicide was cool with her going to Long Island, and reminded her to not let Nico fuck her. But sex was the last thing on Jasmine's mind. She loved sex, but she wasn't a sex machine. And over the past couple of days, she had experienced something she had never experienced before, fucking three different guys within a twenty-four-hour period. She was hoping that her period came so she would have a good excuse not to fuck.

When she got to her and Nico's house, she was glad he wasn't there. The first thing she did was run a warm bubble bath in the Jacuzzi bathtub in the master bathroom. She stayed in the bathtub for more than an hour and a half, periodically adding new hot water to keep the bathwater at a nice, warm, relaxing temperature.

After the bath was over, although it was mid-afternoon, she got in the bed and went to sleep.

Nico came home and woke her up.

"You sleeping?" he asked.

"I was sleeping until you just woke me up."

"My bad."

Jasmine removed the bed sheet from over her head and explained to Nico how she had got home real late because she almost caught a DWI charge with Simone.

"Get the fuck outta here. What happened?"

Jasmine lied and told him that the Bridge and Tunnel officer had allowed her to pull in front of the barrack offices near the bridge to sleep off the liquor.

"He tried to holler at you?"

"No, not at all."

"You lucky then."

She sat up in the bed. "How is BJ doing?"

"He's coming home in two days, but the nigga is fucked up. He has to wear that smelly-ass bag and shit for the rest of his life. A nurse or a health aide-type chick is going to have to come to his house every day and help him clean the bag, so he won't get no infections or nothing like that."

"Poor baby."

Jasmine got up out of the bed and checked her phone. Then she put it in her bag and discreetly started recording with her other phone, which was also in her bag.

"BJ talking about getting back in the mix and shit when he comes home. I didn't wanna crush the nigga's heart or nothing, but I'm saying to myself, BJ, dog, you gotta get out the game. With them kind of injuries, he can't be scrambling on the streets. You know what I'm saying?"

Jasmine nodded.

"We got a shipment coming from the Haitians in two days. They gonna do the drop near that vacant warehouse in Brooklyn Bridge Park, and this nigga saying he wanna be there."

"With a colostomy bag?"

Nico shook his head.

"I just told him that we'll send two of them young-gun muthafuckas from Ish's crew. And since Ish is locked up, we can just move them under BJ and have them report to him."

"What did he say when you said that?" Jasmine asked, putting on her jeans.

"I mean, he's with it. You know he reminds me of one of those boxers that don't know when to hang it up, always want one more prize fight."

"And then they end up punch-drunk and talking with slurred speech for the rest of their life."

"That's what I'm saying."

"I need aspirin. I still got a slight queasy feeling from these Henny Coladas that me and Simone was drinking."

Jasmine walked out of the room as if she could have cared less about what Nico was saying, and he followed her down to the kitchen.

Nico changed the subject to something completely different, having planted the seed of information into her brain. He was ready to sit back and see what that seed would grow into.

The day before Nico's shipment of drugs was scheduled to arrive in Brooklyn Bridge Park, Jasmine met with Agent Gosling at Argentina Steak House, located on Queens Boulevard, not too far from the mall. It was the first time they had met or spoken since the day he had fucked her twice.

When she first walked into the restaurant, Gosling was waiting in the lobby for her. And when he saw her, he walked up to her and gave her a hug, something he had never done before. His 1990s era-smelling cologne was so strong, it almost made her eyes water. She could also smell liquor on his breath. If he tried to push up on her for sex, she was going to tell him that she had her period and a yeast infection. She was not trying to give him the habit where every time they met up he would be expecting to fuck.

"How are you?" he asked.

"I'm good."

"Before we start talking, I just wanted to say, about the other day, it shouldn't have happened. But I also wanted to make sure that I thanked you."

Jasmine just nodded and told him that she understood. The hostess seated them.

"I want you to hear this." Jasmine took out her BlackBerry and played Nico's words from the other night.

Gosling smiled. "When is two days?"

"Tomorrow."

"Why didn't you call me?" Gosling was concerned

that he would have to scramble to get agents in place to help with the raid and the takedown.

"I didn't call you because my gut tells me it's bullshit."

"What if it's not bullshit? We could never get a shot like this again. I want to at least have agents in place."

Jasmine shook her head.

"That's the thing. If it's a setup and Nico spots any agents near that area scoping the place out, he'll never trust me again. Never!"

Gosling thought to himself for a minute. "We have to send somebody."

"Gosling, please just trust me on this."

"I do trust you. Okay, how about this? I know that park, and it's real kid-friendly, right on the water, newly renovated, and everything is visible. So I'll call Agent Battle and have her get four female agents who have small kids. I'll send the agents into the park on different shifts for blocks of like three hours. They'll be in the park with their kids and baby strollers and stuff like that, looking very normal and blending in."

Jasmine felt comfortable with that plan, but she warned Gosling not to send in any unmarked cars and no men, and she also reminded him not to make any arrests or else her credibility with Nico would be shot. Gosling gave her his word.

Jasmine ordered an appetizer and a Sprite. She wasn't trying to hang around Gosling longer than she had to. So within twenty minutes, she was headed back to her and Nico's house.

As it turned out, the next day a drug deal went down in Brooklyn Bridge Park without a hitch at nine thirty in the morning. A young black FBI agent was there near the empty warehouse with her baby, and Nico's young soldiers never suspected a thing. They did see a young black mom taking pictures of her baby, but that didn't seem odd to them at all. What they didn't know was that mother was snapping high-resolution pictures of them as well.

Jasmine was clueless to the fact that she had spared the life of both of her parents.

CHAPTER 46

Nico had to come back to New York when he did because all the people he trusted were either dead, in jail, or injured, and he didn't really know how to move. It was like there were two sets to Ghetto Mafia—his set and Bebo's set. When Bebo had first gotten killed, people from Bebo's set were convinced that Nico had something to do with it. But once Prince had shot up Bebo's funeral, all that changed.

So Nico chose to stay in the safe haven of his house until Prince either got killed or locked up. He wasn't bold enough to go hunt him down and kill him. Nico knew Prince was smart, and he didn't want to slip up somehow and have Prince turn the tables on him.

With all the time he was spending at home, he started to do business on the phone. One morning, about a week after the drug transaction in Brooklyn Bridge Park, Jasmine woke up but stayed in the bed and acted like she was still sleeping. Nico was talking on his cell phone loud enough for her to hear what he was saying. But the thing was, he was talking in code, and she couldn't make heads or tails of what he was saying.

Nico eventually walked out of the room, and Jasmine stayed in the bed for twenty more minutes before making her way down to the kitchen to make breakfast.

While she was preparing waffle batter, Nico walked up to her and kissed her on the cheek.

"What was that for?"

"I just wanted to kiss you."

"What else you want?"

"Whatever you feel like making is cool with me."

Jasmine told him that she was going to make an omelet and hash browns to go with the waffles.

"Let me ask you something," Nico said.

Jasmine looked at him, so he would know that he had her attention.

"We got this major deal going down in Miami and—"

Jasmine stopped mixing the waffle batter and held up her hand for him to stop talking. "Wait, I want to be crystal clear on something. I don't want you telling me anything about what you do, about any drug deals, anything happening in the street, or none of that. Because if you noticed, the past couple of weeks have been so cool, I been waking up and making breakfast. I been cooking dinner. We haven't been arguing or anything. And I realized that it seemed like we went off the track when you lost trust in me and you was thinking I was talking to the police. So the best way to solve that is to just not tell me anything, and then we'll have peace and harmony. Okay? And I'm not saying that in a smart-ass way. I'm just being honest."

Nico shook his head. "You wrong about that. I never stopped trusting you. You always read too much into my moods. I be stressed about all kinds of shit. Muthafuckas trying to gun me down and take over blocks and corners I built up. Shit like that be weighin' on a nigga."

"Okay."

"I need your advice on some shit though."

"So what's up?" Jasmine stopped what she was doing and gave Nico her full attention, her BlackBerry on the kitchen counter recording every word.

"I'm supposed to meet with this Haitian nigga named Patrick down in Miami. All these Haitian dudes named Patrick or Pierre, but this Patrick ain't the same Patrick who runs shit. The Patrick who runs shit got murdered two weeks back. And this new Patrick is the other Patrick's lieutenant. He's like BJ to me. But the thing is, I don't know if he had something to do with his boss getting killed, and I'm going back and forth in my head about trusting this nigga. I don't know if I should find a new connect or just trust this dude."

"Don't do it. He sounds grimy, and you'll go down there and get robbed or killed. It ain't worth it."

"Ain't nobody scared of the nigga; it's just about trusting him."

"It's all the same thing. I wouldn't go."

Nico blew air out his lungs and explained how shit was drying up ever since they lost their FedEx hookup.

Jasmine kept quiet.

"I can't send BJ, and Lo is gone. And I don't trust the young guns on something this big."

"How big is the deal?"

"Low seven figures."

"Damn! How you gonna get that up to New York?"

Nico explained that he had a private trucking company owner who would move it for him.

"See, that's different now. You have to do that deal yourself and be riding in that little sleep-away area that they got on them tractor trailers." She laughed.

"Nah. Once it's on the truck, we good money."

"Well, I say find a new connect. But if you go through with it, don't send nobody else but yourself."

Nico smiled, already knowing what he was going to do about the deal.

CHAPTER 47

When Nico left for Miami, the FBI and the DEA had a team of agents following his every move, since Jasmine had supplied Agent Gosling with the recorded conversation on the drug deal going down in Miami.

The day Nico left for Miami, Jasmine shot over to her Manhattan loft and called Homicide and told him to come meet her there. When he showed up, he wanted to know if she had fucked Nico.

"There was no way I couldn't fuck him, baby. But it means nothing." Jasmine assured Homicide that it would all be worth it in a just a few short weeks, reminding him that after they made their come-up they could ride off into the sunset.

She didn't tell him about the seven-figure drug deal getting ready to go down in Miami because she realized that, for a big deal like that, he would be outnumbered and outgunned. Plus, she wanted the feds to bag Nico, so she could get out of being a confidential informant.

Homicide had never fucked Jasmine in the ass before, but all of a sudden, that's what he wanted. Jasmine had done anal before, but she wasn't a big fan. She didn't want to do it, but she gave in, to avoid any drama with him.

Homicide wasn't gentle at all. Jasmine howled in pain during the ten-minute episode that felt like torture. She knew he was purposely fucking her in the ass hard to send her a message that things could easily go from sweet to sour between them if she ever tried to play him.

After Homicide came inside Jasmine's asshole, he got up and put on his clothes. He told her that he had to leave but would be back later that night or the next day.

Jasmine lay on the bed in serious pain. Feeling a little bit delirious, she didn't even acknowledge him.

Homicide stopped at the entrance to the bedroom door just before leaving. "Hurry up and find out where that stash is at. And you don't fuck that nigga again until you do! A'ight?"

"Okay," she replied meekly.

"I'm not one of these pussy niggas that's out here. Believe that!" Homicide walked out of her bedroom. He slammed the front door so hard, the entire apartment shook.

Jasmine gingerly rolled over from her stomach and lay on her back, a big lump in her throat. She was confident that the feds were going to nab Nico, but now she wasn't optimistic at all that she would get her life back after Nico's arrest. Even if Nico went to jail, Homicide would still be around. She wondered if she had made a big mistake by acting on her childhood crush instead of staying focused on helping the feds lock him up.

She stood up from the bed and saw blood on her bed sheets. She was horrified at the sight, but she knew she had no one to blame but herself for getting so caught up with Homicide.

Nico sat on a street corner in the Liberty City section of Miami, blocks away from a public storage facility, the drugs sitting inside a storage unit, ready to be fork-lifted on to a tractor-trailer in the parking lot.

Meanwhile, there were agents staking out the public storage facility, and agents stalking out Nico, and they were going to take turns trailing him as soon as he decided to drive to the storage facility.

Local undercover cops took turns trailing Patrick as he left his strip club and made his way to the public storage. They all figured Nico would start his engine and make his way to the facility at any moment, but everybody was shocked when they saw Mia pull into the facility in a car she had rented in New Jersey and driven all the way to Miami. Mia had a guy in the car with her—a face no one had seen before.

Federal agents were all in position, but they were told to stand down until the transaction took place. Mia walked up to Patrick's car. He got out, and she gave him a hug, and they walked to her car. She popped the trunk, showed Patrick the money, and then closed it and gave him the keys to the car. The guy in the car with Mia got out and called Nico on his cell phone to give him a play-by-play of everything happening.

Patrick got on his cell phone, and within two minutes

a young black kid who looked no older than seventeen came wheeling a forklift from inside the public storage facility and placed it on the dock right next to the tractor-trailer.

Out of nowhere unmarked FBI and DEA cars swarmed on the scene, as did marked and unmarked local police cars. And suddenly a helicopter was hovering over the facility.

Within seconds, Mia, her male accomplice, Patrick, the young forklift driver, and the tractor-trailer driver were all on the ground and in handcuffs. Then DEA agents locked down the public storage facility and searched every inch of it with drug-sniffing dogs.

As soon as Nico heard the sirens, he knew they had been busted. But in the federal agents' haste to get to the crime scene when Gosling gave the order, the agents assigned to watch Nico forgot about him.

Nico quickly started up his car and got out of Dodge. Once he made it to the interstate, he rolled down his window and tossed all the cell phones he had on him as he tried to figure out exactly where he was heading next.

CHAPTER 48

The raid in Liberty City managed to make national news broadcasts. All of the lead FBI and DEA agents, local police, and federal and local prosecutors held a major press conference, where they had all of the drugs, guns, and cash they had confiscated on display on long tables.

Agent Gosling basked in his glory as he stood behind the microphone and spoke about the case. It was rare for agents who worked undercover in the field to show their face the way Gosling was doing, but as he explained to the cameras, he was going to be retiring from the bureau in a few short weeks, and this major drug bust was the perfect way for him to cap off his career.

Homicide was in a Bally Total Fitness gym working out. Suddenly, he stopped and walked over to the flat-screen, which was tuned to CNN. As he listened, he was seething with anger. He knew Gosling was Jasmine's case agent, from what Jasmine had told him. He stormed out of the gym and sped over to the Brooklyn Bridge and into Manhattan, weaving in and out of traffic until he got to Jasmine's apartment. The doorman knew him and waved to him as he walked to the elevators.

Homicide banged on Jasmine's apartment door, and after a few minutes she answered the door with her robe on.

WHACK!

Homicide punched her square in the face, and she fell backwards to the floor. He stepped into the apartment and slammed the door shut behind him. "You fuckin' lied to me, bitch!"

Jasmine didn't know what was going on.

"Were you fuckin' Gosling?"

Jasmine's eyes got wide. She didn't know where all of this was coming from because she hadn't seen the news. "No!" she shot back.

All Homicide could think about was, had she tipped him off, all the drugs and cash the feds got could have been his. He picked her up from the ground and started to smack her around.

"Tell me where Gosling lives at! I know you were fuckin' him!"

"Baby, what is going on?" Jasmine screamed at the top of her lungs.

"The feds got the stash, and the only way they knew was because you put them on to it. I know it, and don't fuckin' lie to me!" He pulled out his gun and aimed it at her head. "Were you fuckin' Gosling?"

"No, he raped me!" she said, hoping Homicide would go for her lie.

"Get the fuck on your knees right now and put your hands behind your back and face the wall!"

"Why, baby? Why?" Jasmine pleaded, her hands trembling.

"Where does Gosling live?"

"Floral Park!" she shouted.

Homicide knew about the panic button on Jasmine's phone and wouldn't let her get near it. She had told him what he wanted to know, but because she had caused him to lose out on millions, she had to endure a beating that lasted all night.

CHAPTER 49

Jasmine drove Homicide to Agent Gosling's house once she was certain he was back from Miami. They went to the house late at night. She was dressed in a sexy silk robe with nothing underneath. She rang Gosling's doorbell.

"Who is it?"

"Jasmine."

As soon as Gosling opened the front door, Jasmine held open her robe. She had on a lot of makeup on her face and body to cover up the bruises from the beating she had suffered at the hands of Homicide.

"The case is over. You can fuck me the way you want to now."

Gosling didn't even need a Viagra pill for his dick to get hard at the sight of her naked body standing on his front steps. "Come in."

Jasmine shook her head and told him she wasn't coming in until he got naked right there in front of her. "Let me see that dick," she cooed.

Gosling quickly took off his shoes, unbuttoned his shirt, and took off his pants.

"That's what I'm talking about. Stroke that dick for me, baby."

Gosling did just as Jasmine said, not caring if his

neighbors could see him standing naked at his front door jacking his dick.

Jasmine gave Homicide the cue that Gosling didn't have a gun on him when she'd told him to stroke his dick. Homicide, in one swoop, jumped onto the stairs with his gun drawn and forced Gosling into his living room.

Jasmine closed the front door, and Homicide handed her the duct tape and told her to duct-tape Gosling's mouth and ankles, and his hands behind his back.

"So you raped my girl? Once in your car and once on this couch right here?"

Gosling's eyes got wide, as he shook his head no.

"Yes, you did, bitch!" Homicide kicked him in the jaw as hard as he could. "You know I have to kill for that, right?"

Gosling violently shook his head.

"You knew they call her Suicide Pussy, and you still took the pussy. You gotta die."

Gosling was breathing very hard as his life passed in front of his eyes.

"How much money you put in your own pocket from that raid? Enough to retire off, right? Jasmine, this nigga don't wanna talk now, but when he was taking your pussy, he had a lot to say then, right?"

Jasmine nodded.

Homicide turned back toward Gosling, and cocked his gun.

BANG!

Homicide's body collapsed to the floor.

Jasmine had a small .22-caliber handgun that she always kept with her since the night Bebo almost killed her. So when Homicide came up with the plan to go kill Gosling, she hid it in the robe.

"That's right, muthafucka!" She pumped another bullet into his head to make sure he was dead. "This is Suicide Pussy!"

CHAPTER 50

Two weeks after Jasmine had killed Homicide, Gosling officially retired from the FBI. On the day he retired, Agent Battle officially thanked her for all of her efforts as a confidential informant.

And as she handed Jasmine her last check, she told her that her services as a confidential informant were no longer needed. "That's assuming, of course, that you don't want to stay on and help us." Agent Battle laughed.

"Ehhh, no!" Jasmine laughed.

"Open up the envelope and make sure everything is right."

Jasmine opened up the envelope and saw a check for two hundred and fifty thousand dollars. "This is my money?" she asked in disbelief.

"Your money." Agent Battle smiled.

Agent Battle reminded her that, as a C.I., she was entitled to a percentage of what the FBI confiscated, with a cap of two hundred and fifty thousand dollars.

Jasmine, smiling her ass off, couldn't believe it.

"Now," Agent Battle said, pointing her index finger at Jasmine, "you have a clean slate, but stay your ass out of trouble, because if you fuck up, I will come down on you like a pit bull in a skirt."

"Oh, I like that—pit bull in a skirt." Jasmine smiled. "Trust me, I'm done with that life."

"That's what I want to hear."

Jasmine shook Agent Battle's hand, and then she and Agent Gosling walked out of the office together. Agent Gosling told Jasmine that he would walk her down to the lobby.

As they made their way to the lobby, Jasmine was certain that Gosling was going to start putting the screws to her. He held out his hand for a handshake, and Jasmine shook his hand and held on to it.

"You know what, Jasmine? I would have loved to wife you. And I never would have guessed in a million years that I would even be saying this. But when we depart from each other now, we'll never speak again and I think that will be for the best."

"Why is that?"

"Because, we come from two different worlds, and your world is not my world, and my world is not your world. And my circle wouldn't approve of you, and I doubt your circle would approve of me."

"Oh, but I was good enough for you to fuck me, right? You didn't check with your circle of friends on that, right? And I was also good enough to save your life. You know what? Gosling, on the real, you ain't no better than none of these get-money dudes on the street. All you had to do was wish me well like Agent Battle did and then go off on to your retirement. All that other shit you just said was unnecessary. But it's all good. Enjoy your retirement.

Hopefully retirement will teach you how to appreciate people and how to say the words *thank you*, because apparently you know nothing about that." Jasmine turned and walked out of the federal building and never once looked back.

CHAPTER 51

Since Nico was officially on the run and the FBI and the DEA had warrants out for his arrest for a drug conspiracy charge, Jasmine knew he wouldn't be coming home anytime soon. She was planning on moving her stuff out of his house as soon as possible, and was going to have access to her SoHo apartment only until the end of the month.

The day after leaving the federal building, she went to Long Island to get a suitcase and some clothes for a trip she was making to Los Angeles that same day. When she got to the house, she was surprised to see a letter from Mia from a correctional facility.

"What the fuck this bitch want now?" She stuffed the unopened letter into the back pocket of her jeans and told herself she would read it once she got on the plane.

She drove out to Teterboro Airport, where she met up with Shane Wright, a hustler from New Jersey. She had met him when she went into Sway one night by herself, and they hit it off right from the jump. But with all the drama going on with the case, she'd told him she would get with him as soon as she had the time.

Her timing was perfect because, when she reached out to him, he told her that he was going to be flying to

Los Angeles to go to the NBA Finals. Jasmine was never one to turn down a free trip on a private jet.

She hugged Shane and thanked him for not deleting her number from his phone.

"Nah, I wouldn't do that. I liked the fact that you was about something. That nursing shit is the future."

Jasmine felt like she was in heaven as they sat in the plush leather seats with no one else on the plane except for the two of them and their stewardess.

"Excuse me," the stewardess said. "Jasmine?"

"Yes, that's me."

"I think you dropped this when you were coming on board the plane." The stewardess handed Jasmine the letter that had fallen out of her pocket.

"Oh, thank you."

She then told Shane to give her a minute, so she could read Mia's letter.

Dear Jasmine,

I hope this letter finds you in a better place and in better spirits than I am currently in. As you can see from the envelope, I am writing you from jail. I'm writing for a couple of reasons, but I wanted to tell you from my heart to just be smart. While you have your freedom, you should treasure it and value it.

I could have been anything I wanted to be, but now that is no longer the case, and my life will never be the same. Even after I get out of prison, my life will never be the same.

You remind me so much of myself. Jasmine, you are beautiful, smart, and determined, and therefore you can be whatever you want to be. I urge you to take to heart what I am saying and just be smarter than I was.

I competed with you because I was jealous of you. I had a lot of hatred in my heart, and I was afraid my star couldn't shine unless I snuffed out your light and prevented it from shining.

But tonight, Jasmine, before you go to bed, do something that I no longer have the freedom to do. Stand outside and look at all the stars shining and see if you can count them all. What you will find is that the stars are too numerous to count. I was too ignorant to realize that stars can shine together. I didn't have to stop your shine for my star to shine.

Right now I sit here in jail trying to decide if I will testify against Nico. I pray that you will never be in a similar position. What I know is that if you focus on forgiving and not competing, then you won't end up where I am.

I am not asking you to be my friend, but I needed to write this letter to you so I can move on. If you have ever done anything to hurt me, know that I truly forgive you from the heart. I ask you to find it in your heart to forgive me for all the wrong I have ever committed against you. But if you can't, I will understand. But just remember, being unforgiving will have a worse effect on you than on the one you choose not to forgive.

I hope you receive this letter in the spirit in which it was written.

Jasmine, YOU ARE WIFEY!!!

Sincerely and with Love,
Mia

Jasmine didn't know what to make of Mia's letter, but it definitely made her feel good. She put it away and planned to go back to it later.

As the plane took off and lifted into the sky, Jasmine looked out the window and marveled at the beauty of the universe. She couldn't help but keep thinking back to Mia's letter.

Wow! she thought. *Mia actually told me what I'd always wanted to hear her admit. She actually told me in writing, and she actually openly admitted that I AM WIFEY!*

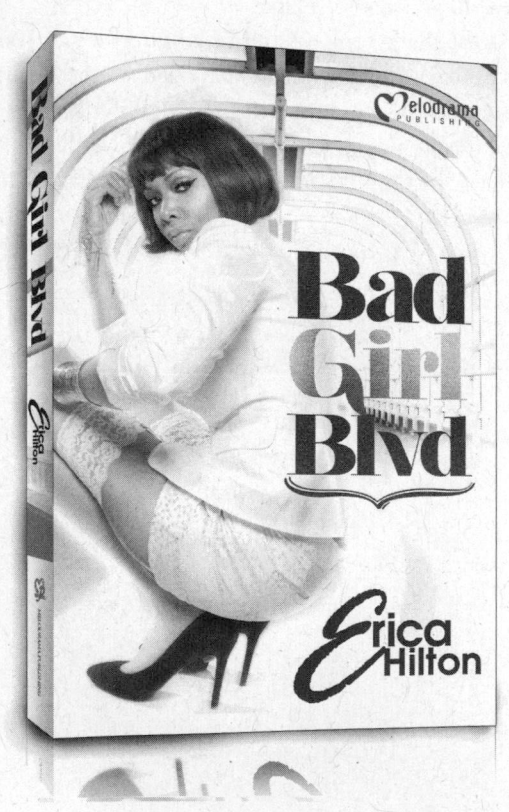

MIAMI, MEET BROOKLYN

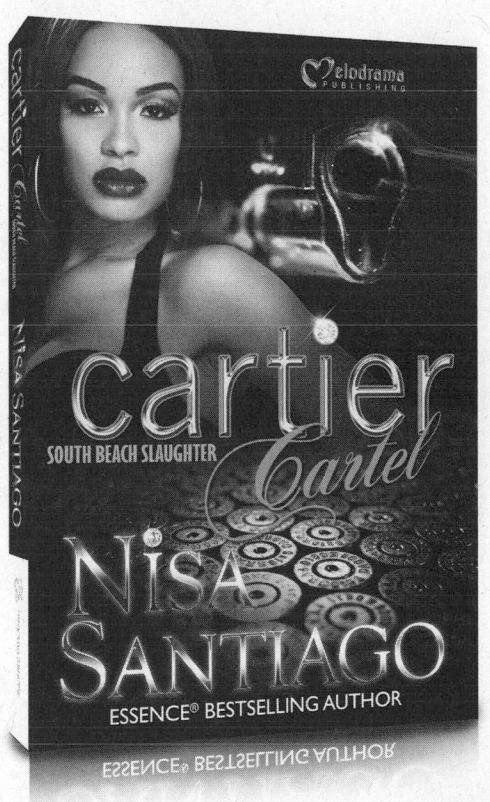

SOUTH SIDE
TO SOUTH BEACH

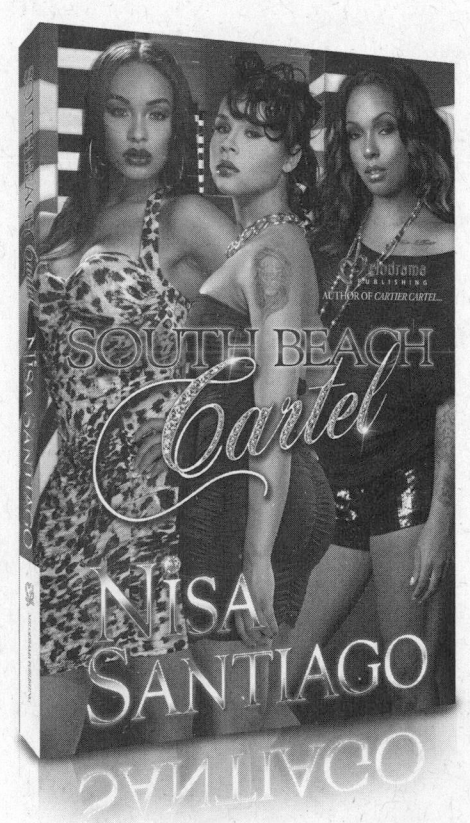